TESTIMONIALS FROM EARLY READERS

I LOVED reading every chapter of this book! Hearing all Faith's stories about how God showed up in her life excites me that He can do the same things in my life! I love how open, honest, and genuine the highs and lows were explained! I was able to relate to every single chapter, and it caused me to deeply reflect on my childhood, growing up, family, college, career, relationships, vision, purpose, and future! I enjoyed her opening my eyes that the blessings I have received are due to seeds others before me have sown and sacrificed. I am so inspired by Faith and her stories of how she continued to let the Lord direct her steps! My favorite revelation I received was right as I finished the book! My faith has increased, and I am ready to load up for the adventure the Lord is taking me on and whoever I can bring with me!!! THIS BOOK W[illegible] ADVANCE THE KINGDOM!!!

- Brittany Keller, Florida, USA

I loved this book from start to finish. There was not a part I did not enjoy, I laughed, cried, and felt Faith's pain as I was reading but I also felt her joy in the Lord through her words and felt her strength and wisdom!

Before this book was presented to me I had been praying for the Lord to give me vision and purpose and this book not only gave me more understanding on what it looks like but has encouraged me in the vision God has for me.

Reading this book has given me a deeper understanding about prayer and interceding for myself and others, I have learned more about who I am in Christ and the Lord has spoken to me more in depth about my spiritual transformation. I have seen the importance of depending on the Lord in every situation and not to compromise who I am for anything or anyone because I am authentically me. I was able to reflect on my own journey and celebrate all God has done and stay steadfast in prayer awaiting breakthroughs on God›s timing, not mine. I was encouraged by faith's stories, victories, breakthroughs, and struggles. She has a way of telling her story like you are sitting right beside her, her words are all God ordained and I felt the Holy Spirit while I was reading. There is deep anointing on, in and all throughout this book! This book is going to help so many people!!

- Jasmine Fryman, Florida, USA

Our lives are supposed to follow the pattern set by Jesus and copied by His disciples - by the set apart followers we read about in the Old and New Covenants. As I read through Unveiling Faith, I resonated with these patterns played out in Faith's life and reflected on my own experience of following the Lord in them. The Holy Spirit rested powerfully but gently on the words as I read through them, encouraging and convicting me at points - there were times I actively stopped reading to pray or act on something in the book. Certain sections or chapters did not resonate as much with me but I see that as a function of diversity: people are different and will therefore connect differently with Faith's life story. I hope, pray and believe that others will be enriched, as I have, by the example Faith witnesses to in her book.

- Benjamin Chua, UK, England

Unveiling Faith has been a blessing and has given me a lot to think about. So much of it was relatable and therefore encouraging. I have yet to see some breakthroughs and prayers be answered and this was a lovely reminder to be faithful even in the waiting.

I loved the Kingdom Themes and explanations of each chapter and how it reflects them.

Overall, I really enjoyed the book. I'm going through a season of uncertainty and change right now, and I struggle with feelings of loneliness and feel directionless and scared. Reading this book at this moment was really encouraging. Again, thank you so much Faith for writing this book, I have no doubt it will be a blessing to many others as well.

- Stephanie Rodriguez, Florida, USA.

Presented To:

From:

Date:

A Spiritual Journey of Transformation

FAITH APIAFI-HAILSHAM

ISBN Paperback 979-8-9864979-1-4
ISBN Hardback 979-8-9864979-2-1

Cover by Alexis Ward at The Visual Republic.

DEDICATION

My beloved parents – The Hon (Bishop) J Apiafi Hailsham and Elder (Mrs.) Violet Hailsham, you gave me a solid spiritual foundation and a reason to write this book.

'My Village' – The Apiafi-Hailsham and Alex-Hart Clan, you make me most proud of my heritage. We are blazing a new trail for the next generation.

My fellow Eagles - Sylvia Mclean, Esther Anato-Dumelo and Margaret Osaghae, you prayed me through the caterpillar and chrysalis years.

My sisterhood of godly strong women, you make friendship a beautiful word.

FOREWARD

REV. RUTHANN CANNINGS

Faith has been willing to allow the Lord to use her in this very personal way to show others that what He did for her, He will do for them. This is a life's journey of discovery and victory in and over the things that can so easily destroy the spirit. Therefore, those who read this book will not only be blessed but healed and restored in their own experience in and of life. This book had been written with love and a deep desire to give others a road map to victory in their lives and their relationship with God, who never fails. Regardless of the road a life may take, it is comforting to know that we are never alone.

Rev Ruthann Cannings
Founder/ Director of 'Arise Ministry'
Conference and Seminar Speaker
Coach
Trained Volunteer Chaplain

www.ruthann.org

TABLE OF CONTENTS

METAMORPHOSIS

Unveiling Faith is a memoir about my spiritual journey.

Like many of us, I grew up praying and dreaming about what I wanted to do and accomplish in my life. I wanted to follow God, build a successful career, have a thriving marriage and family, enjoy friendships and adventures, and bless others both spiritually and materially.

Yet what I discovered is that when you choose the journey of faith, God is not first interested in what you do or accomplish, but in *who you are becoming*.

This is why the life of faith often turns out so differently than we expect—and my life has certainly been no exception. After four decades of life on three continents, experiencing tests, trials, spiritual battles, and waiting seasons, as well as breakthroughs, victories, and miracles, I can say that in so many respects, my story has not been the one I *would* have written—but also that it is beautiful and better than anything I *could* have written.

Of all the lessons I hope to pass on in telling my story, at the center is the paradox of faith. Faith trusts God, even when we *can't see* Him or His promises coming true. Yet it is also by faith that we ultimately *see* God, ourselves, and the world through new eyes of eternal perspective. It is living in this tension that ultimately transforms us and unveils the vision and purpose for our lives.

When I turned 40 and started reflecting on my life, I began to connect the dots of my journey in a way I never really had. I thought about where my life had started, learning to consume the Word, intercede, and grow until I was ready to launch from the land of my birth.

At 20, I remembered hearing the message about the "treasure in the field" and committing my life to seeking the kingdom first. I thought about my "making" at The Call England two years later. I realized that these were all markers of a kind of conception, as though I had swallowed a pill or a seed, which began to slowly grow inside me. Within a period of eleven years, I had a series of dreams of being pregnant and giving birth and each time I did, I felt something growing inside of me and hoped that it had something to do with the fulfillment of my long-standing desire for marriage.

However, it wasn't until 2020 that I finally understood the meaning of these dreams;, I saw quite clearly that what had been growing inside me for so many years wasn't my husband, marriage, family, business, financial breakthrough, ministry or anything external. It was, in fact, *myself.* Like Santiago in Paul Coehlo's *The Alchemist,* I had arrived after a long quest to find that the ultimate treasure I had been seeking was my own reflection, which had been transformed through my journey. It was I who had been born, who had emerged from a chrysalis.

Butterflies and moths develop through a process called *meta-*

morphosis, a Greek word that means transformation or change in shape. There are four stages to this process. First, eggs are laid on plants by the adult female butterfly. Then the eggs hatch into caterpillars. When the caterpillar has fully grown and stops eating, it becomes a pupa or chrysalis. This is the transition phase in which it looks like nothing much is happening on the outside, but big changes are occurring within. The caterpillar encased within the chrysalis actually has two sets of DNA, one for the caterpillar and one for the butterfly. During this stage, the body of the caterpillar essentially disintegrates, the butterfly DNA activates, and the cells of the caterpillar are used to form the new body of the butterfly. The butterfly's struggle to emerge from the chrysalis is critical as well—without it, the butterfly's legs and wings cannot fully develop and enable it to fly. As a butterfly, now an adult of the species, its growth is complete. This is, of course, the stage at which these insects become most beautiful and are no longer bound to crawl slowly along. They have compound eyes, large colorful wings, and can fly far and wide to lay their eggs.[1]

I believe humans, like butterflies, also go through life cycles of transformation as we grow and develop, not only physically but also emotionally and spiritually through the stages of life. However, the timeline of this life cycle is different for each person. Some people develop rapidly and things happen quickly like going through school, university, getting married, having kids, and perhaps going on to become very successful in their field of work. For others, the timeline for these milestones can be quite slow and some may not even happen at the time or in the way we expect. I fall in this second category—the timeline of my life has not followed what I expected, given what I had seen and heard growing up and what I saw happening with many of my friends and col-

1 https://ansp.org/exhibits/online-exhibits/butterflies/lifecycle/

leagues in adulthood. This created a lot of unanswered questions, confusion, and seasons of disappointments and stagnancy for me as I struggled to reconcile my reality with my expectations and make sense of it all.

But all of that changed in 2020. There seemed to be a shift or a breaking of a dam inside of me. I experienced a moment of clarity, an "Aha" moment when suddenly, it all made sense. 2020, the year the world went into lockdown for a pandemic that seemed to fill the earth with the fear of death, was the year that I, Faith, finally emerged from my chrysalis and became a butterfly.

Perhaps, for you too, 2020 brought with it a paradigm shift that now means doing things in a different way. Many are speaking of an awakening taking place, a shift in consciousness, and a way of seeing the world and how it works.

As you begin reading this book, I invite you to reflect on your own life. Questions for reflection have been included at the end of each chapter. The accompanying study guide and journal to this book will be available for purchase in the near future. Details of the study guide release will be posted on *www.faithhailsham.com* and my substack page www.*faithhailsham.substack.com* where you can subscribe for updates. Happy reading!

Introduction
THIS IS YOUR LIFE

In October 2019, I found myself sitting on the beach in the lovely city of San Diego, California. It was a beautiful sunny day, and the waves from the Pacific Ocean were crashing hard. The steady drumbeat of this sound provided a nice backdrop for my reflections as I played with my feet in the sand. As I looked out into the ocean with children and family playing around me, I pondered all that had happened in my life. I was in San Diego on a three-month work trip from London and was enjoying the beauty, peace, and tranquility of Oceanside, where I was currently residing, enjoying the time to reflect away from the busy hustle and bustle of London.

I was approaching "the big 4-0," and although I hadn't yet received the one big desire of my heart to be married and have children, there was so much to be thankful for. My career was going well, my family members were all doing okay, my involvement in church ministry working with young people had been so fulfilling, and I'd done a fair share of traveling and accumulated many life experiences. I knew I couldn't have made it this far without God, who had seen me through every step I have taken on my journey, from my childhood in Nigeria to university and a career in the UK, and now to the US for work. Many spiritual battles were fought and won along that journey.

In light of all this, I felt it would be fitting to have a thanksgiving celebration. I had wanted to have such a celebration in previous years, where all my family and friends could come celebrate with me, and where we could have a thanksgiving or testimony night to talk about all the Lord had done for me and my family. As I hadn't yet had a wedding ceremony, I wanted this celebration to be done in style with my family and friends. So far, it had never come together, but I prayed and believed that if my 40th birthday was the set time for such a celebration, as I sensed it was, the money would come somehow.

The next day, I received a notification that an unexpected payment was being made to me, a bonus from work. This had to be a miracle! There was my confirmation that this thanksgiving party and celebration was meant to be.

Then and there, I started planning a dinner and dance party to be held in London on January 4, 2020, three days from my 40th birthday. Since I was so far away in California, my family and friends stepped in to help. My close friends, Sylvia and Esther, decided to make it a themed party called "This Is Your Life," based on the TV show where they would introduce a celebrity and bring out various people from all stages of the celebrity's life, from school teachers in kindergarten all the way to work colleagues and friends, to share memories and impressions about the guest of honor. I was thrilled at the idea of hearing from so many different friends and family members. Although most of my family lived in

Nigeria, many were planning to attend my brother Emmanuel's wedding in London, so they would already be in town. Everything was coming together!

The Beyond Beautiful Dress

In early December, I traveled from San Diego back home to London to spend Christmas and prepare for the celebration. As the year came to an end and January 4th drew closer, I realized it was going to be nearly impossible to get the dress I'd had specially made in Nigeria to the UK in time for the party. I began shopping for an alternative dress but found none I truly liked at my budget. Then the designer sent me a picture of the finished dress. When I saw it, it seemed all heaven broke loose. As my friend Sylvia exclaimed when I sent her a photo, "This dress is beyond beautiful!" I knew by all means I had to get this dress to the UK. But it was January 2nd, just two days before the party. All the delivery companies I contacted confirmed that it was too late.

I began praying for a miracle and asked everyone to do the same. Family members kept praying and calling to show their support. I remember waking up on the morning of the 3rd, still not knowing how I was to get this dress to me. I knelt and prayed, "Lord, there is a British Airways flight leaving Lagos, Nigeria tonight on the 3rd to arrive in London on the 4th. There is someone on that flight who needs to bring my dress with them to the UK. I don't know who they are, but Lord, You know who they are. Please connect us and let this person not leave without my dress."

Sure enough, by the afternoon, the logistics person in Lagos I hired to arrange the shipping of the dress sent a message that he had found someone traveling on the BA flight on the 3rd. However, this person was refusing to take the dress because he had a connecting flight from London to Scotland, so it would be difficult to get it to me in London as he wouldn't be checking out of the airport. When I heard this, I was overjoyed and thought, "Oh no, nothing can steal this blessing," so I asked to speak to this person over the phone. I explained to him that so much prayer had gone into this dress being delivered to London, and he was an answer to my prayer. I assured him I would find a way to get the dress from him in London. I didn't yet know how that would happen, but I was believing the same God who answered this first part of the prayer and helped us miraculously connect to him would make a way for that dress to make it out of Heathrow airport. I also assured him that if there was no way for the dress to be collected at Heathrow, he could take it with him to Scotland. I was willing to take the risk because I was almost certain the Lord would make a way.

A few hours later, my brother had a genius idea: I would book myself on the same flight this person was taking from London Heathrow to Scotland. I could check in, get to the departure gate, and pick up the package from this man there. When I checked, I had enough British Airways travel miles to book this flight for just £50. I then sent a message to let the person know the updated plan, which he agreed to.

At 5 a.m. on the 4th of January, the day of my party, I arrived at Heathrow Airport, my heart racing every step of the way in excitement, checked into a BA flight headed for Scotland, and waited for the flight from Nigeria to arrive. While I waited, I kept looking out for anyone that fit the description of the man I was supposed to meet, my heart in my mouth.

The moment I spotted him was unforgettable. He was carrying my package–my miracle was in his hands–and I had to rub my eyes twice to make sure I was seeing right because it was all finally happening. When he handed it to me, he told me he was surprised at how far I had gone for a dress and was happy to have been of help. "Beyond beautiful" dress in hand, I messaged all my prayer warriors, informing them our prayers had been answered. Then came the big question—would this dress fit after going through all this palaver? Well, it did fit. Perfectly!

A Grand Celebration

The entire day of the party was full of excitement for me. I had never been 40 and certainly never had a dinner and dance party celebration of this magnitude. It was to be a black-tie event with more than a hundred guests at a beautiful venue. I got my makeup done and then headed to the venue where I had been given a room to get ready. It really did feel like a wedding after all.

When I finally came out fully dressed, friends rushed over to comment on my dress and how I had gone all out for this occasion. The designer had chosen colors for the dress to match the theme of the party. The dress was made of orange and gold sequin lace with gold and silver stones, form-fitting and full length with a trail. An announcement was then made of my arrival to which my friends formed a procession that danced me into the suite. I had chosen a joyful Nigerian song and gave my best shot at dancing in a truly Nigerian fashion to which guests cheered and applauded as they stood up and danced along. The dinner suite was beautifully decorated in shades of cream, gold, and orange. Everything looked perfect and my family and friends had turned up beautifully dressed themselves. My parents, siblings, uncles, aunties, and cousins were dressed in beautiful, colorful attire. Other guests included friends from various stages of my life, old classmates, former and current work colleagues, previous housemates, mentors, lecturer, pastors, and numerous church friends with their family members. I'd hired a Nigerian caterer and the food looked exquisite, featuring traditional Nigerian dishes like jollof rice, fried rice, red stew, fried plantain, egusi soup, ogbono soup, pounded yam, yam porridge, efo riro (vegetable stew), moimoi (beans pudding), suya meat (special Nigerian seasoning), beef, lamb, chicken, and fish. We couldn't wait to dive in.

After the meal, there was a throne set on the stage for me to sit on. I felt quite numb, sitting there watching everything going on. It all seemed like a dream that finally, after so many years of waiting, I was to have a ceremony like this to testify of God's goodness in my life. It was all turning out better than I could have imagined.

As the "This Is Your Life" section commenced, my parents came up to speak about the experience of my birth and how they had seen my life unfold. My dad talked about how they came to give me the name, Faith. After nearly a year trying to conceive their first child, they went to a prayer meeting, where Dad laid his hands on Mom's tummy and prayed for her to conceive. When I was conceived shortly after, Dad decided to call me "Faith," as I was born out of his faith in God. He then announced to everyone that he calls me the "International Queen of the family," to which everyone cheered. My mom talked about her experience of my birth and how she could have died if not for a last-minute intervention by the doctors who performed a C-section to deliver me. Then the three of my siblings who were able to be there—Emmanuel, Violet, and Lydia—talked about their experience of having me as their elder sister. Some of what they said I was hearing for the first time, touching little things like, "We all regarded you so highly that when you left Nigeria for the UK, we took it in turns to use your special plate to eat. We all wanted to use your plate." Afterwards, cousins, aunties, friends from all stages of my life, work colleagues, and church pastors talked about what they knew of me.

One dear childhood friend said, "Faith is certainly a woman of faith. She is an encourager. I went through a devastating and disappointing time in my life where she prayed and encouraged me, resuscitating hope in me. She loves God and desires to please Him and not compromise, which is not easy in this day and age."

A member of my church cell group in London commented, "Faith is a very genuine woman, always willing to pour into others. She is very enthusiastic, rejoicing for others, and pushing them to go beyond circumstances. She is grounded—not seeking the spotlight. However, she remains ambitious, and humble. She is determined, fierce, and a prayer warrior."

A friend from secondary school said, "What makes Faith special is that you can always count on her. Even when we haven't spoken for a while, we can always pick up from where we left off. She's always willing to help, a very good listener, caring, kind, and very serious with her belief in God. No compromise. I also remember on two different occasions where she gave me assistance in applying for two different jobs and I was successful in getting those jobs."

Hearing so many affirmations and testimonies was wonderful, humbling, and a bit overwhelming. The entire event was all I could have asked for and so much more, and as it came to an end, I knew it had been a milestone event in my life, one I wanted to remember and ponder much in the coming days.

Lifting the Veil

In the weeks and months after my birthday party, I reflected on what the important people in my life had said about me and realized something. What my friends, family, classmates, flatmates, work colleagues, and more had shown me was that *my normal, everyday life had been impacting people.* Surely, they all couldn't be making it up or just trying to make me feel good. The truth was that for most of my life, I thought I hadn't really made an impact in the world. I had thought there was so much missing inside me, which had led me to look for affirmation or fulfillment outside of myself. The wilderness and whirlwind season I had been in had impacted my self confidence and trust in God.

Therefore, hearing all these affirming words fundamentally changed my perspective on my life. The conclusion I reached as I pondered all these testimonies was simply that being obedient to the Lord and treating people right, believing and loving on people, are the greatest ways to influence the world around you. Those were things I had practiced since I was a child and came so naturally to me. The way I had lived my life every day was paying off. I was on the right track. I did not have to do something drastic to find fulfillment outside of myself. That in itself was worth so much.

Soon after I reached this comforting and encouraging conclusion, the world went into lockdown in response to the COVID-19 pandemic. I was put on a temporary furlough at my job, giving me space to ponder further about my life and what was going on in the world. It was obvious to me that the world was going through some kind of transition phase, but transition into what? I concluded that the one thing I was really sure of was that change was happening.

Things were not going to remain the same, and we could not remain the same. The only question was what kind of changes would occur? Certainly, many of the changes appeared painful and difficult. People were dying, losing loved ones, jobs, and so much more. Yet God is the master of redemption. I knew there had to be an answer somewhere, especially with the deaths, job losses and so much fear of the world going into recession. Realizing just how fragile and fleeting our earthly lives can be made me wonder what type of mark I would leave on the earth if I was to suddenly depart the world. My desire was to leave "footprints" behind that would guide the next generation in seeking the kingdom of God and more, and I wanted to guide others to do the same, to make their footprints in the sand of life count.

I felt the urgency to look inward for answers rather than externally. What I was sensing was that I needed to dig deep into the treasure wells of my soul, nurture the gifts, talents, and abilities God has given me and step into my God-given assignments.

As I reflected on how to do this, I listened to Dr. Myles Munroe's audiobook, *The Power of Purpose, The Power of Vision,* hoping to better understand what vision was, so I could write one for myself and help others do the same. What I learned took me by surprise. Here were some of the points that struck me the most:

1. Vision reflects what God wants us to accomplish to build His kingdom on earth. This is our purpose.

2. Vision is not merely imagination or a mental exercise—it flows from our hearts and our faith (the ability to see and live from the unseen), and produces courage, discipline, and passion to stay with our assignments.

3. Because it is focused on our unique purpose, vision makes us live a narrow life and keeps life simple.

4. All true visions must be and will be tested for

> authenticity. If you say to the world, "This is what I am going to do," then life is obligated to test that. If your vision is authentic, it will stand the test, and if it isn't real, life will destroy it by opposition. When a vision is authentic, it can handle disappointment, disagreements, confusion, attacks, criticism, people leaving you, talking about you, frustrating you, money not coming in, or people backbiting you. If you believe it and stay with it, it's authentic.[1]

Rather than discovering how to develop a vision, Dr. Munroe's teaching lifted the veil for me to *see the vision I already had*—the vision that has directed my whole life and the way I have lived. Even when I couldn't fully perceive it with my conscious mind, my true purpose had directed me into a life focused in one direction. All the decisions I have made, the vision I have been pursuing for 40 years, flow from my faith in Jesus Christ and my desire to see His kingdom come in me, come through me, and come on the earth as it is in heaven. I have lived a fairly narrow life focused on living out my faith and living to please Him, so He can shape me into the woman He has called me to be. I have been dedicated to the belief that the Lord is my Father and Employer, and whatever I do, I do as unto God and not as unto man.

It was certainly true that this vision had been tested. Living for God and not for man has meant living against the standards of this world and living by His standards revealed in the Bible. The Christian race I have been running has been indeed a tough one, "not for the fainthearted," like my friends and I will say. It's been a long, hard race—sometimes very joyful and beautiful, but many times tough and teary.

1 Dr. Myles Munroe, The Power of Purpose, the Power of Vision (Audible).

As Christians, our fight is always spiritual and not physical. At times, it has felt like every devil in hell was released to test this vision in my life. I have learned to fight in the secret place of prayer with the Lord. That's where the battle is, and I have learned to fight to win on my knees. Thankfully, despite the testing and trials, I have not abandoned the commitments I made to the Lord as a young girl growing up in a Christian family. My vision has been authentic.

As I suddenly understood from the depths of my being what Dr. Munroe was talking about, I burst into tears. I ended up crying for most of the night as it seemed the Lord began to speak to me. The 40 years of my life and all I had lived for finally made sense. The fire in my heart, the roar I felt inside my belly, was now coming to life and becoming clearer. It's funny—someone once told me that I had been misunderstood in my life. At the time, I agreed that I didn't think many people really understood me and the choices I have made. But in this moment, I realized I also hadn't fully understood myself! Now I had indeed caught a revelation from the Lord, and I felt incredibly grateful. I saw that the kingdom of God is truly being established on earth and I had been a part of it all along. All the years and tests of life had truly been worth it.

Why We Seek The Kingdom First

The Israelites spent 40 years in the wilderness before possessing their Promised Land, the land of "milk and honey." The purpose of this 40-year journey was to teach them that God Himself was the ultimate source of everything they needed and wanted, so that when they stepped into a place of abundance and blessing, they would be able to enjoy it and steward it well for generations to come. Their God, not their land, was their "exceedingly great reward" (Genesis 15:1).

Jesus was teaching us the same lesson when He said:

> Therefore I say to you, do not worry about your life, what you will eat or what you will drink; nor about your body, what you will put on. Is not life more than food and the body more than clothing? . . . For after all these things the Gentiles seek. For your heavenly Father knows that you need all these things. But seek first the kingdom of God and His righteousness, and all these things shall be added to you. (Matthew 6:25, 32-33 NKJV)

For the first 40 years of my life, I can humbly but confidently say that I did seek first the kingdom of God, even though in many ways, so much of that time felt like living in the wilderness.

I chose to trust that God would provide for my needs and fulfill my wants, even though in many cases, it seemed like He wasn't—at least in the way I hoped or expected. The most obvious example of this was my desire for marriage. I used to think this would be the earthly crown the Lord had for me, a testimony to the world of the faithfulness and goodness of God. For many years, I contended for this desire in prayer, and finally reached a point of surrendering it fully to Him.

Now that the veil of vision has been lifted on my life, I see that my battle over my desire for marriage, like so many other battles in my life, has prepared me for my land of milk and honey. However, instead of receiving a marriage to a man as the reward of this long-fought battle, what do I have? I not only have a testimony of keeping my vow of abstinence—which many today say is all but impossible or outdated—I have a dance and a roar inside my heart to be part of those who bring the kingdom of God to earth. I have an anointing for prayer, and I get to prophesy and see miracles and healing in people's lives on a regular basis. I can truly say that it is the kingdom of God—not a marriage, or a career, or any other achievement, success, or status I have sought in my life—that satisfies the deepest needs and desires of my heart, because the kingdom is my true purpose, and living for it and in it is by far the greatest earthly crown. The price has been heavy, but I would not give this revelation up for anything else.

It is just this revelation that I wish to share with you in the chapters ahead, for I believe that living in and for the kingdom of God is your true purpose as well and will lead you to your "land of milk and honey." You were created for a life of faith, intimacy with God, prayer, miracles, healing, boldness, and so much more.

Yes, there is a price to pay to enter this life—but then, there is a price to pay for everything in life. The world tries to tell us we will find fulfillment in so many things that fall short of God's best for us and lures us with promises of quick fixes and get-rich-quick schemes. But I have come to learn that anything less than God's best does not satisfy, and all the things that seem to come quickly and easily disappear just as fast. So, we must stop trying to seek a life that does not cost us something. It does not exist. The only question we must answer is, what price will we pay? I can't answer that question for you. All I can do is show you how I have answered it and assure you that any price we pay for the kingdom of God is absolutely worth it.

QUESTIONS FOR REFLECTION

1. God cares about even the little things, like the dress for the party. Has God invited you to contend boldly in prayer like He specifically did for my party and the dress? Is anything stopping you from this?

2. What is something you have given up praying or believing for that perhaps you should have kept on fighting through prayer for?

3. What do you think the people in your life would say about you if you had a "This is your life party?" Would the things they say be different to what you would like them to say?

4. What does the Scripture [Matt 6 v32-33] to 'seek first the kingdom of God' mean for your life? How have you lived this out in your life and what results have you seen so far?

5. How has a major event in your life, such as the global pandemic in 2020, shifted your perspective on life and the kingdom of God?—what changes have you had to make as a result?

SCAN TO SEE
BEYOND BEAUTIFUL DRESS

Chapter 1

FAITH, FAMILY, AND LAVISH GENEROSITY

Kingdom theme: I grew up in a family that was generous in every way, and showed me that it was more blessed to give than to receive. This has defined my purpose my whole life.

THE YEAR WAS 1967. In the early months of the Nigerian Civil War, a woman named Sister Helen decided to visit a family friend in the hospital, a soldier who had been injured in the conflict. She invited one of her relatives, 16-year-old Violet Alex-Hart, to accompany her. When the women reached the man, they saw that both of his legs were hanging in casts, healing from multiple gunshot wounds. However, his condition did not prevent him from taking an immediate interest in Violet.

Violet soon returned the feelings of this young soldier, Jonathan Apiafi Hailsham, and thus began what would prove to be a lifelong relationship. However, what laid ahead for the young couple was the furthest thing from a whirlwind romance.

First, they had to survive the rest of the war. In 1971, they both returned to the Southern Nigerian city of Port Harcourt, Violet from school and Jonathan from the army, and rekindled their relationship. Yet soon, Violet broke it off. She had become a Christian at school, and felt that as Jonathan had yet to give his heart to the Lord, she should not continue pursuing their connection.

A few years later, as Violet was preparing to move to the UK for university studies, Jonathan came to visit her, informed her that he had given his life to Christ, and asked her to marry him. She accepted. But now they faced another challenge: living on separate continents for four years. At first, they wrote each other many letters, and Jonathan managed to make a few trips to the UK to see Violet. He even explored starting a minicab business in London during one of them, but his business ventures back in Nigeria demanded his attention and he gave it up. Then Jonathan's letters began to slow and finally stopped coming. Violet was forced to conclude he had given up on the relationship and decided to move on.

Somehow, the church director of the ministry they both attended in Port Harcourt, a dear friend to Jonathan and Violet, learned of the state of their engagement and encouraged them to renew their relationship. Apparently, this was all they needed to fan their love back into flame, and they finally got married—not once but twice, first in a civil ceremony in Greenwich, London and then in a church wedding in Nigeria. It was now 1978, eleven years since they had met in the hospital.

Violet put off her final exams at university and began married life with Jonathan in Port Harcourt. They were both keen to start a family together after such a long courtship. Yet as they neared the end of their first year of marriage without conceiving, Jonathan began to feel concern. During a church meeting, someone led a prayer for those "requiring the fruit of the womb." Jonathan laid his hands on Violet's abdomen and prayed for God to give them a child.

Shortly after, Violet received the good news: she was pregnant. As it happened, her due date coincided with a scheduled trip back to London to sit for her final university exams, so she and Jonathan planned for their first child to be born in the UK. On January 7th, 1980, Violet went into labor. Jonathan arrived in London three days later and found Violet and his new daughter, the one he had prayed for, waiting for him.

He decided to name her Faith.

Meet the Apiafi-Hailshams

Thus my life began. Like all our stories, mine didn't begin with me. It didn't even begin with Jonathan and Violet, my Dad and Mom, for their stories too were part of a larger, multilayered story—the story of their families going back generations, the story of Nigeria, and above all, the story of the kingdom of God. I grew up learning all these stories from my parents, and they all shaped my identity, my view of the world, and my earliest understanding of my calling and purpose.

Of course, as a young girl, it took me years to appreciate my parents' stories and the long journey they traveled through war (both natural and spiritual), hard work, and much prayer to come together and create the Apiafi-Hailsham family. I was blessed to grow up under the umbrella of their love for God, each other, my six siblings, and me—a love marked by joy, devotion, and generosity. It was this love, above all, that made my early childhood in Port Harcourt rather idyllic.

Port Harcourt in the 1980s was a beautiful place to grow up. The city, which lies in the heart of Nigeria's Rivers State at the mouth of multiple rivers that flow out to the Atlantic, is surrounded by rainforests. My entire neighborhood, as well as our family's property, was like a lush garden exploding with greenery and tropical flowers. Mom enjoyed gardening and, along with many flowers and plants, cultivated dozens of tropical fruit trees, including mango, orange, pawpaw, soursop, guava, plantain, and banana. At one point, we had a pawpaw plantation—one of Dad's many business ventures.

The Nigerian economy was flourishing in those years and Dad's businesses did well. Our home, along with several other houses Dad rented out, was located on a large piece of land he had purchased just after the war. As kids, my siblings and I spent most days outside running around and playing with the other children in this "compound" or "yard," as they are called in Nigeria. (In fact, when I left home for school and began participating in sport, I discovered that all those running games we played had turned me into quite a fast runner!) There was never a shortage of people on the compound—in our house alone, we had up to fifteen people at a time living under our roof, including my grandmother and a number of church members and "helps," teenagers from the surrounding villages who helped around the house in exchange for an education.

My siblings and I were all close in age—after I arrived in 1980, my mother had a child every year or eighteen months till my youngest sister was born in 1989. It felt like my Mom was giving birth all the time, and I loved it, because there was always much celebration when a baby was born. A parade of family members and friends would come by to see the new arrival, bringing gifts and congratulations for all of us. Mom had beautiful babies. Even as a child, I could see this, and many others saw the same and greatly admired my baby brothers and sisters. I remember when one of my younger siblings was born, Mom put the sleeping baby out in a court where family and friends could walk around and admire it. I felt so proud to be the oldest sister of that beautiful baby.

Dad named all of us with two names—one in English and one in our native dialect, Ibani. These names all had spiritual significance and expressed what he heard the Lord saying over each of us as he prayed before our births. However, Dad never called each of us by our actual birth names on a daily basis. He had special nicknames for us, and I can't remember a time when he failed to call us by them—he always had those special names on the tip of his tongue. Other family members and friends gave us nicknames as well, so there were many names to keep track of. I'll give the important ones.

Dad called me Faith because he believed I had been conceived through their faith in God, but also because faith was to mark my life—and it has. My second name is Eretamunosa, which means "the woman of God's time" in Ibani, because Dad believed I was a woman born "for such a time as this." His nickname for me was Dabotuwo, which means "father's daughter" in Ibani. Over the years, he also called me "the Pure Faith" and "The Faith of our Lord Jesus Christ," and now, as he mentioned at my birthday party, he calls me "The International Queen of the Family." My Uncle Owuna, my Mom's older brother, called me "Fatibobosh" my whole life until his death in 2019, but his wife, my Aunty Vicky, still calls me that.

Some family friends also called me "London Faith," both because I was born in London, and to distinguish me from another older girl on the compound named Faith, whom we called "Senior

Faith." Her mother, Elder Mrs. Esther Amiso Alatoru, came to live with us after she became a believer in Christ and faced a lot of persecution. She was pregnant when she arrived on the property, and when her delivery day came, she locked herself indoors, trusted God, and courageously delivered Faith all on her own. Senior Faith happened to be born on January 7th, 1979, and I was born exactly a year later on January 7th, 1980. We were truly like sisters, and Mother Alatoru, who I will always remember as a woman of fervent prayer, was one of my role models of faith. She was a fervent soldier of Christ who traveled across various native fishing villages, preaching the gospel.

My brother, James, born in March 1981, was named after James, the brother of Jesus and Chairman of the Jerusalem church council. His other name is Tamunonye, which in Ibani means God's own. Dad often refers to him as "Chairman of the council."

Esther, the third child and second daughter, was born in May 1982. She was named after Queen Esther in the Bible, and Dad now usually calls her "Queen Esther," though growing up, she was "Esi Daddy's daughter." Her Ibani name, Sopirinye Ibinengi, means, "The gift from heaven is the best."

In December 1984, my brother, Emmanuel, "God with us," was born. His Ibani name is Dagogo, which means "father's namesake," and we all called him by this name at home, as he looked so much like Dad. Dad called him "Daddy's Gogo" all through childhood and into adulthood, but more recently began calling him "The International Billionaire Man of God."

My sister, Violet—Mom's namesake—was born in May 1986. Dad also named her Tamunonengiofori, which in Ibani means, "There is nothing greater than God." My sister was actually the third Violet in the family, as Mom's mom was also called Violet. I guess for this reason she was nicknamed Kalamama, which means "small mama" in Ibani. My Uncle Owuna also had a nickname for her we all used—Koshomeme, or Kosho for short. As the proud big sister, I thought all of Mom's babies were beautiful, but Koshomeme was especially so—if we had signed her up for a baby picture competition, she could have won it. Dad simply called her "The Queen."

David, named after King David in the Bible, came along next in September 1987. His Ibani name is Tamunokuro, which means "the work of God." Growing up, Mom called him "Davido" and Dad called him "David the boy," while my Uncle Owuna affectionately called him "Fat boy" (David was a chubby baby). David was a baby with character. He was always exploring and made everyone laugh.

After David, we all thought Mom and Dad were done having children. There were six of us, three girls and three boys, perfectly spaced in an alternating sequence. Then, towards the middle of 1988, Dad announced during our morning devotions that he had had a dream of a baby girl, who would make us seven in number. Seven was the number of completion, so the Lord was completing our family with this final daughter, who would be called Lydia, after the great lady who helped build up the church of Philippi in the book of Acts of the Apostles. True to Dad's word, in February 1989, Lydia was born. Her Ibani name, fittingly, is Tamunomiekaramam, which means "God has completed His work." Growing up, Dad called her "The Great Lady," and now also calls her "The Philippian Queen."

I found out much later that Lydia was truly unexpected by Mom and Dad and because this was a period of hardship for the family financially, Mom just couldn't see how we could cope with another child. Mom contemplated terminating the pregnancy due to the hardships the family faced. Finally, Mom decided to trust God and tell Dad, and they both decided to have the baby. Mom experienced miracles of provisions with the birth of Lydia, including payment of the hospital bill. Baby Lydia was content with breast milk and grew so beautifully without needing any baby milk to be bought. Mom and Dad saw the tremendous hand of God on baby Lydia, so this strengthened their faith in the Lord to take care of the family.

Lydia was also a beautiful, chubby baby and was loved by many. Ly, as we called her at home, was a favored child. Mom and Dad broke all the rules that applied to the rest of us when it came to Ly. For example, Dad decided we would no longer celebrate birthdays. Once when I was about six years old, I reminded Dad that it was my birthday, and he told me we were not to celebrate birthdays because this was the day we were born into a world of sin. We were only to celebrate the day we accepted Jesus into our lives, which would be called our birthday in the Lord. This was the same response he gave to any other siblings that asked the same thing about their birthday. However, we never celebrated our "birthday in the Lord" anyway, so really this meant no birthdays were celebrated. We just got used to this until Lydia was born. By the time she went to school, to our surprise, her birthday was being celebrated—not just at home, but also in school, which was a dream of ours. Lydia became like the little star of the family. We all loved Lydia and she was a pleasant baby, so my siblings and I didn't really mind that she was favored in this way. Perhaps because there was no doubt that we were also loved, the fact that Lydia was the little star made us all proud of her and did not brood jealousy. Although Dad never celebrated our birthdays, he was very generous in other areas that more than made up for it. As far as I could tell, my siblings and I were happy children and did not have much sibling rivalry.

From a young age, Dad encouraged all of us children to be proud of who we are. One of the first things he taught me was how to write my first name and our last name. The name, Apiafi-Hailsham, has a unique history, beginning with my great-great grandfather, who belonged to one of the ruling houses or clans of Grand Bonny—the Ibani kingdom dating back to the sixteenth century that would become part of the modern Rivers State of Nigeria. During that period, the city of Bonny became a notable slave-exporting depot of West Africa, and my great-great-grandfather, a merchant dealer in palm produce, also bought slaves. However, like some other slave owners, he decided to adopt his slaves as sons and daughters. One of these adopted slaves was my great-grandfather, who after being adopted, was sent to England in the late 1800s to be educated in a town called Hailsham and was apparently so fascinated with the place that he decided to adopt the name of Hailsham as his own. Dad wanted to distinguish *his* Hailshams from the rest of the family, so he decided to hyphenate it with his name, Apiafi. (This is the name he goes by; almost no one calls him Jonathan.) Dad urged all of us kids not to shorten our last name, but to use both.

They say that good fathers instill a strong and secure sense of identity in their children. My father's intentional approach in naming us, especially giving us "royal" names that communicated the nobility and dignity he wanted us to carry, certainly did that. Though we all have grown up to face many challenges and battles in life, we have all remained close and united in who we are: the Apiafi-Hailshams.

Extended Family

Fast forward 10 years after I was born. The sound of car horns and the local market hawkers shouting to invite customers to buy their merchandise filled the air as we arrived at Obudu Street in the heart of Port-Harcourt Mile 1 area. My Uncle Apiri, also known as "Chief Hart," came out to the balcony as he announced 'una welcome' to my mom, siblings, and me as we began making our way upstairs. Aunty Nengi, Chief Hart's wife, appeared behind him as she belted out 'Sisy Lady welcome' to my mom. We finally made it upstairs and into the crowded house. As we got seated, my Uncle Owuna, Mom's elder brother, moved towards us making a funny face at my little brother David as he called out 'Fat boy' - his nickname for him. Aside from the laughter and greetings going on, there was a seriousness in the atmosphere. There had been a negative revelation through a dream by one of the family members of death in the family and so this was a gathering to pray and cancel this negative revelation in the spirit. This was common practice for the Alex-Hart family and all members of the family were present at this meeting to pray through. Mom was the fourth of six siblings, all of whom were very close to each other and to me and my siblings as we grew up. They were all present - uncles, aunties, and cousins. We prayed a lot together as an extended family, and 'Chief Hart,' Mom's immediate younger brother and the medical doctor of the family and our local community, hosted these meetings in his home on Obudu Street in the center of Port Harcourt. This was therefore unofficially the family home for the Alex-Harts. It was always exciting visiting Obudu Street. Everyone came there to seek help or just to be around family.

In Nigeria and Africa, we say it takes a village to raise a child, and that was certainly true in my upbringing. I grew up around my aunties, uncles, cousins, church, and neighborhood community, all of which constituted my "village" and all of whom contributed to the discipline of each child.

Morning Devotions

The thing above all that defined our family culture was the pursuit of Jesus and the practice of Christian faith. We faithfully attended church and participated in many church activities each week. One of my favorite memories from childhood is walking to church and back every Sunday, and sometimes during the middle of the week, with my siblings and the other children on the compound. We all left early to attend the children's service, called Child Evangel, which took place before the adult service. I loved the path to church, which crossed through beautiful fields covered in white sand.

Far more than weekly church services, however, the practice that most shaped my life growing up was the daily morning devotions Mom and Dad led at home. Along with praise, worship, and prayer, these always included a time of Bible study in which we practiced reading, memorizing, and summarizing passages of Scripture from the King James Bible. This study doubled as an education in Christian faith and reading in English. Dad was a master tutor and was passionate about everyone learning to read and pronounce the English words correctly, which is why devotions could take an hour on weekday mornings and sometimes up to three or four hours on the weekend to give everyone enough time to practice. Every member of our household participated, which as I mentioned included a number of people from our church (these were people who had been persecuted and disowned by their families when they became Christians and had nowhere to go; Christianity was still fairly new to the region and was a contrast to the traditional practices that were prevalent then, so many who became Christians found themselves in opposition to their families' hostile attitude towards the religion) and "helps" from the village who, along with us children, began learning to read these morning devotions for the first time.

Mom and Dad encouraged everyone to be active listeners and take in what was being said, memorize it, and be able to talk about it. You couldn't just sit back and be passive during morning devotions, oh no—you could get picked on at any time to answer a question or explain a viewpoint from the passage being read. As I, my siblings, and members of our household grew older, our parents had us take turns leading morning devotions. This involved selecting a few songs for praise and worship, choosing a passage of Scripture to share with everybody, giving a brief talk about what the verses meant to us, and then opening the floor up for everybody else to be able to talk about the verses as well.

The first Bible verse I remember learning at a morning devotion was James 1:25: "But whoso looketh into the perfect law of liberty, and continueth therein, he being not a forgetful hearer, but a doer of the work, this man shall be blessed in his deed." Since memorizing this verse at five years old, it has stuck with me all these years, which shows the power of our upbringing.

Another passage Dad made all of us personalize, recite, and pray over our lives every day was the Magnificat of Mary, the hymn of praise by Mary, the mother of Jesus. Here is how he taught me to recite it for myself:

> "My soul doth magnify the Lord,
> And my spirit hath rejoiced in God my Saviour.
> For He hath regarded the low estate of His handmaiden"—
> *even me, Faith Apiafi-Hailsham—*
> "For, behold, from henceforth all generations shall call me blessed.
> For He that is mighty hath done to me great things; and

holy is His name.
And His mercy is on them that fear Him
From generation to generation.
He hath shewed strength with His arm;
He hath scattered the proud in the imagination of their hearts.
He hath put down the mighty from their seats,
and exalted them of low degree.
He hath filled the hungry with good things,
And the rich He hath sent away empty.
He hath helped His servant Israel,
In remembrance of His mercy,
As He spoke to our fathers,
To Abraham and to his seed forever."
And this is to me and my family forever.
(Luke 1:46-55)

We recited this scripture daily at morning devotions for as long as I can remember growing up, and now I realize what a great foundation of confidence this has given me and my siblings.

At the end of morning devotions, Dad would say, "Good morning, marvelous Jesus family." We would reply, "Good morning, marvelous Jesus Daddy." Then we would go about our day. For Dad, this was who we were—a marvelous Jesus family wanting to live our lives for Jesus. Whenever I did something Dad thought was a great thing to do for the Lord, like defend the gospel or speak to someone about Jesus, he would say to me, "Well done, marvelous Jesus girl." I believe this is what the Lord would say to many of His children today: "You are indeed a marvelous Jesus woman/man."

Rules of the House

In keeping with my parents' passion for building our lives around worship and Scripture, they were also very particular about all matters of character and conduct—how we dressed and spoke, what kind of entertainment we consumed, who we made friends with, and how we spent our time. All members of the household, including our domestic staff and those living with us, had to abide by certain guidelines based on our Christian faith, and if you didn't, you could rest assured you would be in serious trouble.

Some of the rules were very strict. None of us was allowed to touch or drink alcohol. Makeup, trousers, and pants were forbidden for the girls and women; we always wore only skirts and dresses. For a few years, Dad banned us from watching any television. He had a dream of idols being all over the house and decided the TV was taking us away from the Lord. Eventually, he consented to getting a VHS player, but we could only watch movies he permitted. He assigned me to go to a Christian bookstore and buy a selection of Christian movies, musicals like *The Sound of Music* and *My Fair Lady*, children's movies such as *Seven Lucky Kids*, gospel music videos by Hezekiah Walker and Kirk Franklin, and kids praise videos. At one point, we managed to get movies like *Coming to America* and *Police Academy* into the house—I'm not sure how Dad permitted these, but I remember having some good times watching these movies together as a family and all having a good laugh, Dad included.

Secular music (AKA worldly music) was most certainly NOT ever heard in our faith-filled household (I mean….heaven forbid), nor were we allowed to go to secular dances or parties that didn't play gospel music (boo hoo), so I ended up being the good little girl who had tons of gaps in my knowledge of popular culture.

Yes, that was me! That was really my life. When you don't know what is out there, then you don't know what you are missing. So I was actually happy staying within the confines of the Christian culture I was exposed to. For example, one of our Sunday school teachers told us that breakdancing was of the devil. He said that breakdancing had originated from the movements of people burning in hell who had to move in the form of a breakdance due to the pain. Therefore, we were not allowed to dance in a secular way, and certainly not breakdancing. However, eventually all of us kids found ways to enjoy and dance to secular music at parties, and today I love to dance to a good afrobeat, despite this being a no-go area in my childhood and teenage years. I *was* allowed to participate in cultural dance groups from primary school at the age of six up to secondary school, so I can do native dancing quite well and love a good dance to the sound of the African drums.

Over the years, I have come to realize that being Christian doesn't mean we can't enjoy the fun in life, such as dancing and having a good time. This is the distinction between practicing a religion which is about rules and regulations versus cultivating a relationship with the Lord, which is more of a love relationship with freedom to be and express ourselves. But such insights only came with time.

The way we spoke was another big deal at home. Mom and Dad were very particular about making sure we only spoke pleasant and kind words; careless words and swearing or curse words were strictly forbidden. In Nigerian culture, it was common to hear impolite, rude speech, and even insults or abuse, especially toward domestic help. Mom warned us severely against this, explaining that in our family, we were never to speak that way. To this day, I pick my words carefully, avoid curse words, and stay mindful of the words I speak to others. I also learned to speak words of affirmation to others, which was how Dad spoke to most of us. He was always very affirming, even more so than Mom.

Mom also trained us to be peaceful and not get into trouble. She said if you passed someone on the road and they said you stepped on their foot, even though you clearly knew you didn't, you should just say sorry for peace to reign. She said when you say sorry, you have nothing to lose but everything to gain. Saying sorry easily to people became part of us.

Once we became teenagers, no intimate boyfriends or girlfriends were allowed. If any boy ever came to visit me, Dad would question in detail the reason for the visit to ensure there was no dodgy business going on. This was all fine until I turned fifteen and developed my first crush on a friend's brother. I couldn't express this to anyone and learned to suppress the feelings for fear of getting into trouble. Thankfully, I managed to get over the crush after I moved to the UK.

Overall, I was a happy, well-behaved child. My biggest challenge was that I was social and talkative and didn't always know how to rein that in when I needed to. While in primary school, I often received report cards with comments like, "Faith is talkative and can't stay quiet." I remember my maternal grandma always saying, "Faith, you like to go out." It was true—I loved going out to the neighbor's houses to find kids my age to play with. Our next-door neighbors had lots of kids, so I ended up spending a lot of time playing at their house. They also had a VHS player with plenty of kids' movies, such as *Mary Poppins and Chitty Chitty Bang Bang* and in the days when TV and movies were banned from our house, I couldn't resist the temptation to stay over there and watch movies. I wasn't smart about it either. Instead of sneaking out and coming back before Mom and Grandma noticed, I stayed watching movies until someone came looking for me. Then, after having been marched home to receive a whupping, the next day I trooped back to the neighbor's house to do the same thing all over again. This earned me the nickname, "Globe Trotter" from my Grandma—little did she know she was prophesying my future to travel internationally around the globe.

Thankfully, Mom and Grandma didn't try to shut down my curiosity or interest in people. Mom was very much a people's person herself—she would tell me stories about lots of people she had met, either family members or friends, and her stories always seemed so fascinating. She had a genuine interest in the welfare of people and always wanted to check up on them, which was how I picked up that particular trait. Mom thought it was important to know where I came from, as well as my relatives both on Dad's side of the family and hers too, and made it a point to take me to family events like funerals and weddings of distant relatives, so I could get to know them. Given this, it was natural that my social personality and desire to reach out to people and get to know them emerged early.

Spiritual Protection

Nigeria, like any country, had its share of dangers, both physical and spiritual. Mom always covered us children with the blood of Jesus at morning devotions, and anytime there was a threat of something bad, she would plead the blood of Jesus like her life depended on it. I believe it was the blood of Jesus that protected the family from anything harmful happening. I therefore also learned to plead the blood of Jesus if there was any threat of danger.

This habit of praying the blood of Jesus thus became ingrained in me for life. I remember an incident in London many years later. I was walking along a dark alley at Charing Cross in London, an area with quite a number of homeless people sleeping around the tunnels, which could be quite rough. As I made my way to the Tube station, I instinctively knew to be more careful and tucked my bag in more closely. At that very moment, someone started pulling my bag from behind. I was instantly terrified, convinced I was being attacked by a pickpocket. With everything inside me, I screamed, "The blood of Jesus!" at the top of my lungs. The person pulling my bag instantly began apologizing profusely. Lo and behold, it was a friend from church who thought to play a prank on me. He obviously regretted doing this, as he didn't realize he would scare me that much, or that I would scare him in turn with such a bloodcurdling scream. Half joking, he commented that it was definitely a very bad idea to ever cross my path intending to do something bad, as "the blood of Jesus" would totally fight for me. Such was and is my faith in the blood of Jesus, in my head. The blood of Jesus was my invisible pepper spray to be used on anyone who tried to attack me on the road. This was all from my upbringing and Mom's total dependence on the blood of Jesus.

Lavish Generosity

Along with my parents' devotion to faith and a Christian lifestyle, the thing I remember most from my early childhood was their expressions of lavish generosity, not just towards us children, but to so many others, including friends, family members, the extra members of our household, and others who crossed their paths.

Mom, the people person, was always encouraging us to think about others, check on friends or family members, and care about those who were in need. Whenever she went shopping in the market, she picked up items for various aunties and uncles and made sure we took food and money to church members in need. She was always thinking of others and remembering to be generous.

Dad had a great passion for giving to the work of the Lord and philanthropy. He began supporting the Greater Evangelism World Crusade ministry in Port Harcourt years before he married Mom. Though Dad was an entrepreneur with multiple businesses, his first profession was as a land surveyor, and he used his considerable skills to drain a swampy piece of land and turn it into the site of the first branch of Greater Evangelism Church in Borokiri where we lived. By the time we children started arriving, the compound at No. 3 Okarki Street was already an extension of the ministry, a place of refuge for many who needed help.

Dad took in and treated everyone who came to stay on the property like family and even built temporary structures behind the main house in the compound to house some of these people and families. Dad also hosted visiting evangelists and gospel ministers who had come from overseas to minister at Greater Evangelism. He was generous to a fault, sponsored people's education, welfare, and weddings, and was, therefore, loved by many in the ministry and in our community.

All this made me truly proud of Dad as he was always looking to extend a helping hand to those in need and was passionate about financing the gospel wherever he could. My dad was respected by the community and this made me love the gospel even more because I saw him practice genuine faith that was consistent.

Like so many effective parents, my mom and dad understood that actions speak louder than words. My parents won my heart over with actions such as these that I saw them engage in from an early age.

As I mentioned, Dad's businesses did well in the eighties. Shortly after I was born and we returned to Nigeria from the UK, Dad started a business in cocoa and sugar exports based in Lagos, the capital of Nigeria. This required him to be away from home quite often, but whenever he went on a business trip, he always returned with presents for *everyone* on the compound. He bought beautiful dresses for me on these trips on multiple occasions.

Though presents were *not* always a big part of our Christmas celebrations, Christmas was another time where my parents' generous hearts were on display. Dad came up with a tradition at Christmas called "The Lord's Birthday Feast," a weeklong celebration beginning Christmas Day and ending on New Year's Day. The week before Christmas, the family would go on a fast to pray for the upcoming New Year and break our fast on Christmas Day when the feast began. Family members, neighbors, and friends were all invited to join in the celebration.

Sometimes Dad bought a live Christmas goat for the feast. We would gather in the backyard of the compound, where the goat would be killed and roasted on an open-air fire. This was all part of the Christmas excitement. There was a common superstition in Nigeria that those who practiced witchcraft or juju would lure children with money or food and turn them into Christmas goats. We were warned to avoid speaking to strangers, picking up coins on the ground, or accepting food from people we didn't know to avoid this fate. This belief gave rise to such joking phrases as, "Why are you sweating like a Christmas goat?"

Mom was the head chef and all the girls helped with the preparations for the feast. We prepared various Nigerian dishes like fried rice, jollof rice, chicken, goat meat, *ukazi* and egusi traditional soup, and garri (*eba*—a Nigerian local meal eaten with the traditional soups). We then brought all the food out to the dining table, which was set in the middle of the living room with only one chair standing at the head of the table. These were called the Lord's Table and the Lord's Chair, and no one was allowed to sit there until the feast was over. As the head of the family, Dad would say the opening prayer, pull out the Lord's Chair, and invite the Lord to sit at the table. We then cheered that the feast had begun and loaded up our plates. After eating, we danced to Christmas songs around the Lord's Table ("Feliz Navidad" was Dad's favorite), bowing as we passed the Lord's Chair to honor Him. At the end of the night, Dad would say the closing prayer and have the Lord take His leave till the following evening, when the next night of feasting began. After seven days of this, Mom was utterly exhausted, but we all had so much fun as kids with all the food, drinks, and dancing.

However, my favorite childhood Christmas took place when I was about five years old, before my youngest three siblings were born. Mom and the four of us kids at the time traveled on holiday to spend time with my Dad in Lagos. We stayed at a nice hotel called Eco Holiday Inn, with swimming pools and foreign guests, which felt quite luxurious and special. We then had an amazing Christmas dinner at the hotel restaurant. They made such a big fuss about their Christmas special, the "Christmas duckling," that we were so excited when we got to order it.

The best moment of this magical Christmas came when Mom and Dad took us to see Father Christmas and get presents. We joined the queue of people waiting outside the room where Father Christmas was, and my dad paid for us to go in. Then we noticed that there was another long queue of children waiting to see Father Christmas, but it wasn't moving. Dad asked someone why these kids were not going in to see Father Christmas and learned that they were street kids. They had no money, but they formed a line in hopes of getting presents from Father Christmas anyway. I love the faith of those children! Without hesitation, my dad decided to pay for all the children to go in to see Father Christmas. I will never forget how those children screamed with such excitement and joy when they were told they were going to get presents from Father Christmas.

There are certain moments that impact and shape our lives forever, and I can absolutely say that Dad's generosity to those children was one of those moments in my life. To this day, I describe my life purpose as "lavishing generosity," and I know without doubt that this purpose was born in that moment. I was so proud of him and impressed by how much joy he brought to those kids.

QUESTIONS FOR REFLECTION

1. Has your name been meaningful to you? What encouragement, if any, can you take from your name? If you are a parent, did you think through the names given to your children?

2. Do you have any significant (family) role models from your childhood? What was their impact on you?

3. What family/childhood practices, good or bad, have shaped you?

4. What daily routines do you practice in your household to intentionally build up a kingdom focused household?

5. Can you think of anyone you might check in with to see how they are doing?

Chapter 2

THE PEACE RESORT

Kingdom theme: We live in a fallen world full of conflict and tragedy, and this war plays out in each of our hearts. Yet even as we experience pain, loss, and suffering, we have hope that Christ will redeem all as we learn to trust Him in the battle.

WHEN I WAS AROUND EIGHT years old, the peaceful and prosperous "golden years" of my childhood came to an abrupt end. James, Esther, and I came home from primary school one day to a shocking sight. The living room sofas were gone. There were no carpets on the floors or curtains on the windows. As we wandered stunned from room to room, we discovered that the entire house was empty of furnishings.

As kids, we had no way of understanding what this empty house could mean, but much later, we learned the truth. Dad had been in growing financial trouble for some time. My father was a genius when it came to assessing land and determining its potential for development, and had played a key role in various restorative land works in Port Harcourt, creating the Lord Emmanuel Drive, preparing multiple properties for sale in the Abuloma area, and even taking a borrow pit (an excavated area where material has been dug for use as fill at another location)[2] in the Trans-Amadi area and developing an estate from it that now houses over two hundred families.

However, when it came to financing his real estate deals, he sometimes overleveraged himself. Apparently, a number of his real estate deals had fallen through just when he was counting on the financing of the deals to pay his creditors. Meanwhile, his cocoa and sugar exporting business in Lagos had also suffered a major loss when a fraudulent buyer swindled the company out of an entire trailer of cocoa—"419 fraud" as we called it in Nigeria. To settle Dad's business debts, the court had sent bailiffs to our home to seize our possessions.

From that moment on, everything changed for our family. We went "from grace to grass." Bereton Montessori Nursery and Primary School, where James, Esther, and I all attended, soon sent us home because our school fees had not been paid. Against all advice, my dad refused to enroll us in a public school, insisting that we were to be educated at private schools and that God would provide the money. My siblings and I stayed home for two months until our fees were finally paid by relatives. I remember going back to school and lying to my classmates about where I had been for two months, telling them I had traveled to do some exams in my native village in Bonny. Many of my classmates came from wealthy families with big homes, and I felt too ashamed to admit that I had missed school because my fees hadn't been paid. It was my first real experience of shame, and I reacted to it by refusing to show or admit to anyone that we were financially struggling.

2 https://www.merriam-webster.com

But we were struggling, and continued to do so all throughout my primary and secondary school years. Dad kept running his businesses, he made money, and we enjoyed brief periods of feasting. However, Dad never saved any of his profits for tough times believing the Lord will always provide, so when the business dried up, we quickly went from feast to famine. We literally did not always know where our next meal was coming from. Thankfully, Mom and Dad were quite resourceful, so we did some farming of cassava, which produced the main local meal, garri (made from blended and dried cassava), and other vegetables. Dad also frequently took my brothers out to shoot birds, which they brought home for the family to eat. We also continued to receive financial support from close relatives over the years.

A New Home

In the late eighties and early nineties, the Abuloma area of Port Harcourt was mostly undeveloped, in part because ownership of the land was locked up in a land dispute between two native villages. Such disputes were common in certain areas of Rivers State, and some had even ended in tribal wars. However, where most people saw too much risk or a lost cause, Dad saw an opportunity. He predicted that Abuloma was going to be the next up-and-coming part of the city and inserted himself as a negotiator and mediator in the land dispute. He believed in this scheme so much that he sold our compound on Okarki Street and used the money to buy up vast tracts of land in various villages around Abuloma. His plan was to clear these properties, apportion them into layouts, and sell them to landlords to build on.

Amongst the properties Dad bought in Abuloma, he selected about two acres of land to be our new family home. A bungalow and two smaller buildings had already been built on the property, and Dad explained that we would live in these until a larger main house was constructed. We loved hearing his grandiose descriptions of what the house, neighborhood and city would be like in the coming years, his desire to build skyscrapers, and predictions that the area would become a thriving metropolis.

Dad put a fence around our new property with a sign on the main road that read, "The Peace Resort." I think the primary inspiration for this name was his role as mediator in the regional land disputes, and sure enough, he used The Peace Resort as a meeting place for peace negotiations between the heads of the local villages, specifically those in Abuloma and Ogoloma. Many of these negotiations were successful and led to Dad being able to acquire more land in the area. Some of these plots, which he called the Peace Layout, he managed to develop and sell to landlords, just as he had intended. Other properties presented him with many difficulties, as you will hear.

I was already in boarding school by the time our family moved to The Peace Resort, so I missed out on a lot of how daily life unfolded for my parents, siblings, and other members of the household. However, my school was in Abuloma and only about a 15-minute walk from home, so I was able to come home for all holidays and see my family on visiting days. My school friends soon came to know that The Peace Resort was my family home, as it was right on the main road and couldn't be missed. I remember once in school, a teacher wanted to use a hotel as an example and mentioned the "new hotel" along the road called The Peace Resort. My classmates laughed and said, "No, it is not a hotel. It is Faith's family home." The teacher asked me why our residence was called that, and I explained that it was part of our faith in Jesus and my dad's belief we had come to bring peace to the area. Through that experience, I realized that this title could be a way of spreading the gospel, which I liked.

There were other things I liked about The Peace Resort. One was planting a mango seed when we first moved to the property and watching it grow from a seed into a full, fruit-bearing tree that we could all eat from. I was very proud of this achievement. I was away at boarding school a lot during these years at Peace Resort, but was duly updated by my siblings on what I had missed, when I was home for the holidays.

For instance, I was told about a funny incident that captures some of the dynamics of my parents and how they operated in these times. Dad asked the boys—my brothers, James and Emmanuel, as well as Dave and Frank, two family friends who lived with us at the time—to cut the grass in front of the Resort. Their work impressed Dad so much that he ordered a loaf of bread to be bought for each of them—four loaves in total. When Mom found out, she screamed in protest, as a loaf of bread could feed about four people and she thought this was too generous. But Dad defended his actions, saying the boys had done a great job and deserved the bread. He even asked one of the girls who helped around the house to bring some stew for the boys to eat with their loaves. Of course, they ate quickly before anything happened to their rewards.

Such lighthearted conflicts would have been more humorous if they had been the only moments of tension between my parents during our years at The Peace Resort. Sadly, however, apart from Dad's success in mediating the land dispute, a lot of the events that preceded during those years brought the very opposite of peace into our lives.

My Dad, The Fighter

My father has always been a man of conviction and a true visionary, and is compassionate and generous to a fault. He never does anything halfway; whatever he believes in, he sticks with it and follows it through to the end, and he does so, convinced that it will help people and make the world better. However, these personality and character strengths came with challenges and blind spots. To this day, I have no doubt that most of my father's intentions, motives, and beliefs have been right and good. However, the challenge was how he went about trying to convince the world around him that he was right.

Simply put, Dad is a fighter, and he came by it honestly. After his father died when he was just eight years old, his mother, my granny, raised him and his elder brother, my Uncle Kaladar, on her own. With no formal education, she worked hard as a wardress in a prison and also ran a private restaurant business in order to provide for her sons. Granny was a strong fearless woman who was determined to make a good life for her sons and so fought fiercely to ensure her sons got the best education she could afford them. This was highly commendable as a widow trying to survive the 1950s and 1960s in Nigeria. Both at the Okarki Street compound and The Peace Resort, Dad built a small house for Granny, so we children grew up around her and got to know her well before she passed away in 2003 at the age of 101. She took absolutely no nonsense from anyone and never backed down from an argument. I admired Granny's fearless strength to stand up for what she believed.

Once you got to know Granny, it became easy to see that Dad had inherited much of her fighting spirit. As I mentioned in the last chapter, he fought in the Nigerian Civil War (also called the

Biafra War) in his twenties. According to Dad, he had two near-death experiences while on the battle front. First, a bullet hit his right leg and pierced his thigh; the scars remain to this day. The second experience was more frightening. While moving towards the enemy as a leader of his battalion, the enemy camp opened fire and shot him in both legs. They could have easily killed him, but for some unknown reason, the enemy retreated and his life was spared. Even though he did not know the Lord then, Dad believes this was a miracle from the Lord. In total, he sustained seven different injuries in combat, and his bravery on the battlefield earned him the rank of Battalion Commander.

However, the end of the war didn't mean the fighting was over for Dad. He had fought on the Biafra side in the war, which ultimately conceded to the Hausa-Fulani and Kanuri side, who took up political leadership of the nation. The Biafra army was granted amnesty after the war in a truce which was negotiated by notable personalities, including Nigeria's first indigenous president, Dr. Nnamdi Azikiwe, and honored by the Head of State, Yakubu Gowon. Dad stayed quiet about his position with Biafra during the war, so that his life would not be endangered, but at home, he spoke often and passionately about the liberation of the Ijaw people (our Southern Nigerian tribe within the Niger Delta region) and criticized the Hausa-Fulani and Kanuri, whose dominance in the political space has not brought the regional and national development so many desired. He has never backed down from his beliefs about what is best for Nigeria.

Dad actually got involved in politics briefly after the war and was elected president of the Bonny Youth Movement. He was particularly liked due to his charismatic, outspoken, and uncompromising manner in tackling the issues facing the young people of Bonny Island at the time. After a couple of years leading the movement, he stood for elections into the Rivers State House of Assembly under the National Party of Nigeria (NPN) and succeeded to become a member of the House in 1983. His victory encountered fierce opposition, but he fought and the Bonny people elected him. The primary elections, which took place in the Palm Beach Hotel in Bonny, were held three times, and he won all three times. In fact, after his victory, the youths carried him on their shoulders and drove a pick-up van around the Bonny town, chanting, *"Apiafi Hailsham nii wa dogbho,"* which in our native Ibani dialect means "It is Apiafi Hailsham that we want". Sadly, about six months later, the military took over the democratically elected government and dissolved the House of Assembly, effectively ending my father's political career. But again, that didn't mean the fighting was over for Dad.

Having a fighting spirit can be a very good thing. In fact, we need to have a fighting spirit to survive both physically and spiritually in life; however, it needs to be balanced with wisdom, guidance, and accountability. All these taught me the valuable lesson of making room for correction, especially the areas of blind spots in my life.

I saw in my dad's life both the good and downsides of the fighting spirit. In many ways, Dad's extreme personality and drive to fight for his side served him well in the war, in politics, and even in business. Yet when it came to partnering with people in relationships, such as ministry, it became a challenge.

Falling Out . . . Again

As I mentioned in the last chapter, Dad came to Christ a few years after Mom, in 1973. Dad employed a man who was a leader in the Scripture Union as a manager in his land business, and the man shared the gospel with Dad, led him to Christ, and became his first father in the Lord. (I think one of the factors that pushed Dad to the Lord was that his business was struggling at the time and he began to turn to prayer. His manager encouraged him not just to pray for the Lord's help with the business, but to seek Him for His own sake.)

Eventually, Dad made his way to Mom's church, Greater Evangelism World Crusade, because he liked the preaching of Apostle G.D. Numbere of blessed memories. The apostle was always very analytical about the Scriptures and spoke the truth fearlessly. He came to be known as the foremost founder and leader of Pentecostal Christianity in the Niger Delta region of Nigeria. Dad became a devoted supporter of the ministry, especially financially, and was amongst the first set of ordained elders in the ministry. In the early years of the ministry, Dad gave generously and provided accommodation for traveling ministers. He also was involved in helping Greater Evangelism secure various properties on which to build new facilities as the church grew.

Then sometime in the late eighties, Dad had a disagreement with the apostle, which soon escalated into a full-blown conflict. Dad now admits he was wrong to have opposed the apostle in the manner he did, but this disagreement led to a falling out with the ministry and losing many dear relationships and the community we were once a part of.

Dad's conflict with the ministry was followed by other business calamities. This was truly a difficult time for the family due to the chaos and loss this season brought on the family, spiritually, relationally, and financially. Even as a young girl, I felt deeply saddened by Dad's fallout with the apostle. It was a major loss for our family. Our compound on Okarki Street had practically been an extension of the ministry. When we weren't at school, we spent nearly all our free time at church events. I had loved going to Child Evangel and being part of the children's choir. All our friends were from Greater Evangelism, including the apostle and his family. I would never have imagined the day would come when that relationship might be broken. Yet, almost overnight, it was, and with it, much of the life and community I had known disappeared. What was more, it took years and years for our family to find another stable church home.

Peace Church

After Dad left Greater Evangelism, the family 'church hopped' for a few years. This was mostly due to doctrinal disagreements Dad had with a lot of the churches we visited. After failing to find a church he agreed with, and that shared his passion for his doctrinal views, Dad finally decided to start his own church at The Peace Resort, which he called The Peace Church. The consistent members of the church were the members of our household. My brother, Emmanuel, diligently helped set up the church each week, ensured things were in order, and consistently attended workers' meetings. Dad was so impressed that he ordained Emmanuel as an official worker of the church at age 12. I think this was to encourage the rest of his household to be up and doing like Emmanuel, and with time, the other siblings took on roles in the church. In fact, my immediate younger sister, Esther, took up the role of praise and worship leader. But this time set the pace for Emmanuel's ministry, and he later became personal assistant to various pastors and was himself ordained as a pastor. Today, Pastor Emmanuel, as he is known, has founded and leads Nation's Call Church in London, England.

I think for Dad, Peace Church was his outlet, the platform

where he could share his doctrinal preaching and teachings to anyone willing to listen. It was clear that these teachings were so important to my dad that he was willing to do almost anything to stand for them, but for those of us at home, we felt isolated and away from the much-needed community of people a larger church provided.

More Turmoil

Dad experienced ongoing financial and business struggles during this period. Though his peace negotiations had been successful, the logistics of purchasing land from multiple local stakeholders turned out to be very complicated and fraught. Various parties wanted to be settled on various accounts, which meant he had to pay a number of times for the same land.

Sometime around 1994, when I was 14, one afternoon noise erupted from the gate at the entrance to The Peace Resort. I happened to be home at the time and, hearing the noise, ran to the window to see what was happening. About 40 young men were marching toward Dad, who was sitting outside. Stunned, I watched as they seized my father, hoisted him in the air, and carried him back out through the gate, shouting loudly that they were taking him to kill him that very day. Not knowing what to do, I hid in the house and began praying for God's intervention with all my might. We had no telephone or mobile phone at the time, so there was no way of quickly contacting anyone.

Thankfully, one of Dad's cousins, who happened to be walking to The Peace Resort right as this event was taking place, witnessed the whole thing and ran to the police station to report the case. He knew who the young men were—a group of youth from the village of Ozuboko who felt Dad owed them a settlement for some land he purchased, even though he had already paid the elders and owners for it. Despite Dad's attempts to assure the boys that he would settle with them as they carried him off, they seemed determined to kill him that day. Dad's cousin assured the police they would be paid well, so they jumped in their mobile police cars and made their way to Ozuboko junction where Dad had been taken. Thankfully, the police were able to retrieve him successfully before he was hurt.

When narrating his version of the story later, Dad told us he had not been afraid when the boys came. He told them that they would see the handiwork of God; apparently, he sang praises and prayed as the boys carried him to the village to kill him. When they arrived in Ozuboko, the boys were about to take him into the mangrove swamp to kill him, but someone told them "Operation Flush (that's what the police were called) is coming," so most of them were gripped by fear and ran away. Dad urged the remaining gang leader of the boys to leave too before he got arrested, but he initially refused to go and continued to lead Dad toward the swamps. Then for whatever reason, he stopped and ran away. This was the intervention of the Lord—if the boys had successfully taken Dad into the swamps, that would probably have been the end of him. This was a scary experience for me. We thanked the Lord that the boys hadn't spotted me in the house, as perhaps something else could have happened.

Unfortunately, that was far from the end of Dad's struggles with his land deals. Many lawsuits were filed against his purchases. This made life difficult for the family over the years and caused even further financial instability.

The Enemy's Attack

I believe my family are an example of how the area of our greatest strength and calling becomes the greatest area of attack by the enemy. I believe Dad and Mom were clearly called as financiers to advance the kingdom of God. For years, they did this so well together, hand in glove. Dad was a brilliant businessman, experienced so much favor, and was so generous in sponsoring ministry projects, evangelists, traveling ministers, and people in need. Meanwhile Mom was a great hostess who beautifully decorated the home, served the ministers with lovely china dishes she had bought from the UK, and treated them graciously. My parents are people of excellence, and when they worked together, they were such a blessing and were respected by so many people, which greatly contributed to my happy childhood. The fact that our home at Okarki street was a place of refuge for many who were persecuted and played host to many ministers of the gospel gives me so much delight.

However, all of that came to an end with all the chaotic situations we faced. These rough and turbulent times made me determined to work hard to help the family, so we could become more financially stable.

During these times, I found comfort in my friendships, especially my cousin, Suofiri, who would calmly listen to me as I told him these stories. Suofiri was my closest cousin and best friend growing up. We got on well, as I was a talker and Suofiri a listener. He listened to all my stories and waffles without judgment. He was also kind and generous just like his dad "Chief Hart" and would go with me whenever I went anywhere and wanted or needed a companion. I think perhaps Suofiri subconsciously set the bar high for how I think a lady should be treated by a guy. He was a perfect gentleman.

Another silver lining in this season was that hardship began to form my spiritual life like nothing else had. Though we had always prayed as a family, in this time of need and struggle we all began to learn about the power of prayer and see miracles take place. Initially, much of our prayer was focused on praying for God to meet our immediate material needs. Mom would tell us, "You know, we don't know where the next food is coming from, so you better pray." Prayer was really our only hope, so we learned very quickly that everything we needed was dependent on prayer.

QUESTIONS FOR REFLECTION

1. Have you had times of abrupt changes in your life, especially as a child where perhaps you didn't understand what was going on or you felt powerless in doing anything? What were those changes and how did they impact your life for the better or worse? How did your life change? What were the lessons learned from that period of your life?

2. Are there family dynamics in your life you are still trying to understand or process? Are you able to identify the great areas and perhaps challenging areas? How have these impacted your life? Can you be thankful for both?

3. Are you aware of your blind spots and the effects these have on your life, family dynamics, and those around?

4. Role play - What role do you play within your family dynamics? Why do you think you have assumed this role? What events caused you to take on the role(s)? Do you like the role you play? If not, how can you change it?

5. What family setbacks have you faced and how has this shaped who you are today?

Chapter 3

TRAINING GROUND

Kingdom theme: Discipline, social development, spiritual growth, and leadership opportunities are some of the key ingredients essential to discipleship and unlocking our spiritual gifts.

AT 11 YEARS OLD, I left home to attend secondary school at the Federal Government Girls College, an all-girls boarding school in Abuloma, Port Harcourt. FGGC Abuloma was one of the many "Unity Schools" set up around the country by the Federal Government of Nigeria after the Biafra War. These schools were envisioned as centers of academic excellence where national integration would flourish and young Nigerians would be imbued with requisite skills for national progress through capacity building, promotion of leadership, and national unity. Parents were encouraged to send their children to schools outside their state, so they could learn and integrate with the different tribes and cultures in the nation. However, this wasn't the case for me, as

I was accepted in the school within my state.

I was both excited and nervous about the thought of going to boarding school. These schools were known for having strict rules and instilling discipline into students, as well as teaching you to become independent. When you hear the word 'boarding school,' you may be thinking of the posh schools where the elite send their children, such as Malory Towers in the old Enid Blyton teenage novels (if you read those growing up). Boarding schools in Nigeria at the time were quite the opposite. They were federally owned government schools affordable to both low- and high-income families and known for maintaining a high level of discipline. Students were expected to work really hard both ademically and in terms of actual physical labor. There were no cleaners maintaining the dorms or groundskeepers caring for the grounds; we students did all this ourselves, down to cutting the grass to maintain the fields. These boarding schools were tough environments where many parents sent their kids to receive the necessary academic and life training required to withstand life's challenges. Both my parents felt I needed to learn independence and be well prepared for life's challenges. (How right they were.) Mom had attended a boarding school during her secondary school years, Archdeacon Crowther Memorial Girls School (ACMGS Elelenwo), and told me many stories and prepared me to look forward to having my own experiences of being independent. She couldn't wait for me to go, as she thought I needed a lot of training and boarding school was the right place for me to be trained. I was to stay for the full school year of three terms and only come home during half-terms, which were generally a week, and the long holidays between terms. I did understand that due to Mom's experience of the training a boarding school provided, she wanted the same for me.

I vividly still remember my first day at school. As we parked the car and got out, my parents recognized a cousin of mine whom I had never met called Nengi. It was a miracle—practically the first person I encountered was a "friendly face." Senior Nengi, as I learned the senior students were called, gave us a brief run-down of the school, describing where to find the classrooms, standard dormitories for senior and junior students, chapels (one exclusively for Catholics), dining halls, dance/movie hall, Parents-Teachers Association (PTA) hall, sporting field, gardens, and tuck shop where snacks, drinks, and other confectionery were sold. She also told my parents about another cousin of mine, Senior Anita, and then called her over to say hello. Anita was beautiful and very stylish, and I immediately looked up to her, as she was in her final year. She quickly took me under her wing, promising to take care of me in my first year.

After my parents left, I was taken, clutching my possessions in a suitcase, to my dormitory. There I met a number of other Form 1 girls who were waiting in the first room of the dormitory to be allocated a room by one of the senior students. This was really scary, as I knew no one and the seniors seemed huge and intimidating to me. Then another miracle occurred. As I was waiting, I recognized one of the senior students as a girl from my neighborhood. I didn't know her name, but I knew she lived on my street and I had noticed her from time to time when I walked around the neighborhood. However, since I had never actually spoken to her, I was scared to say anything. Then, she looked my way and recognized me.

"I know you! You live on my street at No. 3 Okarki Street."

I nodded yes. She seemed so happy to see me and immediately allocated me to her room, where she was headed. Senior Beimote, as I soon learned she was called, became my "school mother." Back then when you were in Form 1, right at the bottom of the food chain at boarding school, a school mother was essential to protect you against other junior and senior girls who would try to bully or take advantage of you. Senior Beimote was a huge saving grace for me in my first year. I knew this was God watching out for me, even though I felt so far away from home.

Daily Life in Form 1

Although it has been more than two decades since I left FGGC Abuloma, I still recall most of our daily activities. We woke up early, which I believe gave our daily activities a sense of purpose and direction. I once came across a Portuguese adage that says, "Early sleep and early wake up gives health and makes you grow." I have come to understand as I grow older that waking up early sets you up to be productive, while waking up late can make one's day disorganized and even wasted, and I'm thankful that boarding school instilled this habit in us early on.

After the wake-up call, I usually took my bucket to fetch water for my bath. Bathing, like most activities, was a time when many of the senior girls exacted their influence over the juniors. At times, we had to queue to get water, and if you were unlucky, a senior might take the water you had just fetched and pour it into her bucket. Thankfully, we rarely had challenges with having enough water to go around, perhaps because our school was located in Rivers State and was surrounded by many rivers. Since the bathrooms could not accommodate all students at once, we would take turns in taking our baths, which senior students occasionally took advantage of as well. However, no juniors dared argue with the seniors, or they would be marked down for disciplinary actions in revenge, even on fictitious crimes.

After baths, we did chores till 7:00 a.m., then set out for breakfast, which would usually last till 7:30. I miss how we ate together as a family, despite our various socio-ethnic backgrounds of different cultures and habits, which included language, food, and behavioral differences. There was no favoritism, we were all treated the same. However, you had to arrive on time; otherwise, your food might be eaten by others. You had to take your plate to the serving area where you were served your portion of food on your plate and then you brought the food back to your allocated table where you sat with your table members to eat. I can't recall my food ever being eaten, not just because I liked my food and didn't want to go hungry, but because I was rarely late. If you arrived late, it was possible for all the food to have been dished out so there was none left. For those who did have this experience, it was not pleasant or funny; you would see tears rolling freely down girls' cheeks when it happened. The only thing to do in such cases was to fall back on your own provisions. Students often kept *garri*, groundnuts, and *kuli kuli*, a type of snack, in their dormitories, and those regarded as *ajebos* (rich, posh, classy) had Cornflakes, Golden Morn, Cabin Biscuit, Milo, Bourn Vita, and other products. Some students even had canned corned beef, sardine, or Geisha (mackerel), even though canned foods were contraband then. Others would go to the tuck shop to buy stuff to eat.

On Mondays and Fridays, the end of breakfast marked our transition to the assembly; on the other days, we went straight to our classes for morning prep. Classes began at 8:00 a.m., broke for half an hour at 11:30, then resumed till 2 p.m. There was a high level of discipline and orderliness during class hours. Nobody could be found loitering around during classes, or else your name would be written down in secrecy by the seniors, labor prefects, and their spies. The names of noisemakers, those loitering during classes or prep, and those smuggling food out of the dining hall or caught with contrabands were written in a weekly detention book and called out during assembly every Friday. Everyone called would then be punished by doing labor after inspection on Saturdays. Getting your name in the detention book was not funny at all.

At 2:00 p.m., we had lunch, then returned to our dormitories by 3:00. Those who had things to wash like socks or clothes would do so for fifteen minutes or so, then we all took 45 minutes for siesta. Siesta was compulsory, though some students still found their way around it by engaging in small talk (*gist*) or eating food. I loved siesta—it was refreshing after the stress of being in class all day and helped me re-energize my body and soul and refocus my brain for the evening prep, which ran from 4:00 to 6:00 p.m. During this time, we usually had extra lessons, except when we had to do manual labor, or on Fridays because we did not have classes the following morning. These lessons were really enlightening and touched on the vague areas we might have missed during the morning classes.

After evening prep, we had an hour to play in the field or engage in whatever activity we liked—skipping, jumping, running, volleyball, and more. Our field was one of the biggest I have ever seen in my life. The worst punishment one could receive was for the physical education teacher to tell you to jog around it twice!

At 7:00 p.m., we journeyed to the dining hall for dinner, then headed back to our classrooms for night prep from 8:00 to 10:00 p.m. This time was mainly for reading and studying, so we would retrieve our books and writing materials from our wooden lockers and spread out two to a desk that could accommodate three. Senior students, especially those in SSS 3, were assigned as prefects to monitor the classes and curb noise making, distractions, and unnecessary sleeping amongst students.

Most of us would be tired and looking forward to going to

bed immediately after night prep. However, we had till 11:00 or 11:30 p.m. before lights out (this depended on whether the electrician had slept off or not), and the journey back to the dorms was treacherous for us juniors, as we had to look out for seniors who wanted us to fetch water for them for the following morning. An unlucky junior could fetch as much as thirty buckets of water for different seniors! I was so lucky as a junior student because my cousins, Senior Nengi and Senior Anita, who was then in SSS 3, and Senior Beimote, my school mother, all looked out for me and protected me from senior students who could have bullied or taken advantage of me in the school.

Second term, we added some new things to our routines. To prepare for our inter-house sports day, we woke up at 5:00 and then jogged around the school till 6:00 a.m., after which we did morning devotion (being a majority Christian school in southern Nigeria) and chores, took our baths, and set out for breakfast by 7:00. (Devotions were not as spirit-lifting with everyone worn out from jogging.) We also had continuous assessments (CAs) of our academic performance, and at certain assemblies, they would announce the first and last three people in every class, especially the last assembly before holidays. This kept us in check and encouraged us to work hard to come out as top of the class.

Saturdays, along with public holidays, were the best days for us, as they were almost totally free. After inspection, we had time to wash and then attend Protestant fellowship meetings, where we discussed the Bible, counseled one another, and prayed together. Then we would go read in our classrooms (a good way to avoid bullying seniors) or return to the dormitories to do our hair. On Fridays, the social prefect announced the hairstyle every girl was to wear for the following week, with a sample for students to see, then on Saturdays, we created them by helping one another get our hair done. Chosen hairstyles included cornrows woven from front to back (we called these "all back"), woven in a basket pattern, or in the shape of a ponytail. No extensions were allowed, so you had to make these hairstyles with just your own natural hair.

Saturday nights were social nights. I occasionally went to the dance/movie hall to see movies and watch as other students danced; otherwise, I slept or "gisted" with friends. The first Saturday of every month was family visiting day. I always looked forward to seeing my family and at times, didn't even go to the dining hall for breakfast because I expected something better was coming from home.

One important event that took place in the first year was that I officially gave my life to Jesus Christ. I had already made this decision at a much younger age growing up in a Christian home, but when I got to boarding school, I felt like I needed to make a public declaration that this was the path I had chosen, not just because my parents said so, but because it was what I wanted. I needed to make my spiritual life official. So at 11 years old, I publicly declared that I was Christian, and there was no looking back from then on. Even at that age, I was already beginning to understand some of the realities of life and how much we needed God in our lives.

Thankfully, I had grown up watching my parents not only talk the talk, but also walk the walk. Everything they taught us to do was what they did themselves. They didn't say one thing and do another. They were very consistent in their words and actions. I grew up seeing my mom pray about everything and she raised us to do the same. She always stood on the Word of God and was always declaring it. So even though my parents were not with me at boarding school, I had grown up in an environment where spirituality was real and I carried their example with me. I knew I had to live the same way.

Making Friends

In my second year of boarding school (JSS2, Form 2, or Year 8 as it is called in the UK), life became a bit tougher because my school mother, Beimote, and my cousin Anita, who had become like an older sister to me, had finished and left secondary school and I was less protected from the senior girls.

A friend of mine, whom I had first met at a summer camp and became fast friends with at school, began commiserating with me that boarding school was now like a prison. We were facing the hardships of boarding school, such as daily chores that were sometimes hard like scrubbing the dirty toilets, cleaning the gutters, and cutting the grass with a cutlass. However, all of these chores had to be done, and we took them in turns. When some students misbehaved and absconded from their chores, we all served mass punishments. Some students had allergic reactions to the dirty water from the gutters and developed sores on their legs. The lucky students had their parents withdraw them from boarding school, but the rest of us had to learn to deal with it. Bullying by older students was a regular occurrence, (e.g., being sent on complicated errands outside in the dark by senior students). Instead of the second year being easier for us, it was harder because in our first year, we had strong older students like our school mothers and my cousins who protected us from bullying. But as they had now graduated from the school, we faced the harsh realities of learning to survive on our own. My friend and I decided to write to our parents, explaining that boarding life was like hell, and ask if we could become day students (no longer living in dorms, but living at home and attending classes daily). By this time, my family had moved to The Peace Resort, which was only a 15-minute walk from FGGC Abuloma, so I thought my parents would easily agree to this plan. However, they did not respond, despite me sending them multiple letters. My friend, meanwhile, was picked up one weekend by her dad to be taken home from school. I asked if he could check me out of school and drop me at home. He said no, but promised to stop by my house and let my parents know to come and pick me up. That weekend was the wedding of one of my dad's cousins, and the whole family was traveling to the wedding. I really wanted to go and waited for someone to pick me up, but no one came. I was *so* disappointed.

A few weeks later, Mom sent for me to come home and visit. I was elated. Surely this meant Mom was finally going to make me a day student! However, when I arrived at home, Mom sat me down and explained why she had sent for me. Mom had hardly ever sat me down to talk that way, so I knew she was very serious. She told me I was to stop writing letters asking to come home, that she would never allow me to leave boarding school, and that I had so much to learn there. At one point, she started calling on the name of God, and then I knew it was game over completely. Mom was a prayer warrior and did not call on God unnecessarily. When she did, I knew that God heard.

Mom said to forget about the fact that the house was only 15 minutes away and act like one of the girls from out of state, like the girls from Lagos. She said to go back and watch how they coped, knowing they had no choice but to remain in boarding school. They would teach me how to survive.

So, I did exactly as she said. I returned to school and began watching the Lagos girls and others who just got on with it, knowing they had no choice. And I have to say that it worked. I accepted my chores and punishments and got on with life at boarding school. I also think this was where I began to learn the skill of empathy, to see things from the perspective of others and try to understand what they were going through.

I had always been a sociable girl who made friends easily, and with this shift in my attitude, I leaned even more into just being myself and connecting with people at school. Even in first year, I had started to gain a reputation for being friendly, entertaining, and a good storyteller. I was actually a bit of a drama queen—a bit like my paternal grandmother, whom I mentioned in the last chapter. She was a drama queen herself and my favorite person to impersonate for my friends. They roared with laughter as I narrated Granny's antics and imitated the way she danced as she told people off in Engrigbo (Igbo and English). I also remember once coming back from a holiday trip to Lagos and animatedly describing my adventures there, including the privilege of renting movies at Blockbuster with my aunty's card—something we were not allowed to do at home. Some of the girls from Lagos commented that my storytelling made the city they knew well and such everyday events like renting movies fresh and entertaining. I also loved to dance and perform songs from musicals—*My Fair Lady* and *The Sound of Music* were my favorites.

I socialized with all types of girls, from the very popular girls to the really quiet girls' people hardly spoke to. I could talk to them, understand them, and get on with them without having to be influenced by what they did. I knew my boundaries. However, a friend called Boma Tonye, who was a Christian like me, advised me to be more selective of my friendships and pray for the right friends. Each time she saw me hanging out with different types of girls, she would say, "Faith, be careful." After my mom talked to me about staying put in boarding school, I decided to take Boma Tonye's advice and prayed for the Lord to bring me the right friends I needed to do well at boarding school. I still maintained friendships, but just became more selective about them. One was with Baa, another girl whose family home was very close to school but was still required to board. I got to know Baa and her family and frequently visited her during the holidays, as she lived so close to me. Her family arranged to drop us off at the dormitory at the start of the term and picked us up at the end of the term. Baa became like a sister to me.

There was another girl in my year who turned out to be a good friend. Sira and I were in the same class and dormitory. We had also attended the same primary school, so we easily clicked right away in first year. Sira had a big personality, readily spoke her mind, and stood up for herself. She kept her dormitory locker extremely neat and tidy, and her uniform was always spotless and well ironed. She was also extremely hard-working with her dormitory chores. If she was given a chore, no matter how big it was, she would focus and get it done before doing anything else. I saw these as essential survival skills for school and learned to do them from her. I thought Sira was a special person and her courage and confidence inspired me.[3]

In my quest to do well at school, I kept off other distractions by choosing to focus on my studies. I even started sitting at a spare desk in another part of the classroom. I remember putting my head down and studying for a biology test and earning an A, which was a big improvement from the average C grades I had in the past. It surprised me that I could be that good. Pleased with the result, I continued with my new study habits, and my grades continued to improve drastically. In fact, from that point on, I

---

3 The last time I saw Sira was in the UK when she came to do her Master's degree. In 2011, I was heartbroken to receive the news of Sira's death. It shook me to the core as I never thought the day would come when I would get such news about my friend Sira at such a young age. I realized how short our time on earth is and so we have to make the most of the time we have been given as we don't know when we will be called home. Sira, rest in peace and thank you for sharing your short life with us and teaching me some of the great qualities you had.

began to establish myself as a hard-working and high-achieving student.

I remember during one school holiday in my junior secondary years, I visited my Uncle Owuna and his family. He randomly quizzed me: "What is the name of something that light passes through?"

I had just studied this in school. As I took my time thinking, my Aunty Vicky, his wife, tried to help and answered, "Transparent."

"No," said my uncle. "That's something you can see through. Faith, what is the name of something that light passes through?"

They waited. Suddenly, the word came to me. "Uncle, it's called 'translucent.'"

"That is correct." He grinned, as he and Aunty applauded. Then he said, "Faith, you've gone 'international.'"

It was an unforgettable moment for me. Like most Nigerians growing up at this time, I was aware that the ultimate dream and hope after finishing your primary and secondary education was to be able to go abroad for university studies. I was thrilled to hear that my aunt and uncle thought I had the potential to make it that far. Years later when I did, in fact, go "international," I knew they had prophesied over me without realizing it.

My family members spoke positively over my life, which was a blessing and helped shape my confidence and wellbeing growing up. The words spoken to us can either make or break us and affect the way we see or believe in ourselves. We must learn to speak positive words of affirmation over ourselves and those around us to instill the necessary confidence to face life challenges head on.

Another memorable event was when my Uncle Apiri promised one of my siblings a present if they performed well at school and came in the top ten in the class. I overheard this and asked my uncle, "What about me?"

"If you come in number one in your class this term," he said, "I will buy you a present."

I returned to school and all but forgot about his promise, but worked hard, nonetheless. At the end of the term, I finished top of the class. I went back and told my uncle. He was pleased and, true to his word, he bought me a dress as my present. This was a proud moment for us all, and I loved my new, beautiful dress.

Another proud moment was in my fourth year of secondary school, when we had to choose extra courses. I signed up for further math, which a lot of people said was challenging, because I wanted to challenge myself. I focused and studied hard. After completing our first test, I excitedly waited for my test results, feeling I had done well. However, when the results were distributed, mine was not included. Feeling concerned, I went to the office of our tutor, Mr. Abbott, to find out why mine had not been handed back. I vividly remember his response.

"I had to withhold your results so I could meet you in person," he said. Then he produced my exam, where I saw an A+ written at the top. Mr. Abbott told me how impressed he was by my score, and that he would be watching out for me in the future.

These experiences solidified for me that if I put my mind to something, no matter how difficult the task seemed, I could accomplish it and perhaps exceed even my own and others' expectations. This insight was fuel for me for the future, and it is true for us all that when we put our minds to something, we can surprise even ourselves as we are not always aware of our abilities until we put our mind and effort to work. Put the work in and soon enough, you will see the results.

Leadership Roles

The junior dormitories at boarding school housed girls from Form 1 to Form 3, and the senior dorms housed Form 4 to Form 6. The three junior dormitories were called Jasmine, Lily, and Ixora houses and were run by senior students called Room Heads. The four senior dorms were Bluebell House (blue), Alamanda House (yellow), Lavender House (purple), and Primrose House (pink). Each junior student was assigned to a senior dormitory when they joined the school, so you knew where you would end up. Your senior dormitory also determined the color of your day wear (worn in the dormitories after classes in the evenings and weekends). I was assigned to Bluebell House in Form 1 (though I lived in Jasmine House through Form 3), so my day wear was blue. Competitions and school events were done by houses. Whenever we had an inter-house sports competition day, the houses competed against each other in different sports like running, long jump, high jump, shot put, javelin, marching, and more.

In Form 4, I moved from Jasmine to Bluebell House. I soon discovered that I was once again at the bottom of the food chain, now amongst the seniors. Fourth years got sent to do all the "dirty" work that no one else wanted to do. A number of girls who lived in Port Harcourt became day students to avoid all this work, but for those of us who knew that our parents would not allow it, we had to learn to deal with it. I think this only made us more resilient.

Towards the end of Form 4, I was picked, along with five other classmates, to become a room head in Jasmine House. This was my first key leadership role during secondary school. It was a saving grace to be a room head, as we no longer had to cope with the difficulties of being in senior dorms. However, it had its challenges. There were eight rooms in the dormitory, which housed about a hundred sixty students. I was responsible for two rooms. It was my job to delegate chores to the junior students and ensure they were done. This meant learning to instill discipline in them, not harshly, but by talking to them kindly yet firmly and showing them respect and fairness. If they did their assigned chores, then it was all good. If they didn't, they were disciplined to ensure they understood this was not accepted. I found that, even at 14, leadership came naturally to me, perhaps due to having younger ones I learned to help nurture from a young age. My fellow room heads were also hardworking and fair, so we worked well together, learned teamwork, and did a good job managing our house.

Towards the end of Form 5, when leadership was being handed down from the Form 6 students to the Form 5 students, most of us room heads were chosen to be school prefects or captains in various capacities. I was assigned to be a house captain/prefect for Bluebell House. We, together with three other prefects, were responsible for the welfare of Bluebell house and managing the Form 4 and Form 5 girls to ensure order and a smooth running and cleanliness of the dormitory. This was the toughest task I faced before leaving school. I was dealing with older and tougher girls, who were stubborn and tried to make life as difficult as possible for the leads. I therefore worked closely with my counterparts to ensure we carried out our job successfully. All the skills I had learned from Jasmine House came in very handy, as I had learned to be very firm and take drastic actions in some cases to ensure discipline.

Looking back, I see how I was being prepped for the life ahead of me through these leadership roles. I took my duties and responsibilities in school so seriously that even though I lived so close to the school, I was one of the last ones to leave the dormitory to go home on holiday. I also made lifelong friends, whom I am still in touch with after over 22 years since graduating from school. In fact, as I prepared to write this book, I reached out to a number of my boarding school friends and classmates to ask them to share their memories of me at FGGC Abuloma. They described me as being hardworking, confident, very focused but not uptight, relatable, able to talk a lot, and able to deal with many types of personalities and characters. They knew I was God-fearing and spoke out for what I believe.

Here is what my friend and senior prefect of our 1997 set, Chinyelu, wrote about her memories of me:

> Though it's been over twenty years since we last saw each other, I still remember that first glimpse I got of you almost thirty years ago (JSS 1) in Jasmine House. Yes, I remember a tall, dark, pretty girl in a neatly ironed A-shaped (I think) Bluebell daywear, with a voice I still think was babyishly funny. I remember the countless times I noticed you patiently standing by the tap, waiting for your turn to fetch water. I remember the times I witnessed you opposing wrong behaviors and ideologies amongst our peers, despite your age. I remember your natural hair and how I thought I had understood what having a round face meant just by observing how your hedges were perfectly formed in axis. I remember those bow-like legs of yours that I thought were discolored towards the ankles. I remember you in quadrangle prayers—always present and enthusiastic. From these initial observations, I simply concluded that Faith was a church girl and must have come from a prim and proper, morning-and-night-devotion family.
>
> I remember when I had to work with you as Jasmine

House room heads. I remember how your voice, no matter how hard you strained it, could barely be heard at the gate when you did the countdown for the girls to either assemble or vacate the hostel. I remember all the mornings and even the six of us—you, Courage, Onyinye, Lidadi, Tariye, and me—bathed at the slaps. I can't forget the way you usually tied your striped towel to your chest, swinging your young figure eight so easily with your empty bucket dangling in your hand. I remember the times you and Courage insisted we prayed together as room heads. I doubt if you ever broke any rule as a room head or, did you ever join us when we skipped prep, made and ate *ebange* and concoction rice (which could have got us into serious trouble if we were caught)? Did you contribute your Geisha or sardine or spices? I can't remember.

Three things I can't forget about you: organized, spiritual, and a quiet spirit. Your Bluebell day wear remained ever below your knees till I last remembered you. You'd rather counsel junior students than bully them, you walked away from drama as much as I remember and could argue out your point to finish when you mean to drive home your stance. I saw you study hard, focused like you already understood life's depth, and I saw you so disciplined and mature.

I don't know what you do now, but my impression was that you were going to end up a counselor or a teacher. Truth be told, you were a formidable model to reckon with. I can't really remember just the two of us gisting or sharing moments alone, but I noticed and admired you from a distance. I have no doubt you're living your best

life now, Faith dearest.
- *Chinyelu Lily Chimuanya nee Ugochukwu*

It's interesting how people observe you from afar without you knowing. Even when I wasn't aware of it, people were watching my life and testimony, the grace of God on my life. It makes me even more grateful for my years at FGGC Abuloma. Through both the ups and the downs, I learned habits and virtues that have become part of my daily life till now—orderliness, compassion, empathy, the resolve to be diligent in the pursuit of excellence, and integrity in the face of temptations. True to its vision, FGGC Abuloma developed me as an accomplished female, and I am proud to be an alumna of one of the most prestigious secondary schools across the nation during my time. I am forever thankful that my mom encouraged me to embrace life at boarding school, even when it was difficult.

Exams

At the end of Form 6, we took our GCSE O-level final exams in preparation for university. Having been a strong student with top grades through school, I expected to perform well. Admittedly, my house captain duties made it difficult for me to dedicate consistent time to studying for the exams, so I resorted to cramming in the final weeks leading up to them, but I still felt confident that I could put in a good performance. However, during the exams, particularly during math and physics, I panicked and froze, which was ironic since math was one of my favorite subjects.

When I came to check my results, I was told I couldn't get them until I paid the balance of my school fees. However, my food and nutrition teacher, who regarded me as one of her best students, went and checked my results for me as she was hoping

I would have made an A in her subject. I happened to bump into her, and she showed me my results. I was shocked and disheartened to see that I only had one A in Chemistry. The rest were Cs, and I had only made Passes in math and physics, which were unacceptable for the courses I needed to take at college and universities. I couldn't believe it at first and thought maybe it was all a mistake. I decided to go home and pray for a miracle. I told my parents I couldn't get my result due to the outstanding fees to be paid and prayed that night for the Lord to reverse and give me better grades by the next day. However, on getting to the school the next day, settling the balance of my fees, and checking my official results, I saw to my dismay that the results were still the same.

I brought the results home to show my parents. Dad's immediate conclusion was to blame my responsibilities as house captain for not giving me enough time to study. In the moment, I didn't agree with him, but later as I considered the situation, I had to admit he was right. I remember asking the Lord why He would let my leadership duties jeopardize my exam results and not reverse my results. However, as my life has unfolded, I have come to see that the life skills I learned at boarding school have been critical in my journey. Meanwhile, not being able to go straight to university also turned out to be providential. During the year following boarding school, I was able to attend a prep course and ultimately take the Cambridge O level GCE exams, where I got the grades I needed for college. However, that year at home ended up shaping me, especially spiritually, like nothing I had experienced before.

QUESTIONS FOR REFLECTION

1. Looking back on your own education or early training, where can you see God preparing you for your role in the present?

2. What key experiences during your early school years have had a lasting impact on you?

3. I mentioned how I wanted to leave boarding school and return home. Was there ever a time when you felt like things were too difficult and it would be easier to give up, how did you face the challenge? Were there people in your life that encouraged you to do your best and not give up?

4. Have you encouraged others when they were close to giving up?

5. Is there a time in your life where you can now see that God's hand was clearly on you, even though at the time you couldn't see it?

6. What is something you've had to work hard at to achieve?

Chapter 4

LEARNING TO BREAK THROUGH

Kingdom theme: Our destinies lie on the other side of impossibilities, because God wants us to learn to partner in prayer and faith with Him, the God of the impossible.

I'll never forget the day in fourth year when Mom came to visit me at boarding school. I was fifteen at the time. She sat me down and told me that she and Dad were thinking seriously about sending me to London for university. When she asked what I thought of that plan, I was ecstatic.

"Yes, I want to go to London!"

The dream of moving to London for university studies had been growing in my mind since I was a little girl, hearing Mom tell me of her experiences living and studying there. I was fascinated by her descriptions of the electric trains that went so fast they could close on you if you didn't get out quick enough.

Then, in secondary school, I quickly learned that many of

my classmates shared the same dream of studying abroad, as did many young Nigerians. Following the oil boom of the 1970s and '80s, international opportunities and scholarships had become widely accessible and desirable for university students. Companies like Shell Nigeria offered scholarships as Corporate Social Responsibility, and many scholarship recipients finished with sterling performance in their respective fields—medicine, engineering, education, arts and humanities, science, and more.

My mom and her siblings, my Uncle Owuna and Aunty Data amongst others, were all scholarship recipients and studied at universities in the UK. They grew up in a highly academic family, as both their parents, my grandfather and grandmother, were teachers. My grandfather, Mr. Alexander Barasitamunopiri William Hart, was the preeminent schoolmaster and headmaster in the famous Bonny Government school for most of his career from 1929 to 1960. He was known for his disciplinary actions on tough students, molding them into shape such that several prominent figures in Bonny took delight in placing pupils under his care. Most of these pupils went on to become high achievers in our society. He was also a bandmaster extraordinaire and played several wind instruments, such as the trumpet, trombone, bugle, flute, and clarinet with a fine touch. He was responsible for the introduction of the now famous Bonny "Abara Dance" (a type of traditional dance) to the school. With his usual dedication and perfection, he trained the first abara team, which then represented Bonny in Enugu in the Eastern Part of Nigeria in 1956 during the visit of Queen Elizabeth II, the incumbent Queen of England and the former British Colonies, and they won first prize. Meanwhile, my grandmother, Violet Ezekiel Hart, was a school teacher at Boyle Memorial school in Bonny until she retired to focus on raising her own family. The academic heritage set by my grandparents encouraged Mom and her siblings to work hard and laid the foundation for their ambition to get to the peak of their careers.

After secondary school, Mom got a job immediately as a Radiographic Technician at the General Hospital in Port Harcourt. At that time, Nigeria was flourishing with the proceeds from crude oil, and jobs were already waiting for graduates, even those with secondary school certifications. This was also a spiritually rich time for Mom, as she and her friends were pioneering members of Greater Evangelism World Crusade, which quickly attracted young people to its open-air revival meetings. Many gave their lives to the Lord during this period, including my dad. Then in 1974, Mom was granted a scholarship for in-service training in London, UK. After accepting Dad's marriage proposal, she traveled to the UK to commence training at the School of Radiography, Memorial Hospital, Shooters Hill, London, which was part of the Woolwich and Bexley Area Health Authority where she studied up to 1979.

Mom's eldest sister, Professor Alexandra Data Hart, earned multiple degrees on her way to becoming a Professor of Human Nutrition. She received a number of scholarships and finished her studies in 1987 with a PhD in Nutrition from Southampton University, UK.

Mom's brother, Pastor Roland Alex-Hart (FCA, FCTI & AMNIM), (my Uncle Owuna) was an A student and a high achiever. He received a scholarship from Shell BP in 1970 to study GCE A levels in the UK. He attended the Loughborough Technical College, Leicestershire, then went on to the University of Swansea, Wales and obtained a BSC degree in Mechanical Engineering in 1974. He then trained as an accountant in London, where Mom joined him as she came for her studies. My Uncle Owuna was also present at my birth in London before finally returning to

Nigeria in December 1980, where he continued his profession as an accountant.

Growing up, I loved to imagine following in the footsteps of my mom and her siblings—getting a scholarship and completing my university studies abroad. However, my desire was to remain abroad to work, marry, and raise a family, while giving back to Nigeria through humanitarian activities. From the moment Mom told me that she and Dad wanted to help me get there, scholarship or not, my hopes and plans for life after school all became centered on one goal: moving to London.

However, two years after that conversation, when I finished secondary school and moved home with my family, it seemed that my dream had become all but impossible.

The Mountain

My poor O-Level results meant I needed to retake the exams if I hoped to qualify for university studies. My only option was to try and take them through an alternative examination service, but this was expensive and a bit tricky to find one that was reputable and honest. By this point, the Nigerian economy was declining after those oil boom years, which meant scholarship opportunities were diminishing and becoming much more competitive. Bribery and corruption had begun to proliferate as people began to take advantage of vulnerable students desperate to achieve an undergraduate degree. To study in Nigeria meant I had to take the Joint Admission and Matriculations Board (JAMB) exams for entry into university. However, this became a real issue for me when my results, along with those of everyone who took the exams at that exam center, were withheld twice due to suspected exam malpractices. Exam malpractice had become so rampant that unfortunately even when you refused to participate, you were still penalized for it, and there was no way of separating yourself from these malpractices at the exam venues. These were some of the challenges I faced in Nigeria, which only confirmed to me over and over again that my future was indeed abroad in the UK.

I began to formulate a new plan. I would renew my British passport, secure the finances to travel to London, find work there, and take the necessary courses and exams for university. However, when I told my parents this plan, I was shocked and dismayed by Dad's response. He told me flatly that they did not have the money to send me to London, and what was more, he did not want me to go anymore. In fact, he had decided he no longer liked the UK because of what he judged to be its negative influences on Nigeria (the British had handed over the leadership of Nigeria to the North, and Dad felt this was the reason for what he called the "Oppression of the South," where we came from), and wanted me to renounce my British citizenship.

It was a massive blow. As I have shared, living away from home at boarding school had shielded me to a great degree from the turmoil and financial struggles afflicting my family due to my father's fraught land deals and church conflicts. The only times these realities intruded were on those occasions when Mom had pulled me aside, often at the end of a holiday just before I returned to school, and said, "Faith, you need to start praying, because we don't know where your school fees are going to come from. You should also start rallying your uncles and ask them for some money." Obediently, I had prayed for the fees to come through and reached out to Mom's brothers to ask for their support. The money somehow came through every time. My uncles were always so generous and would give me the money if and when they had it.

Now these financial struggles, along with my dad's passionate and determined ways, my lack of exam results, and the state of the Nigerian economy and education system, all seemed to loom before me like an impassable mountain, blocking my way to the longing I had carried for so long. I had never been in a situation that felt more hopeless. There was only one thing left to do: pray.

There are times in our lives where things really feel hopeless and we can't see how God can make a way; this was one such time for me. My dad was truly a force to reckon with. You could never win an argument against him, so it felt hopeless trying to break through to my father to convince him that this was the future God had for me. Prayer had always been my fallback and especially so now that I could see no other way out. Everything was dependent on prayer; there was no plan B.

Testimony of Prayer

Mom was my first and primary instructor in prayer. She not only encouraged us to pray, but also showed us how to be a person of prayer and the Word. Her personal testimony of coming to Christ had always impressed me because it showed how her life of prayer and intercession came to be.

She told us that her heart first began to seek God after hearing the story of Nicodemus asking Jesus, "How can one be born again?" at church. This question lingered in her heart, and she began to pray to God, even though she didn't yet have a relationship with Christ. She specifically asked God to help her catch up in school, as she was years behind due to the war interrupting her studies. She gradually improved in her studies (even once coming third in a class with a lot of boys, who were all shocked how well she had done) and was able to return to her all-girls boarding school. She had to believe it was God who had helped her.

Then one day in the school dormitory, Mom was sitting chatting with four other girls when one of the girls stopped another girl passing by, who happened to be Mom's cousin, Iyingi. The girls asked Iyingi about her conversation with a student teacher, Mr. Sokari, who was one of the officials of the Scripture Union (SU) in the school at the time. Iyingi explained to Mom and her companions that Mr. Sokari (now known as Professor Sokari) had said they were all sinners.

Mom and the girls were shocked and exclaimed, "What! We are all sinners?"

When Iyingi nodded yes, a sense of conviction seemed to fall in the room. Curious, the girls asked, "What did Mr. Sokari say we have to do?"

"He said to kneel down and ask God for forgiveness and that's it—you will be forgiven."

This sounded too easy to Mom and her friends. They decided to track down Mr. Sokari and hear for themselves the proper process for being saved. When they found him, he led all five girls to the Lord in prayer. It was a defining moment for them all. Mom told us she had never experienced so much joy. Together, they started attending Scripture Union parties in school, where they began to learn how to study the Word, pray, and build their relationship with Christ.

One day in her final year at boarding school, Mom heard a preacher speak at a school service on the topic of prayer and fasting. The man taught that you could ask the Lord anything and be rest assured He would give it to you. If you added a day of fasting to it, this would intensify your request, he explained. Then, if you fasted for three days, the intensity would rise to a much greater level.

Mom was riveted by this teaching. At this time, her mother,

Mama, was ill and unable to work. Mom committed to fast for three days—no food or water—and prayed for Mama to be healed. On the last day of the fast, she decided to visit one of the Scripture Union leaders in the school, a fellow classmate, and ask her for prayer. The girl looked a bit puzzled to see Mom, but prayed with her anyway.

That evening during the Scripture Union meeting, this girl came up to share a testimony. She said she had been lying on her bed when someone had walked in, stood at the head of her bed, and said, "I am sending somebody to you. You should pray with her." She jumped up from the bed, but whoever it was had disappeared. The room was empty. As she was contemplating what had just happened, Mom walked in and asked that they pray together. Mom was so encouraged by this, as it confirmed that God was, indeed, listening to her prayers and had even sent an angel to speak on her behalf.

Towards the end of the fast that evening, Mom gathered her friends who had given their lives to the Lord to pray with her. While they prayed, one of the girls burst out speaking in tongues, although they had no idea what this was. It turned out the girl had not only received the gift of tongues, but also the interpretation of tongues. She began prophesying over Mom, saying: "The Lord says He will show you great and mighty things."

True to this word, Mama got well after Mom's prayer and lived long to take care of all her children. She spent most of her life afterwards with Mom and our family. Mom felt God gave her divine favor with Mama's recovery and she was able to enjoy Mama for a good number of years.

Just as wonderfully, Mom had the chance to lead many of her family members to the Lord. In 1971, she brought a preacher home to the family house, where she stayed with Mama, her maternal uncle, and other uncles and aunties. About ten family members were present that day to listen to the preacher. Their hearts were touched and convicted by the Holy Spirit, and all gave their lives to the Lord, including Mama. Mom was overjoyed. Mama, who had a beautiful voice and had been singing hymns for a long time, said, "Now the words of the hymns seem brand new, like I had never sung them before."

Along with these miracles and breakthroughs, Mom had also experienced spiritual warfare over the years. One of the most intense seasons of warfare occurred during her years studying in London. It ultimately fueled her prayer life and led her to more spiritual breakthroughs later on. Her experience ultimately foreshadowed my own, and I came to understand that I would need to push through similar barriers through prayer.

Hearing these stories growing up had shaped my understanding and conviction that God was real, that our fervent prayers and fasting matter to Him, and that He will answer our prayers in miraculous ways. Yet now that I was facing my own impossible situation, I had to access a deeper level of faith to pray and believe that God could move the mountain before me. Thankfully, along with Mom, God brought people alongside me to encourage and equip me with the courage and tools I needed. I have found this again and again through my life, that in times of desperation, God will bring the necessary people around us and the tools required to break through. We just have to be obedient and tap into these provisions and not seek to get answers in our own ways.

Learning to Intercede

One of these people was a girl by the name, Otonye, whom I knew from secondary school. Otonye was the chapel prefect during our final year at school. She always seemed confident in who she was, took her walk with God very seriously, and was not shaken by anything. I was most impressed by a story Otonye once told me about an injustice she had endured as a young girl. In her final year in primary school, she ended up the best student with merit at her school, and thus won acceptance to our boarding school, FGGC Abuloma. Then, shockingly, she learned that her acceptance had been revoked. She later discovered her results had been sold to someone else. Her family did not have the resources to fight this injustice in the courts, so there was nothing to be done. Though she wept and wept over this wrong, she did not give up and attended a state-owned school for a year and then reapplied to FGGC Abuloma and got in. I could not believe Otonye had gone through such a difficult experience at 11 years old and was encouraged by her faith in the Lord and her persistence. After secondary school, we stayed in touch and she introduced me to her sisters, Geri and Belema. These three women, the Dago sisters, shared a firm faith in the Lord, and we soon became fast friends. I discovered that they each had their own struggles and impossible situations they were dealing with, but they consistently responded to this by turning to the Word and prayer. I always felt encouraged by talking with them.

Otonye and her sisters also invited me to attend a student fellowship with them called Faith Power. Most of the students in the fellowship were in university, but there were others like us who had just finished secondary school. I had never met a group of young people who were so vibrant in the Lord. As I got to know people there and heard them share their stories, I discovered that almost all of them were also facing incredibly tough battles. Yet they were choosing to turn to God in prayer and worship to fight these battles. It was at Faith Power that I first remember us experiencing such an anointing in prayer and worship that we sang the same song for almost two hours.

Another person who brought me crucial encouragement and teaching in this season was a minister, Rev. Victor Uzosike (now Bishop Victor Uzosike) who I refer to as the Reverend. He was the patron of the Hallelujah Praise Club at FGGC Abuloma. I was a member of the club for many years and served as president during my final year. I got to know the Reverend well, as he supported the club members and organized meetings to bring words of encouragement to us students. At the end of my final year of school, we held a meeting for all the Exco members with the Reverend and had such a powerful time of prayer to send us off into the world. I still remember this meeting vividly, as it was a profound time of worship and commissioning. I believe this prayer provided a covering to sustain me and help me maintain my spiritual grounding as I launched out into the world after secondary school (high school).

After finishing school and moving home, I happened to attend a Hallelujah Praise event at our sister school, FGC Port Harcourt, as a guest. I saw the Reverend there and ended up confessing to him all the difficulties and obstacles I was facing in trying to get to the UK. I explained that my dad had said no to even getting my UK passport and certainly no to traveling, and even if he had said yes, there was no financial means for any of that to happen. I'm sure I couldn't hide how discouraged I was.

After hearing this news, the Reverend told me he would like to schedule a meeting with me, and I agreed. When I arrived at this meeting, the Reverend explained that he had brought me there to explain the principles of intercession.

"Your type of serious challenge needs intercession to unlock the answers," he said. "Here is what you need to do. Go into your room and closet, shut the door, and begin to pray. Pray with everything inside of you. Pray as if your whole life depends on it. Do not accept this situation as it is. People will wonder what is going on and ask you questions, but don't hold back. Let them hear you. It's no longer business as usual."

So, I went home and did exactly as the Reverend had said. I went into my room, shut the door, and began to pray. I first asked the Lord for the gift of tongues, my prayer language, and told Him I would not come out of the room until I received it. About an hour later, I started praying in tongues. I was the first one in my family to receive the gift of tongues. My family all came to hear me pray. Even Dad came to hear me and later spoke to me about it and congratulated me.

After my family left, I continued to intercede. As the Reverend had instructed, I prayed like my life depended on it. I was so loud that my family members came back to my room and asked me what was going on. I told them I was praying for a breakthrough. I had to call down heaven.

For the next two months, I interceded daily in my room for two to three hours. I also began fasting. As I prayed, I could see a mountain in my mind's eye. I knew I had to get through this mountain. I had learned some warfare songs in secondary school, and I sang them over and over. One had words like, "Mountain, you've gotta move in Jesus' name" and I sang this over and over again.

Another song had words like, "I am giving up no grounds because I now have a cause to fight for."

I also sang one about "Giants in the Land." This had words that meant "even though there are giants in the land, I am going into the promised land" - just like the children of Israel in the Bible did with their march into the promised land during which they saw the walls of Jericho come crashing down and the giants in the land conquered.

The same worship anointing I had experienced at the Ministry Faith Power seemed to fall on me in my room as I sang these songs. I would sing them and pray for hours, just building up my faith and trusting God. As I engaged in warfare, I felt like this was necessary for a breakthrough for the family and not just for me. We had been through so much hardship and challenges, some of which were generational, and I knew in my heart I had to break out of this cycle. I was contending for our future. Being the firstborn of my family, there was no other option or plan B. This had to work! My future was at stake. I was tired of the difficulties and struggles we had faced as a family and wanted to see a future for myself and my siblings. I had to pray! I also felt like I was contending for my calling and purpose, which was beyond going to London. God had a great plan and purpose for my life. I felt this deep down and knew London was a part of it, so I had to contend for it.

When we battle in prayer this way, we must keep our eyes focused on the Lord and stand on the Word of God and as we do we begin to see God for who He really is.

Through this time, the Lord strengthened me and showed me I *would* be going to London. I had this confidence in my heart that I would soon be traveling. I began to see myself being and living in London, and my mind became fixed on London. I prayed that He would provide the finances for my ticket, upkeep, and a place to live, and give me favor in my Promised Land of the UK.

It's very important when we are praying to break through in a situation or area of our lives that we persevere in prayer to the point where we begin to visualize the breakthrough. Our vision changes and we begin to see through our eyes of the spirit (faith) what is to be. This visualization is a necessary step to breakthrough. At this point, most of the victory has been won in the spirit and then we pray to see the completion, which is the physical manifestation of what we have already seen through the eyes of faith.

Breakthrough Begins

After about two months of this focused intercession, the first breakthrough came. My dad agreed that I could renew my passport. I think when Dad saw how much I had prayed and how hard I was working to go to London, something shifted in his heart. Of course, I knew it was the Lord working behind the scenes.

Then He brought another answered prayer. Some finances had come in, and my dad offered to pay for me to study with tutors and take the Cambridge GCSE exams there in Port Harcourt. I was so encouraged and determined to get the scores I needed for university. I dedicated myself fully to my studies for about three months, took the exams, and sure enough, got all the grades I required for college. This really strengthened my hopes for going to London and my heart was even more set on traveling.

I had my passport and exam results—two seemingly impossible obstacles had been cleared! The final obstacle was securing the finances to travel to the UK and make living arrangements there. I continued in intense prayer over this for a few more months. I also reached out to several of my well-to-do relatives and asked if they would consider sponsoring me. Somehow in my mind, I concluded that this was going to be the way God would answer my prayer. However, relative after relative apologetically told me that they didn't have the means to sponsor me. The day after the last relative turned me down, I felt this crushing sense of disappointment. In my mind, the battle was over. That was it—I wasn't going to the UK. Defeated and discouraged, I gave up and stopped my intense prayer.

A few weeks later, I was at an in-home session with one of my tutors (I decided to retake Additional Maths Cambridge GCE to improve my grade), and he started telling me about his life. He was a Christian and decided to share his faith with me. I had said nothing to him about my financial difficulty or battle I was facing, yet what he told me was directly applicable to my situation. He told me that he was an orphan and had been raised by an uncle. He became very dependent on his uncle as his main source of sustenance. Then, one day, his uncle could not provide something he needed. In that situation, he heard the Lord speak to him: *"Your life is not in the hands of your uncle. Your life is in the hands of God."* From then on, he solely depended on God and not on his uncle or anybody else.

His words immediately stirred my spirit—I knew this revelation and word was for me. It was as if the Lord sent this tutor specifically to minister to me. As soon as I left the class, I went straight into my bedroom prayer closet to do business with God. I first asked the Lord to forgive me for trusting and putting my faith in man, rather than Him. Even though I had been praying, my response when my prayer was not answered in the way I expected showed where my faith had been. I then recommitted to putting my full trust in God. I said, *"Lord, I thank You that my life is not in the hands of any man, any relative, and not even in my parents' hands, but my life is in the hands of God."* I also said, *"Lord, this time I don't care how You will do it. All I know is that You will do it in whatever way You want to do it. My eyes are completely on You."*

Sometimes we think we are trusting God, but really, we have put our trust in other things we are hoping will produce the answers to our prayers. We think we know the means or timeline in which God will answer our prayers, but we are completely wrong. That's exactly what was revealed to me that day. I had the wrong mindset, so the Lord was teaching me a necessary ingredient to the journey of faith: *total dependence and trust in God–all eyes on God.*

I then began to intercede and sing my warfare songs again, but this time, I went back into battle with my eyes completely on the Lord. I stood on Matthew 17:20: "Assuredly, I say to you, if you have faith as a mustard seed, you will say to this mountain, 'Move from here to there,' and it will move; and nothing will be impossible for you" (NKJV).

After about a month of praying like this, I felt I needed to start taking steps of faith. Back then, you could go to a travel agent and make a flight reservation without having any money. When the travel dates approached, you would pay to confirm the date, or cancel. I decided that was my step of faith. Without having any money or idea where the money would come from, I decided to visit the travel agent and reserve a date. I asked a friend who was in a similar situation to come with me, and we both reserved travel dates. When her family heard what she had done, they laughed, said the money was not coming from them as they had none, and told her not to do ridiculous things like that. Well, the date we had reserved approached and the money hadn't arrived, so we of course had to cancel. I told my friend that we should go again and reserve another date, but she said, "Absolutely not." She wasn't going to do it if her family thought she had gone crazy. I tried to convince her not to listen to others, urging her that when the Lord provided and she traveled, everyone would see why she did it. But she couldn't bring herself to take that step again, so I decided to go by myself. I carried on booking my dates and canceling (thankfully, the travel agent was gracious to me to keep on letting me do this), and kept praying and fasting.

After about six cancellations, my dad called me and asked if I had any travel dates booked. I said yes, I had just booked a date in May 1998. He said he was in the midst of a land transaction that had miraculously come through, and once the sale was complete, he was going to give me the money to purchase my ticket. Sure enough, the money came in, and my dad not only paid for my ticket—he also gave me money to buy things I needed for my trip and pocket money for when I arrived. I was going to London! It felt like a dream, but this was real and I was so excited that I couldn't contain myself. I danced for joy praising the Lord for His faithfulness in answering my prayers. My breakthrough had finally come in full, and I knew this was not only an opportunity for me to build myself up, but also to then assist my family and pave the way for my younger siblings. I was the first one in my family who had been born outside Nigeria, and I had sensed that this was a sign and gift of God that I was always meant to "go international." (My dad even jokingly told me to go to the hospital where I was born in London, introduce myself to the doctors, explain that I had been born there, and offer to support if they needed anything. It was the sort of eccentric and outgoing thing *he* would do, which made me laugh.) My parents, family, and friends all had high hopes for me to make the most of this gift and opportunity.

I was now at the point where it felt like a dream that I would be traveling, I was full of excitement, could hardly sleep and kept imagining what London was really like. When the breakthrough finally comes, what do you do? Rejoice, take it with two hands, step in with confidence and a new level of faith into your promised land and expect to see God in ways you hadn't seen Him before the breakthrough. This was exactly what I decided to do, I had prayed and waited for this, I was ready. What a great place to be!

Stepping into the Promise

I began preparing for my trip. I initially decided to live with a relative in the UK, but a week before my flight, this relative called and told me that the landlord would not allow a second person, so I needed to find somewhere else. My mom turned to her old contacts from when she lived in the UK to see if any of them would take me in. One of her old friends, who lived on the outskirts of London, decided I could live with her until I got myself settled. Thankfully, I was able to push my flight out a bit to accommodate this.

On arrival at London Heathrow, my parents had instructed me to call my Uncle Apiri (Chief Hart), who was doing some medical studies at the time in London, and he would give me directions to where I was to stay. I made the call. A friend of Aunty Data's, known to me as Aunty Liz, who was hosting Chief Hart in London, instructed me to get on the Underground and come to her house, and then they would assist me in getting to my final destination. However, on arrival at her home, Aunty Liz decided I would live with her and her family instead.

This was the biggest breakthrough up to this point; I had prayed through where I would live, and God gave me immediate favor with Aunty Liz. When God grants you favor, He opens doors that no man can open or shut, which is why it's important we completely rely on Him. The miracle with Aunty Liz was a door of favor I would never have been able to open on my own because I didn't even know who she was, but God knew her and spoke on my behalf. It was the first, but not the last time I would see how the Lord can go before us and speak on our behalf.

Aunty Liz's home was interesting and fun. The Arsenal football (soccer) stadium was within walking distance, so I got exposed to the world of football straight away and saw all the craziness of the Arsenal fans (called the Gunners) when they won a match. The household was a big one for UK families, as it included five of Aunty Liz's children, her niece Sue, Uncle Chief Hart, Aunty Liz, and me. I shared a room with Sue, and we got on well.

Aunty Liz had a bubbly personality and was very hardworking. She worked long hours to take care of her family and when she got home, she expected the house to be in order—I quickly discovered that if it wasn't, she had a real go at everyone. Therefore, we endeavored to ensure the house was in order when she came back home.

I found favor with Aunty Liz, so thankfully she was always lenient with me and we would spend hours talking. She believed in me and became one of my biggest cheerleaders and encouragers. She really made me feel like I could take on this new world of London I had come into. She also came to admire my faith and confided in me, asking for prayers from time to time. Aunty Liz also gave generously when asked and never held back, which fueled a heart of generosity in me even after leaving my home in Nigeria. It was also great having my uncle around. I soon felt quite at home having a family member there who I had grown up with. I realized the Lord had set up this household for me, so I could easily settle into this new country and environment without so much difficulty.

Aunty Liz's eldest daughter was Chi, who was fifteen at the time and what I thought of as a typical London teenager. She loved using a lot of makeup, doing her hair, and dressing up, and had garage music playing in the background in her room at all hours of the day. She also had a lot of friends who came round to visit. I soon came to discover that underneath all the makeup and teenage behavior, Chi was a really sweet and caring girl. We became friends and she would listen, intrigued, as I told her about my life in Nigeria. Although Aunty Liz was Nigerian, Chi and her siblings were all born in the UK and hadn't had much exposure to life in Nigeria.

My roommate, Sue, was a hardworking young lady. About a few months into sharing a room, Sue came to me one day and asked for the address to the church I had started attending. She ended up attending a service and came home and announced that she had given her life to the Lord. What a testimony! I was overjoyed, as I had been praying and now those prayers were being answered. In no time, Sue began to talk to Chi about giving her life to Jesus, and very shortly after, Chi accepted the Lord and started attending church with me.

At some point, Chi told me that when I first arrived at their home from Nigeria, she saw how different my lifestyle was due to my faith and she was so sure that I would eventually change to be more like her. Lo and behold, instead I ended up influencing her life to change for the better through her receiving salvation and giving her life to the Lord. Chi became passionate in her faith for the Lord. This was definitely the Holy Spirit at work.

Over the years, I've learned that when we pray for our family or friends to receive salvation, we must persevere, even when we can't see any change happening because the Lord is working behind the scenes. If we are not in a hurry but linger and do not give up our praying, we eventually get to see the result of our prayers. If you are still waiting for family or friends to be saved, keep praying and loving them and as they see Christ through your actions, trust that the Holy Spirit will bring about the change. I never preached to Sue, but the Holy Spirit spoke to her through my actions at home and she was won over to the Lord. Sue wasn't one that could be convinced by words. She needed to see action and proof.

In the midst of all these answered prayers, I had not forgotten the Reverend, Victor Uzosike, whom I hadn't seen since that meeting where he taught me intercession. One of the first things I did when I arrived in London was to write him a letter, filling him in on how I had followed his instructions and prayed and fasted, and how God had answered prayer after prayer and moved the mountain in front of me. I posted it to the address I had, not knowing if he would receive the letter or not.

Sometime later, I received a letter from my sister, Esther, who was attending FGGC Abuloma and was a member of the Hallelujah Praise Club. She said that during one of their club events in school, the Reverend shared a great testimony with all the students that got them all screaming and hailing. He narrated the story of how he had met and prayed with me, the former president of the club, when everything seemed hopeless about God making a way for me to travel to the UK. He never heard from me again until he received my letter from London. He showed them the letter and they were all amazed. He then encouraged all the students that the Lord could do the same for them. Esther described what a beautiful moment it was, with everyone praising God for what He had done. Some came to her asking more about my testimony, which she confirmed as true. Her letter truly encouraged me too as I hadn't anticipated just how much my testimony would impact others. It was my first big lesson in the truth that there is usually a line of people behind us in whatever battles we are facing. As we break through, we pave the way for others and encourage them to also trust God and take the leap of faith before them.

QUESTIONS FOR REFLECTION

1. Have you ever faced an 'impossible' situation? Did you bring it to the Lord in prayer? Would you do the same, given another such situation in the future?

2. If you are honest with yourself, are there any areas of your life that depend on man and not God?

3. What obstacles have been in the way of your purpose, how can you make sure these don't stand in your way?

4. Can you name at least three different times God made a way when it seemed impossible? Have you taken the time to thank him? Takes a few minutes to thank God for unexpected breakthroughs.

5. Knowing that your breakthrough paves the way for others and encourages their trust in God and their faith, how does that change the way you see the battles you face?

6. Is there an area where you are trying to breakthrough to be the first in your family to achieve? This is an area you are pioneering for your family and future generation, bring these before the Lord and begin to pray for breakthrough.

Chapter 5

STEWARDING OPPORTUNITIES

> **Kingdom theme:** On our journey to fulfill our calling, we will often need to redefine success to align with God's definition.

London was a fascinating and wonderful place for a teenager "fresh off the boat from Nigeria," as some would say. I loved it all—the hustle and bustle with lots of people, the London double-decker buses, the Underground, those electric trains Mom told me about, the corner shops stocked with flavors of sweets and crisps I had never seen before and the high street shops that all looked so beautiful. I just couldn't get enough of London. I listened to classical FM every day and absolutely loved it. I had dreamt of this since I was a child.

Of course, I hadn't come to London as a tourist. This was my land of opportunity, the place where I had come to train, work, and fulfill God's calling on my life. During all those months of prayer and intercession that had opened the way for me to come here, a vision had been forming inside me, a vision for who I was called to be, how I was called to live, and what I was called to do. I wanted to train for a career that would allow me to support my family back in Nigeria and the work of the kingdom. I wanted to find a husband and raise a family of my own. I wanted to be part of a vibrant church community, grow in my faith, serve in ministry, and grow as a leader. I wanted everything God had for me.

I didn't know how the vision was all going to unfold. I didn't have a scholarship to university, jobs, or any other opportunities already lined up. But I did have two things. First, I had the testimony of all the miraculous breakthroughs and signs of God's favor that had gotten me to this point. This gave me incredible confidence that what God had started, He would be faithful to finish. I also had a set of values, beliefs, and convictions that had been instilled in me about what it meant to live with a biblical work ethic.

I understood from the Parable of the Talents (Matthew 25) that God had given me abilities and opportunities to steward through hard work, and I was accountable to Him for how I invested these gifts. I wanted to get to the end of my life and hear Him say, "Well done, good and faithful servant" (Matt. 25:21). From the Parable of the Workers in the Vineyard (Matthew 20), I had learned that I did not work for man, but for God. I knew that no task or job was beneath me if that was where God had given me the opportunity to serve, and I was to do it with all my might (Ecc. 9:10) and "with all [my] heart, as working for the Lord, not for human masters" (Col. 3:23 NIV). Even scrubbing toilets and floors was preparation and a stepping stone for what laid ahead, so it was important that I did my best at it. I also trusted that hard work, excellence, and a good attitude would lead to favor and promotion. As Proverbs says, "A man's gift makes room for him, And brings him before great men" (Proverbs 18:16 NKJV) and "Do you see a man [who] excels in his work? He will stand before kings; He will not stand before unknown [men]" (Proverbs 22:29 NKJV).

Finally, I understood that the road ahead of me was going to be filled with challenges and obstacles that would test my faith and resilience. However, if there was one thing the previous year had taught me, it was that the true battle was fought in the secret place of prayer, worship, and intercession. That was where I aligned my heart and mind with the truth and stood in authority of the Word and God's promises to me to command my mountains to move. If I broke through in the secret place, I knew the breakthrough would come in whatever circumstances I was facing.

With these convictions in place, I hit the ground running to start my new life. The first task before me was finding employment. I managed to secure a position at a fast-food outlet at the Natural History Museum. I faced a bit of a dilemma when deciding to take this job, as it would require me to wear a uniform made up of trousers and a top. As a typical girl from Nigeria from a strict spiritual background, I never wore trousers and didn't use any makeup. It had been quite an exposure moving in with Aunty Liz, where they all wore trousers freely and used makeup. Even seven-year-old Helly wore nail polish. I decided to discuss this decision with everyone at home—should I take this job and break the rule I had lived by, or look elsewhere for a job? They all tried to convince me that there was nothing to it and I wouldn't be sinning against God by wearing trousers. Knowing that this was our background, my uncle also explained to me that it was okay to wear trousers, as sometimes it was needed out of necessity. He talked about when he had to work in Scotland in the mountains where it was so cold you had to wear a few pairs of jeans to keep warm. I thought about it and realized that there was nowhere in the Bible that said trousers were wrong. It was more of a cultural view, which I didn't need to observe anymore. I realized that the city of London, a melting pot of various cultures and beliefs from all over the world, presented a perfect opportunity to become more open-minded and ask myself why I did and believed things I did. Was it because it was what the Word of God said or was it a cultural or religious practice? God wants us to enjoy a relationship with Him without the restrictions of imposed cultural practices that may place unnecessary limitations on our lives. Therefore, I decided it was okay to wear trousers and accepted the job.

The Natural History Museum was a beautiful place to work. The dinosaurs were spectacular to look at, but the best part was meeting people from all over the world and becoming exposed to their cultures and how they thought. My work colleagues were teenagers or young adults like myself from various parts of Europe like France, Spain, and Italy who had come to either improve their English or spend time traveling. I also loved watching and meeting many of the tourists who visited the museum and lined up to get lunch from the cafe. The cafe was a bit like McDonald's, and we had to be quick on the tills to keep the long queue down. I was nervous at first, but soon got the hang of getting the orders out quickly and became one of the fastest on the till. One memorable experience from this job was that I frequently got compliments on my name, as I wore a name badge. I had never really thought much about my name and definitely did not think it was anything extraordinary until these compliments started coming in over and over. American tourists, in particular, would tell me, "Faith—that's a beautiful name," or "That's a lovely name." I was struck by the value people around the world put on having faith. The word meant so much to them, not just to Nigerians or my family. This experience opened my eyes to the value of what I possessed, not just my name but my faith in God.

I soon outgrew this job and spoke to Aunty Liz, with whom I was residing, about my desire to do something else. Aunty Liz believed I was more than capable of getting a better job, and challenged me to go to Oxford Street (one of the busiest high streets in Central London) and walk from one end to the other, giving my CV to stores and applying for jobs. She assured me that if I did, that I would get a job before the end of the day. So, on my day off, I did exactly that. I set out early with copies of my CV (resume) and began handing these out to the various shops on Oxford Street.

I came across a shop that seemed to me to be the most beautiful shop on the high street. It was a soft toys and cards shop and had an eye-catching display of gorgeous plush toys in the shop windows. I immediately decided this was the store I would like to work for. I went in, spoke to one of the employees, and was able to fill out an application and secure an interview date right away. During my interview, they asked me why I wanted to work for this company. I described my first impression of the store, how beautiful I thought it was, how it stood out amongst all the other stores, and how I knew immediately this was the place I wanted to work. The two interviewers looked at each other, apparently amazed and impressed, and offered me the job on the spot. This experience taught me that in job interviews, it's best to speak from the heart sincerely with passion, and this insight has served me well ever since. And of course, I know this was also a result of praying for God's favor with work.

I started as a sales assistant in autumn of 1998, just as the shop was preparing for the Christmas season. I made lots of friends in the store, all around my age or slightly older. I soon discovered that not many of my work colleagues shared the same Christian values I held on to. I remember one day everyone got talking about sex. I was so shocked when they started high fiving each other over when they had lost their virginity. When they found out I was a virgin, they suggested that keeping my virginity was old-fashioned and stupid and that I should get rid of it quickly. I knew these teenagers were either living in ignorance of the Word of God or were completely deceived. I decided to stand my ground in the Lord and be a light to these young people, so they could see Jesus through my life. I did this primarily by showing kindness and treating everyone with respect. I also talked about church or God and even invited friends to church when I had the opportunity.

Thankfully, I was able to find a good church where I started to meet and form friendships with other believers—Kensington Temple (KT), London City Church, a major Spirit-filled Pentecostal and Charismatic church based in Notting Hill, London. As I was now attending college part-time in the evenings during the week, and worked every day, including Sunday mornings, I decided to go to church on Sunday evenings. When Aunty Liz discovered I was returning home from church alone late on Sunday nights, she was very concerned, as she had heard horror stories of young girls being attacked and murdered on the streets of London. I was more concerned about not being able to go to church, which was a lifeline to me, so I started praying and asking the Lord for His solution.

One day at a church service, I met a family called the Lambos—Mr. Taiye, married to Bunmi, and their baby daughter, Joanne. I shared this issue of my travel home from church with them and asked for prayer. After we prayed, the Lambos decided to become the answer to my prayer! They agreed to drop me off at home every

Sunday after church, even though the church was in West London, I lived in North London, and they lived in South London. Aunty Liz was thrilled. This was another example of the favor of God and His power to answer prayer. The Lambos became good friends as I got to know them better. They were people of integrity, committed to serving God and open to being used by Him. When Taiye told me about his work ethic and how he worked hard no matter how he was being treated by his employer because he worked as unto the Lord, I knew I had much to learn from this family. He told me a particular time when he was mistreated by his employer who made him work very long hours, did not pay him anywhere near enough, and was rude to him. He focused on doing a great job and maintaining a good attitude. When he eventually left that job, he was able to secure a few offers that doubled his salary right away due to all the experience he had gained working so hard for very little pay. What a way to represent the kingdom of God! To this day, the Lambos are like family to me.

Meanwhile, I carried on interceding for my family back home in Nigeria. My heart was still very much with my family, as I knew they were still going through a lot of financial hardship and challenges. Aunty Liz and her family had to get used to hearing me pray and worship for an hour or two different days of the week. I also wrote many letters to my family and received responses describing how they were all doing, which I cherished. In one letter, my brother told me that some ministers had come to pray with the family to break strongholds. As they prayed, they received a revelation from the Lord that my dad had a child who was not present there. My dad confirmed that his eldest daughter was away in the UK. The minister said the revelation was that this daughter was interceding strongly for the family and that the Lord was hearing her prayers. My family was so happy to hear this that my dad instructed the family to always pray for me at morning devotions, which they started doing daily. I was very touched when I heard this story, as it meant my prayers were indeed coming up to heaven and making a difference. I decided to pray even more for my family for things to turn around.

This reminds me of the scripture in the book of Revelations that describes our prayers as being collected as incense in golden bowls in heaven. If our prayers are being collected as incense in heaven before the Lord, we cannot give up praying. [Revelation 5:8 paraphrased]

Promotions and Pressures

After a year of working as a sales assistant at the Oxford Street shop, I decided to apply for the role of cashier. When I didn't hear anything from the management, I started looking for another job. I applied for a position at the Home Office, went through a tough interview, and was told they were planning to offer me the job. In the process, they sent a reference request to my employer, which prompted them to approach me and ask why I wanted to leave. I explained that I had wanted to move forward, but since I never heard back regarding the role of the cashier, I had decided to look elsewhere. They immediately offered me the cashier job, which I jumped into right away. Later, the Home Office called to tell me that they were withdrawing the job offer, as I hadn't yet been residing in the country for five years, a requirement I hadn't been aware of. This turn of events was yet another miracle I thanked the Lord for.

I worked as a cashier for a year, and then in 2000, I realized it was time to move on from working at the shop. Auntie Liz had encouraged me to target the banks, saying they liked to hire smart people like me, and she turned out to be right. I found an advert for a job in retail banking, applied, and was offered the job after the interview. It turned out my experience as a cashier and sales assistant were transferrable and matched what they were looking for. I started at the bottom as a machinist, processing checks, was trained to become a bank cashier within a couple months, and after two years, became a personal banker.

My life was very full, as I worked full-time and studied part-time in the evenings. One of the challenges I faced was going to university after completing my HNC (Higher National Certificate) at college. At that time, I hadn't been in the country for over three years, and the first university I applied to had a rule that I couldn't be classed as a home student and had to pay overseas student fees, which were much higher. I had no way of getting this money. I remember crying and pleading to be allowed in as a home student, but to no avail. They told me I either had to pay the overseas fees for my part-time studies or wait until the following year. It occurred to me that one easy way out would simply be to lie on my application form and say I had been in the country for over three years (I was close by this point), but I knew I couldn't do that. In the vision for my life I had received back in Nigeria before coming to London, the Lord had shown me that one day I would become a leader. I had to do things the right way to ensure my records were kept clean. I imagined the press trying to dig up any skeletons in the cupboard, and I wanted them to only find a clean cupboard. More than the press, I had to keep the records clean for the Lord, so He could be pleased with me and use me for the plans and purposes He had for me. I therefore chose to do things the right way, and even though it was hard, I knew it would pay off in the end. I had learned that these small victories in life are the ones that train and propel you to face your giants and defeat them.

I didn't want to set myself up for a bigger failure down the road.

I applied to several other universities, and as I prayed, I received a response from London Guildhall University, who accepted me in 2000 into their part-time business degree as a home student! Thrilled, I dove right away into university studies while continuing to work full-time at the bank. I also got more involved in the cell ministry at Kensington Temple, which meant my community of friends and support network grew tremendously.

I will always be grateful to Taiye Lambo for giving me some good counsel that helped me resolve a very difficult situation in 2001. My dad had sold a piece of land in Port Harcourt to some buyers based in the UK and instructed them to pay some of the money to me to help with my school fees, which they did. However, due to complications with the land, they decided to pull out of the deal and requested I pay the money back to them. Dad wasn't in a position to send any money across, so I wasn't sure what to do. They kept calling and abusing me over the phone, threatening to call Scotland Yard and report Dad and me as fraudsters.

Terrified, I shared the situation with Taiye, who advised me to find a way to raise the money to pay these buyers, as it would be the best way to eliminate this issue. I knew this was the honorable way to handle it by taking responsibility and sorting it out, though I had nowhere near the amount of money and no means of raising it anytime soon. So, I began praying for a miracle. Soon after I started praying, I learned that my employer had decided to give grants and scholarships to students, and that I was eligible for one. I applied and received the grant, which was about the same amount required to pay back these buyers. The Lord had made a way! I paid the money back in full and have never heard back from them to this day. Praise God! I learned the valuable lesson of taking responsibility for situations and being honest in my dealings with people and this has always paid off.

Given my family's ongoing financial struggles, they were constantly on my mind, and I was always looking for ways to help them improve their situation. Around this time, in 2002, my brother Emmanuel was finishing secondary school, so I wrote to him encouraging him to study Information Technology (IT) at university as this had very good prospects for the future and a lot of young Nigerian men I knew in the UK were moving into IT careers. I also counseled Emmanuel to behave himself and take his walk with the Lord seriously. To my surprise, he wrote back to me sometime later, informing me he had listened to my advice and enrolled at university for an IT degree. I was so proud of Emmanuel and grateful to think that somehow, I had influenced him despite being so far away. It encouraged me to continue praying for my siblings and not take any part of their lives for granted.

In 2004, I decided to do my final year full-time to complete it in one year, which turned out to be a huge challenge, as I had to attend classes one full day during the week, as well as evening classes, while continuing to work full-time at the bank.

As my study workload increased, my bank began driving targets quite hard for personal bankers, as this was how our performance was measured both individually and as a branch and group. We were advised that if targets were not hit, this could lead to disciplinary action. The pressure of struggling to meet my target while studying full-time became incredibly intense, and at one point, it got so bad that I decided to shave off my hair, which I hadn't done since junior secondary school. I was discouraged, but it still felt like the right representation of what I was going through. This act was like a baring of the soul, sort of like the sackcloth and ashes instances in the Bible (Esther 4:1).

Eventually, the stress became so bad that I began contemplating leaving work to finish my studies and met with Pastor Amanda Dye from church to get counsel about this. As I reasoned with her, it became obvious that I would have no means of financial survival if I was to leave my job, and I knew that leaving my studies was not an option. She therefore counseled me to do my best to get through the year, as I would graduate in a matter of months. This encouraged me to keep going. Through experiences like this one, I learned to seek godly trusted counsel when making critical decisions or in times of trouble. This has always led me to the right path and is part of the reason I have been able to stay levelheaded. Some of the best godly counsel I have received have been from my pastors, mentors, cell leaders and trusted godly friends.

During this period, I received a phone call from an old friend from church whom I hadn't seen for a long time. This was my prophetic friend who said the Lord had prompted him to call me, and that he had a word from the Lord for me. He talked about some great things the Lord was going to do with my life, and then he said the Lord wanted me to know He cared about me so much—up to the hairstyle on my head! That was profound to me. This friend had not seen my new hairstyle, so he had no way of knowing I had shaved my hair. I knew the Lord was trying to communicate to me that He was present with me and cared about every detail of my life, including the hairstyle I was lamenting about. This encouraged me to keep going and not give up on either my job or studies. The Lord sends help and encouragement into our lives just when we need it. He is a very present help in times of trouble! This also was a reminder to be obedient to the Lord when He gives us a word for someone to deliver it faithfully. That word could be the lifeline for the situation that person is going through, as my friend's words were for me.

Post-Grad Life and Career Unfolding

In 2004, I graduated from London Guildhall University (which by this time, had merged with North London University to be called London Metropolitan University) with a 2:1 (second-class upper or an equivalent of a 3.7 over a 4.0 GPA score). I was so glad to have achieved a good result, though I really aimed for a first class (4.0 GPA). Considering everything else, this result had to be good enough and I needed to be happy with it.

In this season, I also became close friends with Sylvia, another girl whom I had met at Kensington Temple. I discovered that Sylvia lived close by, so we started spending time at each other's places. I got to know Sylvia's family, and we had many movie evenings and chill-out times. We also constantly encouraged each other in the Lord, and motivated each other as we sought the Lord for jobs and direction. It was a great comfort to me to have a friend who was as strong spiritually as I was, wanted to do things God's way, and was in a similar place in life.

Sylvia was fun-loving with a big personality, and she taught me a lot about how to have fun as a Christian. Sylvia had done Film and European Studies at Durham University and introduced me to different types of movies, including psychological thrillers, sci-fi and dramas, teaching me how to read these movies and understand what was going on. Over the years, we even found the Lord speaking to us through movies like *The Lord of the Rings*, *The Incredibles*, and *The Game*, and used these to preach to the youth and young adults we came to lead in the youth ministry at KT. Sylvia also worked on my outfits, teaching me to dress more in style with the current fashion. This, combined with makeup lessons from another friend, Nadia, brought me up to date in the modern world.

Another key friend I made during this time was Esther. I first met Esther at the youth ministry of Kensington Temple. I had never seen her before and thought she must be new, so I decided to go speak to her. After the service, I introduced myself to Esther and invited her to my cell group, but she said she was busy and couldn't make it. I persisted in trying to make small talk with her, but she just seemed uninterested. Undaunted, I got her number and promised to check up on her. This was a season in church when we were encouraged to reach out to those visiting or attending the church for the first time, make them feel welcome, and ensure they get plugged into the church.

Over time, I got to know Esther a lot better, found out she was very different from my first impression of her, and we eventually became the best of friends. Her nickname was "Queeney Empress," and I came to discover that this was more than a mere term of affection. Esther was named after Queen Esther in the Bible, and she had a profound understanding that she too was a queen, the daughter of the King of Kings. As a result, she walked in a high level of identity and confidence, which soon began to inspire and rub off on me. She also had a big personality, a love of beauty and excellence, and great attention to detail. Esther was, and still is, a big dreamer. When I first began to share my "big" dreams with Esther, I thought she might flinch or look at me like I was crazy. Instead, she told me my dreams should be even bigger! Esther soon became my dream partner and one of my biggest cheerleaders for steps of faith I was taking.

Along with providing me with a home and these dear friendships, the Lord also opened the door for my first post-grad job, and in an unlikely way. When I started job hunting after returning to the UK, I had hoped for a high-flying job in a

London investment bank. However, as I began applying, I soon realized how competitive these jobs were and that getting one was likely to prove difficult. So, I prayed and asked the Lord to guide my steps and signed up with a number of recruitment agencies in hopes that they could find an opportunity for me.

One day, one of these agencies called and asked if I was interested in a temp job covering the position of a receptionist at a small IT firm for a week. At first, I said no, wanting to focus on securing a graduate job, but the agency insisted it would only be for a week and I would earn good money. Well, I needed money, so I took the job. During that week, I did my best to take the receptionist role seriously, make friends amongst the thirty or so employees at the firm, and be as helpful as I could with whatever needed doing. At the end of the week, I mentioned to a couple of my new colleagues that I would not be returning, as I needed to find a more suitable position. They asked what type of job I was interested in and I said a graduate position in finance. They responded by telling me the Chief Financial Officer (CFO) at the firm was looking to recruit an assistant, since it was just him in the finance department. At first, I thought they were joking, as it sounded too good to be true. But later that day, I saw the CFO, asked him if he was indeed looking for an assistant and he said he was! I expressed my interest and he told me to send him my CV (resume), which I did later that evening. The following week, the CFO called me and said he had spoken to the COO, and they had come up with a package to offer me. Pleasantly surprised, I quickly accepted the offer. A one-week temp as a receptionist had indirectly been my interview for the graduate position I had been looking for! To me, this was yet another miracle, a sign of God's favor, and an answer to prayer.

When I started the job, I still had my eyes on investment

banking and hoped this experience might make me more competitive in that field. However, I eventually came to see that this job and career path were really the best for me. For one, it allowed me to maintain a good work-life balance. I had time to study in the evenings for my accounting professional exams and still be active in church with cell ministry, youth, and young adults. The CFO taught me how to run an accounts department from the very basics of the ledgers, both purchasing and sales ledgers, up to preparing the management accounts. This was a great opportunity and advantage for me as a budding accountant, as most places required much more time before they moved you up learning the various parts of the finance department.

Soon after I started the job, an incident took place that convinced me the Lord had planted me at this company and given me favor there. The company offices were situated around the Old Street/Moorgate area in London. One day, the CFO sent me to cash some money from the bank to be used to pay some wages. As I left the bank with the cash, I saw a friend of mine who worked across the street from the bank, and crossed the street to say a quick hello before walking back to the office. As I neared the Old Street Tube station, a lady approached and told me there was a stain on my winter coat. I looked behind me and saw that the bottom of my coat and trousers was covered in some kind of creamy substance. In shock, I accepted the lady's offer to help me try to clean it off. I took off the coat, hung it on some railing and started trying to wipe off the substance, which I realized was ice cream. Soon, a gentleman joined in helping me and the lady. After a few moments, both the lady and gentleman announced that they needed to go. I began to gather my coat and handbag, intending to return to the office and hopefully find a way to get the rest of the ice cream off my clothes there. That's when I realized my handbag had been opened. Horrified, I saw that the money I had cashed from the bank was gone. I began to panic. What was I supposed to do? How could I go back and tell my new boss the money had been stolen? What if they thought I took it? Could this cost me my new job?

I decided to call my friend who worked across the road, and he came straight away to meet me. I told him what had happened and my plan—I would go to my bank, cash the money from my account, and give it to the company, as I didn't think they would believe me. He wisely convinced me to first go to my company and report what had happened. He walked me to my office, as I was still in a bit of a shock and promised to wait for me as I went inside. I went straight to the COO, as the CFO was not in, and explained what had happened. I showed him my stained clothes and described how the money had been taken from my bag without my knowing in all the confusion. The COO responded by asking if I was okay and apologizing that I had to go through such an experience. He told me not to worry about the money and said they really should have sent someone with me to the bank anyway. He then told me to take the day off, go home to rest, and send my clothes for dry cleaning and expense it to the company. I couldn't believe it. I was so amazed and grateful. I knew this was the favor of God on me and that this was definitely the company I was supposed to work for.

This was another lesson in the power of honesty, integrity, and speaking the truth despite the perceived consequences. Speak and stand on the truth because, like the Scripture says, *"The truth will set you free"* (John 8:32b). I have proved this to be the case over and over in my life.

I ended up spending nearly three years with that firm and enjoyed my time there. I learned a lot from the various friends I made at the company. I also started a small Christian fellowship at work with my colleague who became a friend and we called it "God at Work." The COO was supportive of this and we got to pray for the welfare of the company and gave encouraging words to the COO when we had the opportunity to. This employer also sponsored my accounting studies in preparation to become licensed as a chartered management accountant (CIMA).

The next job I secured was filled with a lot of challenges but the blessing from that tough job was that I was able to start a Bible study group with a few of the ladies I had met there. We met at Café Nero once a week, and it was so lovely sharing the Word with these ladies and seeing them grow. There was one member of the group, Namali, who I knew had not yet accepted the Lord, though she was clearly hungry to know Him as she had agreed to come to the group. I didn't feel a need to force anything on her. I simply prayed for her, asking the Lord to minister and speak to her, and only spoke to her about the gospel when she asked and seemed to have an interest. I knew the Lord was taking her through a process. After I left the company, I ended the Bible study but continued to pray for Namali. One day, she contacted me and asked if I could meet with her. We met at a restaurant and she told me she had been trying to find answers regarding the purpose of her life and felt that she should ask me and that I would know the answer. I knew right away this was my answer to prayer. I said yes, I knew the answer. I spoke to her about Jesus and asked if she wanted to pray to receive Him. She said yes, and right there I prayed with her and she gave her life to Him. I left the restaurant walking on air, rejoicing and praising God that this precious soul had come to know the Lord.

Not long into a three-month contracting role afterwards, I began looking for a permanent position. At drinks with old work colleagues, one of them, Kevin, began telling me how he had increased his salary by almost fifty percent when he had left our previous workplace. Inspired by his determination and success in advancing his career, I decided to take a leap of faith and look for a job that was on the next level in my field. I began informing my recruitment agencies that I was looking for a job that paid £8,000 more annually than I was making and included a study package. Most of them tried to discourage me, telling me that a position like this would be nearly impossible to get. However, I was determined and kept praying. I believed that if the Lord made it possible for Kevin, then the Lord could do the same for me too. At one point, I told the agents to stop calling for jobs that were below my expectations and ignored all the numerous emails they sent for jobs I didn't want. I focused on only agents who listened to me and tried to find me exactly what I wanted. I also asked my friends who were my prayer partners and my cell group in church to pray with me. This was a walk of faith and I was determined to see it through.

One day, I finally got a call from an agent who told me she had found the job she thought was what I wanted—a part-qualified accountant role. This job paid my desired salary, included a good study package with study leave, and also offered free travel in London. This was beyond my expectations and I knew this was the job for me, so I immediately began praying and asking all my prayer partners to pray for me to secure the job.

After an interview with the hiring manager and a tough second interview with the Finance Director (FD) of that division within the company, I got my answer to prayer and was offered the job. This job was truly a blessing to my life.

A New Home and Updates from Home

After living with family, friends, and flatmates for a decade, I began dreaming and praying about owning my own flat. I had been working to put my finances in order for a couple years, using Dave Ramsey's "Money Makeover" approach to retire a debt "snowball" I had accrued through investing in some small side business ventures. I managed to pay off these debts in full by the end of 2008 and started researching ways to purchase a property. Thankfully, I was able to find a much cheaper place to rent temporarily, which meant I could save a significant amount a month towards a down payment. But given housing prices, it initially seemed impossible to imagine affording a place in London.

I was starting to feel pretty hopeless until a colleague of mine started telling me how he bought his flat in Stratford, London and talked me through what to do as a first-time buyer, which included researching for apartments and applying for government housing assistance. I did all of this and began researching properties, praying the whole time for God to lead me to the right place for me. I remember one day just being so frustrated with the search process that I went to the park during my lunch break at work to pray. Right after crying my heart out to the Lord about providing a place, I had a call from a property developer I had seen and really liked inviting me to come and view the show flat. My colleague, who was my prayer partner at work, prayed with me and told me to spend some time in the show flat, declaring that the property was going to be mine. She reminded me of the scripture, Joshua 1:3: "Every place that the sole of your foot will tread upon I have given you, as I said to Moses." I took this to heart and after the sales manager had shown me the flat, which I loved, I asked to view the flat on my own. I went in and had a prayer session in the flat, touched the tables, walls, and finishings as I declared that every place the sole of my feet tread upon was mine, that I would be moving into this development, and that this was all going to come together. After I was satisfied that I had completed this task, I went back to the sales office, where the sales manager began completing all my paperwork for the flat. Even the specific flat she encouraged me to choose was perfect for me. I applied for a loan to purchase the property, and after a few obstacles that were removed as I kept on praying, I was granted my full loan to purchase my flat and moved in late 2009.

Finding My Personality Fit

In 2011, I finally completed my CIMA exams and became a member of the Chartered Institute of Management Accountants (CIMA). Ironically, as I was in the process of achieving this major milestone in my career, I was also beginning to question whether I wanted to continue my career at all. I had been working as a divisional accountant for years by this point, and was feeling bored, unchallenged, and ready for a different experience. So, I began a journey of self-discovery to find out what career I should really be doing to feel better fulfilled.

I decided to take a Myers-Briggs test to learn more about myself and see if this might give me any insights into what I needed to change at work. The results of the test showed that my personality type is quite project orientated. I thrive when I have short-term goals and wins and then move on to the next project. Mundane and repetitive tasks, on the other hand, are a horrible fit for my personality, which explained why I was feeling the way I was in my current role, as it was filled with such tasks.

With this insight, I decided to explore the option of working in project accounting, and soon came upon an advertisement for a secondment (temporary job placement) for a project accountant at my own company. This job was the next level up and required more experience than I had, but I decided to apply, and once again got all my friends and cell group praying. About two weeks later, the hiring manager called me, told me I was the only one who had applied for the job, and invited me to come interview for it. I was pretty surprised, as our company was restructuring and downsizing at the time and I assumed many people would be applying for any available positions internally to secure their employment. I took this as the Lord saying, "I've got you. This is your job." Sure enough, I went for the interview and got the job.

It didn't take long in this new job to recognize that I had found the type of role that fit my strengths and personality. I thrived in this environment with the interactions and problem-solving required across teams. Being a people person, I enjoyed communication on all levels and was able to resolve issues just by personable and effective communication. I also had a great manager and senior managers. God gave me favor with them, and they opened doors of opportunity for a long-term role in project accounting with the company.

When I became fully qualified as a Chartered Management Accountant (CIMA), my company offered me a pay raise. When I spoke to my colleague and shared this news, he asked, "And you accepted their first offer?" When I said yes, he explained that his wife is a great negotiator and never accepts the first offer. This got me wondering if perhaps I had shortchanged myself. I prayed about it over a weekend and asked the Lord what to do. I knew I had to go back and put down a counter offer, so that's what I did. My manager ended up meeting me halfway between my offer and his, which I saw as a win-win. It was an important lesson that there's always room for negotiations. Ever since, my slogan has been, "You don't ask, you don't get."

About four years into my project management role, things became difficult at work. Management changed, recruitment was put on hold, my team shrank, and I found myself taking on more and more responsibility until I was doing the job of four people. It was simply unsustainable. When I asked to be compensated for all this extra work, I was told it wasn't possible under the terms of my employment—only contractors could bill for all the hours they actually worked. So, I took a week off work to get away, pray, and decide my future. The comment about contractors had caught my interest, and the more I thought and prayed, the more I knew that contracting was the direction I needed to head toward. It would be a huge step of faith, but I felt this boldness to take it. I knew I had reached a point where I had let the circumstances around me get the best of me. My life's vision and purpose had become dim, and discouragement, disillusionment, and burnout had set in. I needed this kind of step of faith to renew my life's vision and goals and reset my focus back to the future God had for me. I knew I had more to accomplish and do—ministry, international travel, and more—and I couldn't allow fear or my current situation at work to hold me back.

One of the practical things I did to rejuvenate my spiritual energy and vision and strengthen my faith was spend time in prayer and worship. As I worshiped and praised in my time with the Lord, I could see the Lord being magnified and my faith level began to increase. I began to see God's vision for my life again and I knew that He had so much more for me, and I couldn't stay where I was. I received a fresh revelation of how great God is, and this level of faith drove back any fear that would have tried to stop me from taking the step of faith.

By the end of my week off, I had decided to hand in my resignation at work, with one month's notice. I had no job or contract in sight. Some colleagues thought I was crazy or wasn't telling them something, so I explained that my confidence was in God and the future He had for me. I started learning all about contracting through some friends who were contractors, set my expectations high, and worked towards establishing myself as a contractor. Within two months, I had secured a temporary contract through a friend. This opened the door to a big long-term contracting role, which was exactly what I had prayed for and more. This contract doubled my previous salary, which compensated for all the hard work and late nights I had to put into my previous role. I was also able to establish a good work-life balance in this role and focus on building up other areas of my life. This was truly a blessing from the Lord that no man could have given to me.

This contract went on for about two and a half years, coming to an end in early 2017.

After three months of searching, funds were getting low and I was getting desperate for the Lord to provide a new contract. One day as I was praying, I remembered a prophecy I was given a few months back about a job opening that would open the door to me traveling. I listened to the recording of this word, and my faith was stirred up. I began to pray and declare this word in prayer, calling this job forth. After prayer, I felt the need to decide what area I would like to specialize in if I was to travel. Immediately I knew systems implementation. Therefore, I went to meet with a recruitment agent the next day and informed them that this was my area of interest. Right away, the agent said he knew of a job that traveled around the world doing systems implementation. I knew this was my job! As I was given more details, I immediately fell in love with it and applied for the job. It took about three months before the interviews were set up, but thankfully, I was able to secure a temp contract with the plan that I would switch over to this other job once they started the process. As I prayed and got all my close friends and family praying into this international job, the interim contract I secured was dealing with systems implementation, which eventually gave me a good footing to securing the international job three months later. It was yet another perfect setup by the Lord.

My faith was always the bridge between where I was and the next level the Lord had for me in my career. I needed to apply my faith each time to get to that next level. I have come to learn that God has so much more for us than we expect of ourselves so we cannot settle for less. It's amazing what God has waiting round the corner when we take those steps.

Through all of these ups and downs with my career, I was able to hold fast to the Lord because of the exciting and life-changing ministry I was actively participating in, including a new type of discipleship, and cell ministry that bore great fruit.

QUESTIONS FOR REFLECTION

1. Take some time to reflect on your own journey. In what ways is it different to what you had planned for yourself? In retrospect, can you see God's guidance and protection over your life?

2. How did you deal with the frustration when things didn't go as expected? In what way could you handle it better next time?

3. When contemplating big decisions, are you seeking wise counsel?

4. Can you think of any areas of gifting God is calling you to grow in? Is there anything stopping you from stepping out in that, or moving onto the next assignment?

5. Have you ever been tempted to "take a shortcut?" If so, was it worth it? If not, what did you learn?

Chapter 6

THE EASY FRUIT

Kingdom theme: True discipleship leads to serving, supernatural ministry, and raising up disciples.

DURING ALL THE UPS and downs of my employment journey, I was steadied and strengthened by the inner healing I received at my church, Kensington Temple. My first experience of inner healing was at Kensington Temple when they started putting on Encounter Freedom weekends (healing retreats). We were encouraged to prepare for these weekends by fasting and prayer, so we would go in expecting to have a real personal encounter with God. My first Encounter weekend was just for the youth ministry and was led by the senior pastor, Colin Dye. I was excited for what the Lord would do, and it turned out to be transformational.

The pastor invited us to imagine our lives being played out as a movie before our eyes. I was shocked to recognize issues with my dad, which I never realized were there. The years of challenges, financial stress, and spiritual warfare our family faced due to the actions of my dad all played out before me, and I realized I carried a lot of shame because of those experiences. I wept and wept, and finally was led to forgive my dad.

Pastor Colin, who walked me through that powerful experience, was one of the reasons I started attending Kensington Temple (KT), London City Church, in 1998. I thoroughly enjoyed the "revival meetings" held at North Acton (the main church building was based at Notting Hill) and found them refreshing, especially as I had just come from Nigeria and wanted somewhere where I could feel the presence and fire of God.

Soon after I started attending KT, I joined the kids' ministry and volunteered in the crèche for a few months. One day, I came to the church's primary building in Notting Hill and discovered that some young people were having a meeting in the basement hall. I got talking to one of them and found out they were all part of the youth ministry. They invited me to the meeting, which was called M'Pact, and I happily did, thrilled to see so many young people around my age. I started attending these M'Pact ministry meetings regularly, and in 1999, I left the crèche to join the youth ministry.

Everyone involved in KTYM (Kensington Temple Youth Ministry) was passionate and radical for Christ. Daniel and Linda Stenmark, the youth pastors, were from Sweden, and had the fire of God in them. Daniel had been part of a band in Sweden called "Repent"—that said it all. There was a high level of spiritual discipline in terms of prayer, orderliness, and structure within the ministry, and emphasis on holiness, purity, sacrifice, and being sold out for God. I knew this was my tribe of people and immersed myself completely in the ministry, attending both the services and

Tuesday morning prayer meetings at 7 a.m. About twenty or more young people would turn up for these meetings and pray powerfully. I never missed them, taking the Underground train before work to attend even when I lived a bit further out in Southeast London. Through these prayer meetings, coupled with my own personal times in prayer at home, my prayer life grew tremendously.

I remember Daniel mentioning how some days he would rush home after work to spend time with the Lord. He could just be hours with the Lord and loved every minute of it. I understood this, as I would also come home to spend time with the Lord in the secret place in prayer and worship and could go on nonstop for hours. My roommates, the Dago sisters, came to understand that prayer was so important to me. I took everything—I mean everything—to God in prayer. If I was angry or upset about something, I had been trained by my mom not to let myself have outbursts of anger, but to deal with issues and emotions in prayer. Every time, the Lord would calm me down and strengthen and soothe my heart. My mom had told me that as a child, I got angry quickly and started to react, but she would stop me right away and tell me to control the anger. Sometimes, I felt like I had this trapped anger inside of me and sometimes felt like I was about to explode. Prayer was my outlet where I could really be myself and just pour out my heart to the Lord. I cried, worshiped, felt the Lord's presence, and heard Him speak to me. Prayer was always my go-to.

I also became part of the worship team of KTYM as a backing vocalist and enjoyed every bit of it. We had rehearsals during the week in the evenings, which I ran to after work before my part-time evening studies. Many of us on the team had to fit this commitment in with our busy schedules—I remember my friend, Bola, would travel to places like Scotland for work and would literally come from the airport to rehearsals. But that was how committed the team was. Our hearts and souls were totally in it.

The G12 Vision

Somewhere around 2000, KT adopted the G12 Vision discipleship model as part of its vision for church growth. This model, developed by César Castellanos in Bogotá, Colombia, is based on Jesus' example of nurturing and training twelve disciples. The church forms small groups of twelve people called "cell" groups, due to the emphasis on multiplication. The cell groups were typically homogeneous—male leaders led groups of men and female leaders led groups of women. The expectation was that the cell group would train the members to become leaders and eventually plant their own cell groups. If you as a leader successfully trained twelve cell members to start their own cell groups, those twelve leaders would multiply into 144 people, which was called your "downline" or "tribe." If every one of those 144 succeeded in starting a cell group, the "tribe" would multiply to 1,728 members.

G12 was a very powerful model of multiplication for the church because it kept you from having to focus on so many people. You only had to focus on your primary twelve members, and then they did the same with their twelve, and so on. This helped to prevent new believers from falling away due to inadequate discipleship. Every believer is a fisher of men, but when we cast out our net to catch people, we want to be sure those who make a commitment to know Christ are not left on their own, but instead are trained up to spiritual maturity and eventually become leaders and fishers of men themselves.

The G12 vision was summarized by four steps called "the ladder of success," the process of evangelism that ensured the saved soul was not lost:

1. Win
2. Consolidate
3. Disciple
4. Send

So, firstly, you won someone to the Lord. Then you took them through "Consolidation," which focused on helping them get to know the foundations of their newfound Christian faith. This step included the "Encounter Freedom" weekends. The "Disciple" step was taking them through training to become leaders themselves. And finally, "Send" was sending them out to win souls and eventually starting their own cell, thus activating the multiplication factor.

I believed 100% in the G12 Vision, or "cell ministry" as it was later called, and even tried to raise some money at one point to visit the church in Bogotá, so I could see how the church had grown over there, but it didn't come together amid my busy work and study schedule. However, I completely immersed myself in the G12 Vision, and each time Pastor Colin called for meetings to impart the Vision into our hearts, I was there taking in every word. This Vision was all about people, which meant as a people lover, I was in my element. Even with my full schedule, I endeavored to attend every meeting possible, as this was where my heart really was, and ministry energized my life. Part of what I loved about the cell ministry was the mobilization of Christians from being passive to being active members of the body of Christ. In the cell group, every believer had the opportunity to grow and use their spiritual gifts. I felt this made the church more enjoyable and varied, as you could experience so many people taking active roles rather than just a few ministers doing all the work.

I was one of the first to join a cell group in the youth ministry led by a young lady called Vikki—a one-in-a-million leader who was passionate for God, lively, interesting, and creative. Even when we were the only two who showed up for meetings, we prayed over the empty chairs and prophesied for our members to come forth. Like me, Vikki believed completely in the cell ministry and was very much a visionary. She started to plan for our tribe long before we had one. She told me she could see the primary 12 being formed, and in time, our full tribe or downline, and even envisioned us running our own Encounter Freedom weekends, as well as a school of leaders. I completely agreed with her vision and was excited to see it happen.

Within a short while, Vikki had trained me up as a leader, and I planted a cell group in the year 2000. I therefore became part of Vikki's "downline." We had about 12 downlines in the youth ministry, which we called "tribes." The leaders of each tribe named them according to the vision and gifts the leader believed would mark their people—for example, "Pillars of Faith," "Kingdom Seekers," and "PH2 (Plundering Hell, Populating Heaven)." Vikki felt that prayer was the DNA of our tribe, so she called us "The Generals of Intercession," inspired by Cindy Jacob's book *Possessing the Gates of the Enemy*, which she loved dearly. We loved to pray and intercede and we had a chant for our tribe, which we did during some of the youth meetings: "Generals of Intercession, yay, yay, yay!"

Vikki and I ended up working together hand in glove for 12 years. By 2012, just as she had envisioned, Vikki was leading the largest downline in the youth, with over a hundred young women. She had an ability to draw young people in and just love and nurture them. Even with that big number in her downline, she never forgot anyone and was always checking in and following up on her leaders and members. Vikki's cell was quite international, which was a reflection of the large group of international students in London who became part of the church and the cell ministry. This gave us more exposure and a wealth of experience and knowledge about other cultures. At the time, KT was made up of people from over 100 nationalities, a truly diverse congregation and reflection of the City of London. It seems the nations of the world came to KT and then took all they had learned back to their nations. We kept in touch with some of these diverse women after they returned to their countries.

We made the cell interesting and engaging by going out to the streets to evangelize by giving out lollipops and words of knowledge (one of the spiritual gifts mentioned in 1 Corinthians 12:8) to strangers and offering to pray for them. However, Vikki's emphasis was always the intercessory spirit and the heart for discipleship. One of her beliefs was that "the multitude was on the inside of us." She emphasized that the pressure was never on us winning souls, but on being prepared and committed to take care of people when they came to know the Lord. She encouraged us to see souls in our mind's eye, know they were coming, and prepare our hearts to make the sacrifice of time and energy it would take to disciple them. Were we truly ready to pay that price?

Our tribe was in charge of step two in the "ladder of success" —Consolidation—which was a very sensitive part of the cell vision. This was the ministry that made sure that after a person gave his or her heart to the Lord, someone would follow up with them via phone calls and home visits, take them through some foundational teachings of Christianity, and prepare them to attend an Encounter Freedom weekend where they could encounter God and get set free from things holding them back. This would prepare them to start being trained up to become disciple-makers themselves.

The cell ministry gave us young people the opportunity to serve and minister in a way that perhaps we would never have been able to. We stepped into it, our faith grew, and we began to do the impossible. We prayed about everything and saw so many answers to prayers. At one point, we even had a testimony book where we all wrote our prayer requests and put in our answers to prayers, so we didn't forget. One of us would take the testimony book home each week and pray over the prayer requests for more testimonies to be recorded. We had testimonies of cell members getting jobs, promotions, financial provision, healing, restoration of relationships, marriages, exams success, and much more.

Within the cell, we encouraged the members that they could discuss any issues without being judged and didn't need to hide anything. Therefore, the young ladies knew they wouldn't encounter criticism if they were open and honest, but only love, a listening ear, and godly counsel. A lot of the courage to be vulnerable and go deep with one another came from the inner healing we were all experiencing as a result of the Encounter Freedom weekends we had been on. As I was writing this book, I interviewed a lot of my friends from cell groups and many of them talked about how special and deep that season of fellowship was.

I loved evangelizing and being able to share my faith with those around me. When I graduated from the leadership training in KT to start leading my own cell, I wrote an article in the KT church magazine, *The Revival Times*, called "Giving It All up for Souls." Though I was working full-time in retail banking and studying at university, I was completely sold on the gospel, and my heart was passionate about winning the lost in London.

In the early 2000s, KT had an annual conference called "Harvest for Europe." I particularly enjoyed these and took time off work each year to make sure I was part of the full conference.

One year, one of the guest speakers, an American minister, gave a talk on the Parable of the Hidden Treasure: "Again, the kingdom of heaven is like treasure hidden in a field, which a man found and hid; and for joy over it, he goes and sells all that he has and buys that field" (Matthew 13:44 NKJV). The minister said that he had "bought the field"—he had given up everything for the kingdom. This profoundly resonated with me. Right there and then in that meeting, I made the same commitment to "buy the field" and give everything up for the kingdom of God. At the time, I probably didn't realize the price to be paid—none of us really can—but my heart was set on it. I meant it with all my heart and have carried that with me everywhere.

When I planted my cell in 2000, I started by doing home visits as new believers were referred to me. I loved home visits because I got to know so much more about the person and their environment, which made it easier for me to truly connect with and also minister to them. I often got to meet the person's family and gain their trust too, which meant I could have a relationship with the whole family and not just my cell member. This connection made it much easier for my cell members to be committed to our cell group and receive their family's blessing to freely attend our weekly meetings, as well as other church meetings. Jennifer was one of our first members, followed by Joko, with whom I met at her home at first, as she couldn't make it to church or cell meeting due to work. From there, my cell grew steadily, though not rapidly as members—again, most of them international students and travelers—came and left.

Despite having many members around only for a short time, I loved interacting with such a diverse group of people from all over the world. These interactions opened my understanding to other people's cultures and challenged some of my cultural beliefs I had thought to be biblical. For example, I grew up in a church culture that viewed drinking alcohol as a sin. Through my exposure to other cultures, I learned that the Bible doesn't condemn drinking, but drunkenness. Therefore, I decided that though I didn't want to drink myself—I just didn't like alcohol very much—I could be comfortable with my friends drinking and take a sip from time to time without feeling like I was committing a sin.

My Mentor and My Making

In 2002, two things happened that forever marked and influenced my spiritual life and growth. Early in the year, I started praying for godly mentors, asking the Lord to bring the right older women around me from whom I could learn from. Just a few weeks after I began praying for this, one of the KT pastors, Rev. Ruthann Cannings, came and spoke at a youth meeting. Rev. Cannings was a beautiful black lady who was very elegant and carried herself gracefully yet was also bold and fierce for the gospel and spoke with such confidence. I knew this was the lady I wanted to mentor me and therefore decided I would speak to her after the service and ask her if she would do so. I was so excited I could hardly contain myself. After the service, there was a long line of young people waiting to speak to Ruthann, but I took a seat and waited patiently, determined that come hell or high water, I was going to get my chance to speak to her. Finally, my chance came. I introduced myself and asked Ruthann if she would become my mentor. Wonderfully, she agreed and thus began a long, beautiful mentoring relationship that continues to this day.

I have been so blessed to have Ruthann in my life teaching me how to be a godly woman—a woman of integrity and no compromise, who stands firm with the Lord despite the situation. Ruthann's love of God is displayed in her speech and everything she does. She declares the truth with incredible boldness and is admired by many. She carries a beautiful anointing with fragrance like a sweet perfume. A lot of the way I have decided to live my life has come from the life lessons I have learned from Ruthann through spending time with her, receiving her counsel, and just observing her life. Next to my mother, Ruthann is my role model, and I view her as a spiritual mother.

In July 2002, I attended The Call England. The Call was a movement started by an American minister, Lou Engle, to bring about national revival. Prior to this event, there had been several of these meetings in America, like The Call DC, where young people and church leaders came together for an entire day to fast, repent on behalf of the nation, and pray for revival. In KTYM, we started preparing for The Call England some weeks before the event by attending evening events at Westminster Chapel, as well as our normal youth services, where radical youth pastors spoke to us, calling us to repentance, purity, and prayer. These sessions saw a lot of young people running up to the front to recommit their hearts to the Lord. I still remember a youth pastor from the States, Judah Smith, speaking at the youth service about purity. I soaked in this message and others he preached and also bought his tape series on purity and listened to them all. I truly dedicated my life to the Lord and wanted the Lord to use me for whatever He saw fit.

The Call took place at the Reading Stadium in Reading, England. Church leaders from all over the country and the United States led us in prayer throughout the day, and various worship bands led us in worship. At one point, our youth pastor, Daniel Stenmark, called a few of us from KTYM to go up to the stage to pray. I was thrilled, though also a bit nervous, to have been picked as one of the intercessors. But Pastor Daniel, as well as others, had observed that I had been praying with a new level of boldness and authority at our morning prayer meetings. He recognized that God was doing something in my intercession that needed to come out at The Call.

Before walking out to the big stage, we were taken to several rooms, where we were prayed over by a prayer chain of intercessors, finally passing through a prayer tunnel leading to the stage. All these prayer warriors laid hands on us, prophesied over us, and prepared us to get to the platform. For me, this was life changing. I had never experienced this sort of prayer chain and I felt so charged up spiritually. When we finally got to the stage, we were pleasantly surprised to meet Cindy Jacobs, an American prophet and intercessor we had admired so much—the inspiration for our cell group tribe, Generals of Intercession. It was a big deal to meet the woman who had been like a mentor to us through her books and ministry.

As we got on the stage, we felt such a strong presence of the Holy Spirit. I knew this was a whole new level of ministry for me. To my surprise, I was the first to be handed the mic after another minister had prayed. As I walked up to the front of the stage, I knew this was a call on my life. God had set me apart to be an intercessor, not just for myself or the people in my life, but for the nations. I was part of what He was doing to release revival, bring in the harvest, and establish His kingdom on earth as it is in heaven, there in England and around the world.

When I reached the front, I fell to my knees under the power of God and began to pray like my whole life depended on it, crying out for people to be set free and experience healing, restoration, and revival. As I did, it felt like I was in a spinning wheel and everything was spinning as I prayed. I then handed over the mic after praying. Someone later told me they saw me on TV praying, as it must have been broadcasted on one of the Christian channels. I knew that this was it—my life could never be the same. Somehow, this event had marked my life for good. I therefore refer to The Call England as part of my "making." I will never forget this experience. Even years after The Call when I felt down spiritually, I would play the promo song that was used for the event and feel the presence of God afresh. I know seeds of prayer were sown into the grounds of England that day, which will grow and bear fruit in years to come.

Inner Healing

As I mentioned at the start of the chapter, I went through a powerful transformational experience on my first Encounter weekend (healing retreat). After hearing a particularly profound teaching Pastor Colin gave on "The Divine Exchange at the Cross", he led us through a physical act to enable us to receive our exchanges on the cross, and encouraged all of us to read *The Exchange at the Cross* by Derek Prince. Here are some of the things Jesus came to exchange with us:

1. Jesus was punished that we might be forgiven.
2. Jesus was wounded that we might be healed.
3. Jesus was made sin with our sinfulness, that we might be made righteous with His righteousness.
4. Jesus tasted death for us that we might share His life.
5. Jesus was made a curse that we might receive the blessing.
6. Jesus endured our poverty that we might share His abundance.
7. Jesus bore our shame that we might share His glory.
8. Jesus endured my rejection that I might have His acceptance with the Father.

9. He was cut off that we might be joined to the Lord.
10. Our Old Man was put to death in Him that the New Man might come to life in us.

Through this teaching, I came to understand that while I knew Jesus had died on the cross for us and forgiven our sins, I hadn't yet personalized it. In particular, I had not exchanged my shame for His glory or my poverty for His abundance. I walked through verbally making that exchange, and it was powerful! Wonderfully, the healing work God had begun in my life carried on after the Encounter weekend. For example, though many around me may not have sensed it, I struggled quite a bit with self-consciousness, especially when I was on the platform with the worship team, which was linked to the shame I had carried for years. After exchanging that shame for His glory, I began to walk with new confidence, and my self-consciousness fell away. I knew that when people saw me, they weren't seeing my shame, but the glory of God. My heart was opened in a new way to the love of God, my spiritual eyes seemed to be open in a new way, and I felt the Lord begin to show me fresh glimpses of my future and the things He would do with my life. Through this, I began to feel a genuine inner transformation.

These experiences showed me that inner healing is all about appropriating the revelation of the cross to dismantle the strongholds in our lives that hold us back from experiencing the fullness of who we are called to be in Christ. Strongholds are systems of beliefs and behaviors that are rooted in agreements we make with lies (2 Corinthians 10:2-5 NKJV paraphrased). The enemy gets us to make these agreements in moments of pain and trauma, then they come to define our reality. For example, thanks to the stronghold of shame in my life, I had actually come to believe that "self-conscious" Faith was who I truly was. When the Holy Spirit led me back to the experiences where that shame took root in my life, helped me renounce those lies, and brought healing to those original wounds, I could finally receive my true identity in Him—a bold, confident woman of God.

On the other side of these initial healing experiences, I became more passionate than ever about my faith and sharing it with others. I had a testimony! I couldn't wait to tell people, "This is what Jesus has done for me. He has set me free from unforgiveness and shame." The reality of my salvation had gone from head knowledge to heart knowledge at a much deeper level.

When the opportunity came to be trained as a guide or facilitator for the youth Encounter Freedom weekends, I jumped at the opportunity. I still remember the first weekend we led as youth leaders. We met weekly to pray and fast, and for three days before the retreat, we did an even more stringent liquid fast, which we broke on the opening Friday night. That particular weekend was so full of the power of God. We saw many young men and women being set free and delivered. Aunty Liz's daughter was at this retreat weekend and it was a gem to see the Lord do a great work in her life.

From that time on, I became fully invested in the Encounter Freedom weekends, helping organize, lead, and sometimes financially sponsor teenagers who couldn't afford to pay for themselves. It was priceless watching young people get changed and set free. I saw young people come to the weekend emotionally closed up due to wounds and brokenness, but by the end of the weekend, they were worshiping and praising God freely and coming forward to testify of His goodness. Unforgiveness was particularly a big issue a lot of people struggled with, so the session addressing forgiveness was usually where the majority of the breakthrough took place as they chose to let go of their hurts and forgive.

After seeing the results in people's lives, I became convinced that everyone needed to experience these weekends. Whenever I received a new cell member, I started praying for them to be open to attending one, as I knew this would set them free through the healing power of the cross and set them on their journey to becoming leaders. I also began praying that one day my family members back home in Nigeria, especially my sisters and cousins, would experience the Encounter weekends and come to be set free of life issues. I wanted them to catch this fire of God I felt inside of me and the excitement of total self-abandonment to the Lord.

Many years later, in 2011, these prayers were answered. I was able to sponsor my sister, Esther, to live with me in London while studying for her Accounting Qualification. In the same year, my cousin Biebele (also known as Bibi) also joined us from Nigeria to study for a master's degree. The three of us lived in my flat and they both became part of KTYM, joined a cell group led by my friend Sylvia, and attended an Encounter weekend where they both experienced profound breakthroughs and grew in their faith. I was thrilled! Not only had I prayed for this to happen, but had also mentioned to Sylvia that if any of my female family members came to live in the UK, they should be in her cell as I knew that she could really nurture them, which was exactly what happened. What an answer to prayer!

In 2013, we organized an Encounter Freedom weekend that was particularly memorable. Firstly, there was such a unity of heart amongst the leaders in praying and working towards the Encounter. We decided to deal with very critical issues facing young people and talk about issues usually not talked about enough in church, such as:

· Identity, the root of the issue
· Sexuality (including fantasy, pornography, masturbation, sexual abuse, incest, and rape)
· Body image, beauty
· Rejection
· Singleness and virginity
· Sexuality for men
· Work/drive to succeed/competence
· Forgiveness
· The Holy Spirit

By the end of the weekend, we saw so many young people walking in new freedom. Person after person shared about how they had gotten to the root of problems and strongholds, forgiven abusers and others who had caused them pain and hurt, experienced healing from emotional trauma, received freedom from anger, and received assurance of the future, revelation of God's love, the infilling of the Holy Spirit, and messages from God. (See appendix 2 for details of specific testimonies).

Another young lady also shared with me how she had been so impressed and moved by witnessing the unity between the leaders, me and my three friends, Sylvia, Esther, and Margaret. She said she saw us like a present with four corners being unwrapped and had decided to call us "The Four Corners" because we made a complete package. From then on, Esther, Sylvia, Margaret, and I began to refer to ourselves as "The Four Corners." As we did ministry together, we were later known by some of the pastors as "The Fantastic 4." I have to say that I'm not sure if we lived up to these names, but it was certainly the grace of God that gave us these experiences and opportunities to reach out to others.

My sister, Esther, attended this weekend, and through it, began her inner healing journey. I knew my sister had been through a lot of trauma growing up, which is why I had prayed for her to come to the UK, so she could experience healing and restoration. At eighteen, Esther had become pregnant out of wedlock, which was a great shock to our family. My father did not take this well at first and was very punishing toward her, depriving her from eating and spending time with the family, and even asking everyone not to speak to her. Teenage pregnancies were seen as shameful and much frowned upon back then in Nigeria, and it was especially scandalous for a good girl from a Christian family coming from an all-girls secondary school. As the news spread, so did gossip. However, Esther stayed strong and kept attending university, refusing to allow the pregnancy to deter her until she had the baby. In June 2001, she gave birth to a bouncing baby boy. Thankfully, by this time, Dad had come around to accepting Esther and her son and called him Obed after King David's grandfather in the Bible, the son of Ruth and Boaz. In fact, Obed became Dad's delight when he was born and all his anger towards Esther completely disappeared. However, Esther's life as a single mother had not been easy, and like many women in Nigeria, she hadn't had the resources there to pursue inner healing and had simply coped the best way she could. Obed stayed back in Nigeria with my parents, while Esther was undergoing her studies in the UK.

I had no idea how deeply hurt my sister had actually been, as I had been away from home for so long. Through the Encounter weekend, Esther began dealing with these issues and wounds, which took a lot of courage. Opening up the pain of the abuses she had been through caused her to spend many nights crying. All I could do was pray over her. The trauma was not all going to be dealt with in one weekend. Eventually, Esther was able to get counseling and the much needed help she required to take her through her healing journey.

One of the eye-opening moments of the retreat came as we dealt with unforgiveness and forgiving those who had hurt us. I was shocked when Esther came to me to talk about how much my actions in boarding school had hurt her and had caused some of her issues. When Esther entered boarding school two years after I did, she expected more care and protection from her elder sister, which unfortunately she didn't get. For example, I didn't always respond to Esther's cries for help or sometimes I was impatient and curt with her. I wasn't understanding enough at the time how much more sensitive she was to the hardships we suffered in school. On reflection, my own struggles to cope with the challenges of boarding school left me less than sympathetic to my sister's needs as I wanted her to figure out her own way to cope, as I had. I didn't always take the time to listen to her, so I was unaware of the struggles she was facing. As she shared these feelings with me, my heart broke to hear all that she had to go through. We were able to deal with these issues and forgive.

This was a big lesson for me in leading these Encounter weekends and taking young women through emotional healing. Up to that point, I hadn't really considered that I could have contributed to someone's pain and emotional wounds. I understood the need to be aware of the consequences of our actions, as sometimes we can hurt others even without knowing it. I also had to forgive myself and accept that I am only human with many imperfections. Thank God for Jesus that He has taken our imperfections, so that we can have His perfections.

My cousin, Bibi, also attended the weekend and had a powerful encounter with the Lord. She was able to start to deal with issues that had come to the surface since being in the UK. After that weekend, she attended a series of counseling sessions and other healing meetings and received healing and freedom from things that had been holding her back. This led Bibi to start a foundation in Nigeria called Bella Foundation, which supported the Ministry of Women's affairs and raised awareness on protecting children from abuse. She also gave some talks in her church and a few other places in Nigeria on the same topic.

In 2015, Bibi and I went to Nigeria and ran a one-day women's retreat in Port Harcourt with our family and friends and some good testimonies came from the women who received emotional healing. This was another answer to a prayer I had prayed from the early 2000s, that my family and friends would experience the power of God to bring inner healing to their lives. I know there is still so much more to come in this.

Through her own healing journey, Bibi also felt led to make a commitment and vow to the Lord to keep herself pure until marriage. I remember when she came and handed me a letter to the Lord and asked me to hold it for safekeeping. I very gladly did so and kept praying for her. In 2018, God brought a strong man of God into her life whom she married. What a great testimony to crown the work the Lord had been doing in Bibi's life.[4] I was able to send her off from my home like a proud mother. I couldn't have been more excited for Bibi's wedding and marriage, yet at the same time, I was longing for God to answer my own prayers for a husband and a family. It would take me some time to develop my own testimony in the area of singleness and marriage.

4 Bibi wanted me to end this story with her own words about me: "You are a role model to me and I have learned a lot of life skills from you which is still helping me today."

QUESTIONS FOR REFLECTION

1. Are you being discipled by someone? If not, is there someone you could seek to be discipled by? Are you discipling someone? Pray and ask the Lord to send you someone to be discipled by and someone you can disciple.

2. Can you make your own example of a cell group in your life, even if your 12 consists of your own household, family, friends, or anyone? How can you start to disciple them?
If you did have a tribe group, what name would mark the vision and gifts of your tribe (this could apply to your household or family, too)?

3. Is there anything - anything at all - that you need to take to God in prayer right now?

4. I took everything - I mean everything - to God in prayer." What kind of things do you bring to God in prayer? Do you bring your anger, frustration, and disappointments to Him, as well as your dreams, desires, and excitement?

5. Have you ever had a transformative moment like I had at The Call England? Do you ever take the time to reflect on it? This could be a 'first love' memory that marks the foundation for your life in Christ. Just as I liked going back to the promo song from The Call, do you find it helpful to remember a marker of change in your life from darkness to light? Can you find motivation from these to carry on and look forward to the hope ahead?

Chapter 7

DESIRE AND DISAPPOINTMENT

Kingdom theme: None of us can avoid testing and trials, sacrifice, and obedience. These are what shape the interior depth of trust and character like nothing *else.*

I PUT THE ISSUE of singleness and marriage in the same category as loving and serving the Lord. Both are matters of the heart. The Bible says, *"For where your treasure is, there will your heart be also"* (Matthew 6:21). My treasure and heart have been in the kingdom of God since I gave my life to the Lord. I surrendered to Him absolutely everything concerning my life, including who I would end up with in marriage. At 17, I declared to the Lord, "My life is not in the hands of any man. My life is in the hand of God." That has been my anchor ever since, and I know I can always go back to the Lord to inquire about any struggles or disappointments, in the area of longing for marriage and any other areas, rather than blaming or depending on any man.

I started praying for marriage when I was 19, as I became more aware that I would like to be married one day. I already had young men who had approached me concerning marriage, but nothing came of these offers, as they were either not born-again Christians or I did not think we were meant to be together.

There was one particular guy I really liked who was very interested in me. This was my first "temptation." I felt such an attraction to just go out with this young man. However, he wasn't a committed Christian and had a complex situation—I'll just leave it at that—which I knew would be too difficult to get involved in. I knew deep down it wasn't right and I had to say no. So, even though my body was almost saying yes, my mouth kept saying no, and I prayed earnestly that the Lord would help me fully shut the door on it.

I had to learn self-control through this experience, as a young woman with so much love and desire on the inside waiting to come out and be expressed. Even Aunty Liz, whom I lived with at the time, was surprised that I would say no, as she knew how much this meant to me, but I knew in my heart this relationship was just not right for me and more importantly, that it was not what the Lord would want for me. This was the beginning of "putting God first" for the sake of my love for Him and wanting to please Him above all else. I had to choose between the Lord and this man, and I chose the Lord. I had to dig in my heels and endure this short-term, difficult "loss" for a much longer-term gain, as I knew the Lord had some good things in store for my future and I was truly excited and confident in that future. It *was* painful, but as I leaned on the everlasting arms of the Father, it made my love for the Lord much stronger and fiercer than before. I am a naturally passionate person with a tendency for extremes, so I either really believe and give my heart completely to something or I don't do it at all. It's almost "all or nothing" for me in matters of the heart, so the experience I had in making a choice between the Lord and this man was my process of learning to guard my heart.

As I mentioned in a previous chapter, in 1999, at 19 years old, I started working for a card and soft toys retail company during the Christmas holidays. Valentine's Day soon followed and was one of our biggest sale periods. For weeks, I was surrounded by people coming to buy Valentine cards and presents for their loved ones, as well as friends buying and receiving Valentine presents from boyfriends and girlfriends. As I worked on the shop floor, I couldn't help but ask, "What about me, Lord?" But I knew I had to just take my eyes off all of that and focus on Him, even as I was in the store full-time watching all the excitement and listening to all the love songs playing in the background. I knew I could trust the Lord even with this area of my life and that He could truly give me the best love story.

During this period, I met this wonderful friend who became an older sister to me—Big Sis Tola. Tola and I found out we were not just both from Nigeria, but had lived in Port Harcourt, attended Federal Government colleges, and had some mutual connections, so we clicked straight away. For me, this was a God arrangement to find a sister-like figure in such a workplace. Tola saw that I was quite naive, took me under her wings, and began to open my eyes to the ways of the world. I remember meeting a particular guy in the Tesco's down the road. I began going to Tesco's for lunch in the hope that I could see him and chat with him. (When I got my next bank statement, I realized I had spent so much of my money at Tesco due to this "Tesco guy.") He was interested in me and I liked him a lot, but Tola advised me that if I went out with this guy, I would most likely compromise my standards as a Christian. I absolutely did not want to compromise my standards and told Tola this, so she said that settled it—I could not have a relationship with this young man. Despite my flesh screaming for that, I knew I had to hold back and die to that desire. I am thankful to Tola, whom the Lord used to support and strengthen me and give me perspective in an environment where most people were doing the exact opposite. It was the grace of God that kept me from going against the grain and helped me stand my ground.

From my teens, I practiced these Scriptures fiercely—*"Abstain from all appearance of evil"* (1 Thessalonians 5:22 KJV) and *"Flee youthful lusts"* (2 Timothy 2:22). These verses were a "lamp unto my feet " in those days. I did not even give myself the opportunity to come into compromising situations. I had to learn to be discerning as I matured into a young adult. Once I discerned something that was even slightly off, I would change course and walk somewhere else. If anyone tried something against my will, I would leave the situation, avoid them completely, speak to someone for counseling, or go into my prayer closet and pray. I fled at all costs, even if it meant moving house. Somehow, God gave me the wisdom from a young age to be radical about every area of my life and not to compromise or give any room to the enemy.

I think perhaps a part of this came from having a strict father. He encouraged us his children to keep ourselves for the Lord and serve Him, including guarding ourselves against sexual sins. I saw some of my older relatives get into serious trouble at home when they were thought to have behaved inappropriately. This helped me make up my mind to fiercely guard against falling into compromising situations that could lead to sexual sins. I decided to "set my face like flint" (Isaiah 50:7 KJV) in this area. I said, "God, I do not ever want to be caught out." I'm grateful for the lessons the Lord taught me because they worked.

About the age of 22, at a youth conference in London, I made a signed covenant to keep myself pure, to completely abstain from sex and kissing, and wait for my first kiss at the altar when I got married. I had read books like *Passion and Purity* by Elisabeth Elliot that encouraged me in my vow of purity. I also read *When God Writes Your Love Story* and *When Dreams Come True* by Eric and Leslie Ludy and completely agreed with all they said about "complete self-abandonment" to God. Leslie decided in addition to abstinence to have her first kiss at the altar, and I wholeheartedly agreed with this and decided to add that to my covenant to the Lord.

I didn't just sign the piece of paper the pastor at the conference gave to us—I signed on my heart, and years after the paper was lost, I carried this covenant inside me. I did this because I had such a deep love for the Lord and wanted to give Him everything possible I could offer up for His glory. I didn't really tell people about this covenant, though, as firstly I thought it was private between me and the Lord. I also didn't want to be criticized, as I knew this was a bit of a radical step. But I thrived in being radical for the Lord, so for me, this was the obvious way to live my life. In a way, I lived a very narrow life. I knew exactly what my mission was for the Lord and that drove every aspect of my life at home, church, and the workplace.

Not the One

In my early twenties, a young man expressed his interest in me. He respectfully went through all the right channels to express his interest, which impressed me. We finally went on a date. He was very respectful and nice, but for some reason I didn't understand, I became so nervous during the date that I couldn't eat any of my food at dinner. My anxiety persisted throughout the date, and by the time I got home, I was so agitated I couldn't sleep.

Unable to put my finger on where this anxiety was coming from, I finally decided to go to counseling. As I talked about the experience with the counselor, we uncovered the reality that I was carrying a deep fear about marriage connected to living through the turbulence of my parents' marriage. The counselor prayed with me, taking my pain and trauma to the cross and exchanging it for Jesus' peace and healing. I received the truth that what my parents lived through didn't have to be my story and felt such freedom!

However, despite feeling much better after counseling, I still didn't feel settled about continuing to date this young man. He kept pursuing me and clearly liked me, but I just didn't feel the same conviction that we were a match. One day as I processed my thoughts and feelings about the relationship with a close friend, she stopped and said, "Faith, this should be simple. Just answer this question: If this guy today says to you, 'Marry me,' would you say yes or no?"

I hesitated. "Well . . ." I began to explain that if certain things changed, I could see marriage being on the table, but she interrupted me.

"No, don't think about if anything changes," she said. "Just think about right now, as things are. Just say yes or no."

"No."

"Then there's your answer."

And she was right. As soon as I said no, I felt better. I had been feeling so much pressure to say yes and make this guy work, but once I had confessed my true feelings, that burden had lifted. That ended things with the young man. I learned a valuable lesson from the situation—to trust how I feel deep down and not ignore those feelings, as they are part of who I am and the Holy Spirit can speak to me through them. I remember a few friends challenging me about my decision as they felt this young man was a great guy, but I had to follow my heart. I had a strong sense of conviction in my heart that the Lord was fully in control of my life and the path I was on. Even though I didn't fully understand all that was in my heart, I trusted the Lord that He would guide me through as I depended on Him. I felt the Lord give me a word after I knew the answer was a "no," the verse, *"He has made everything beautiful in its time"* (Ecclesiastes 3:11a NKJV). I read it as a promise that "He makes all things beautiful in its time," and I felt a deep sense of peace with this word that the Lord would make things beautiful in my life concerning marriage at the right time.

Around this time, I was getting to be good friends with Mary, one of the girls I met at the church. We confided our hopes and dreams for marriage to each other and began to pray regularly together for our future husbands. I introduced Mary to a guy friend, Alex, at an event we all attended. Alex was the guy I liked at the time, but I hadn't said anything to him, as I thought the guy should make the first move if he was interested and I wasn't sure he was interested. Alex once joked with me that he felt my husband would be an angel dropped from heaven in the form of a man. I laughed and thought to myself, *If only he knew what I was thinking—he could be that man.*

When I introduced Mary to Alex, I went all out talking up Mary's good qualities, because I was proud of her. Alex joked that I was trying to sell my friend to him, but I said, "No, I'm just speaking the truth."

Sometime later, Mary and I were hanging out chatting and decided to tell each other who we liked. She asked me to go first and I confessed I liked Alex, that things were looking favorable in terms of us potentially getting together, and that he just seemed really nice. After a few minutes of going on about him, I was stunned to see tears welling up in Mary's eyes. Immediately concerned, I asked her what was wrong.

"You're just so lucky," she said. "He sounds great and his family really does seem lovely."

"Well, I don't know if anything is going to happen." I laughed, a bit perplexed by her emotional reaction. "I just like him. What about you? Who do you like?"

Mary seemed a bit flustered and was still crying. She told me she was interested in a pastor who was recently divorced and she didn't feel hopeful that he was interested in pursuing another relationship. I presumed this must be why she was crying so much. We talked about him for a bit and then moved on to other subjects.

Some days later after a church event we attended, Mary came to my flat for a sleepover, opened up, and said, "Faith, I have a confession to make. The reason I was crying the other day was because I actually like the same guy you like, Alex."

"Okay . . . wow." I didn't see that one coming at all. What did one do when two close friends liked the same guy? I stood in silence for a while to take in what Mary had said. I felt this was definitely a test of our friendship. Of course, I realized this was the reason Mary didn't want to tell me in the first place, but she felt convicted for lying and confessed the truth. I also felt convicted as she shared this, that I shouldn't have been too presumptuous about the chances I thought I had with Alex. I later scolded myself over talking too much. Why did I keep going on about this guy to Mary, not knowing she also liked him and thought from all I had said I had a better chance than she did, which is why she was crying? I was grateful for Mary's honesty, as I knew this must have been difficult to admit. That night as we talked about the situation, we felt a Holy Spirit moment where we laid it before the

Lord. We were not going to let the fact that we liked the same guy ruin our friendship.

Sometime later, Alex contacted me and asked if I could give him Mary's contact details. As painful as this was to my heart, I went to her and said, "Mary, I think he is interested in you. He asked me for your number, can I give it to him?" I also explained to Mary that she had my blessing to pursue the relationship if she wanted to, so she agreed. I knew I had to release Alex from my heart and not hold Mary back from what could potentially be for her, even though it was what I desired also. I knew to keep my heart right before the Lord, I had to act in love towards Mary and give her my blessing without any resentment.

In no time, Mary and Alex were dating. I won't lie; it was painful that Alex picked her instead of me, but I knew I had to guard my heart from bitterness. I was happy for Mary—at least one of us was now in a relationship. Though it meant dying to my flesh, I chose to protect my friendship with Mary and trust that the Lord had someone in store for me who was better than any guy I could have picked for myself. I remembered the word the Lord had given to me, that He would "make all things beautiful in its time" concerning my life, and this gave me a sense of peace in the midst of this emotional storm. Deep down, I also felt that a guy interested in me would pursue me, and if he didn't, then he was not for me. I felt that in this case, and I therefore wished Mary the best in her relationship with Alex. However, it was a tough period for me, as it was rare that I liked a guy as much as I liked Alex. I also remembered my revelation from the Lord that "my life was not in the hands of any man—my life was in the hands of God," and this strengthened me to trust that the Lord had the best in store for me. My friend, Bunmi, was a big support to me during this season, encouraging me that mine would come.

In the end, Mary and Alex broke up, but in another year or so, she met her husband and got married. We had been praying for our husbands together for two years at that point, and I figured that now that her prayer was answered, it was my turn next. I even received a few prophetic words at church about marriage. My hopes were high.

Out of the blue, I received a call from a childhood friend in Nigeria, Luke, whom I hadn't spoken to in years. We began to catch up, and after a few long phone calls, he confessed that he was interested in me. I don't know why, but for some reason, it was like this lightbulb flashed on and I just knew he was my guy. He was a Christian. He knew Scripture. I knew and loved his family, and they were close to my family. This was it. Everything fit. I told Luke that I liked him too, and that was that—we were in a relationship, a serious relationship. In no time, we were unofficially engaged, and I began making plans to come home to Nigeria for Christmas to see him.

As the trip approached, I began to feel nervous. By now, I was 25 years old and hadn't seen my family for seven years. I didn't know how it would go being with them after so much time. I had also received a cautioning word from a friend who expressed her concern at how quickly Luke and I progressed with our relationship without really knowing each other. However, I felt comfortable with the pace we had been taking and reasoned that if this was from the Lord – which I felt it was – things would work out.

The trip home went well at first. It was wonderful to see my family and finally meet my nephew, Obed, who was four by this time (he was the first to spot me as I walked across the tarmac at the airport to meet the family and cry out, "Aunty Faith! Aunty Faith!"). I also had the joy of being a bridesmaid at my friend,

Amina's, wedding, which was especially meaningful as she had a close shave with death on her way there. She had been booked on a domestic flight in Nigeria from Abuja to Port Harcourt, but at the last minute, was removed from the flight. Despite begging to be allowed to fly, she finally had to accept this decision and ended up taking an overnight bus to Port Harcourt. Upon arriving, she heard the terrible news that the flight she was supposed to have taken had crashed, with only two survivors out of 109 passengers. At her wedding, we all celebrated and praised the Lord for sparing her life.

Both my dad and pastor from home were pleased by my relationship with Luke. Luke and I got to spend some time talking and getting to know each other. We really did like each other and began planning towards our wedding. Though another friend cautioned me that things seem to be moving too quickly with Luke and encouraged me to slow things down, I didn't think this was necessary.

After I returned to the UK, Luke and I progressed with our relationship and it soon became evident that we actually had rushed things without getting to know each other well. Of course, the challenge of a long-distance relationship was a part of it. I sought counseling from my church pastors at KT. They encouraged me to slow down, put the big decision of marriage on hold, and get to know him more. They said that time is a revealer, and I believed if I gave things enough time, things would come out and give me the confirmation and clarity I needed. This was a truth I carried from this point on, that time was indeed a true way to test friendships, relationships, and other things in life. If it could pass the test of time, it was a good indication that it was meant to be, and therefore I didn't need to rush things.

Unfortunately, as much as I hoped for it, my relationship with

Luke did not pass the test of time, and after we broke up, we never got back together. I was devastated and wrestled greatly with this because I truly had believed Luke was my husband. We had even bought engagement rings and started wedding plans. I kept asking the Lord, "What happened? I thought I had heard You. I had all these Scriptures confirming that this was it. I wanted this." I wasn't the only one, either. My dad in particular was completely convinced that Luke was supposed to be his son-in-law. This created quite a bit of tension for me, especially when I returned to Nigeria the following year to officially break things off with him. My dad insisted that I was making the wrong decision.

I decided to seek more counsel from our family pastor in Nigeria, who had been all for the relationship. I explained the situation, how Luke and I had been so sure this relationship was meant to be, yet things were just not working out for us to progress to marriage.

The pastor said, "Faith, you have to hear God for yourself. It doesn't matter what I, your father or anyone else says. We can make mistakes. In fact, I once had a mentor I regarded highly encourage me to go on a particular path because of a dream he had, but this ended up being an error as things went horribly wrong." He went on to explain that thankfully, God had saved him from that situation, and that as he discussed the dream with his mentor, it became clear that the dream had actually been a warning, not an encouragement. His mentor had got it wrong and had to apologize to him. It was a lesson that we need discernment and especially that each of us has to hear God for ourselves.

Next, I went to my mom to discuss the decision with her. She also told me I had to hear from God for myself. I was the one who would be in the marriage to Luke, not my dad. She explained that before marrying my dad, she had asked God to send her confirmation that this was the right decision, and she got every confirmation she asked for. Years later, when things became difficult in the marriage, she returned to these confirmations and took courage from them that God was still in the marriage and she needed to stay and make it work.

I took all this counsel to the Lord in prayer and trusted that in time the Lord will guide me through it all. In the end, it was clear that this relationship was not to be. Though it was painful, this helped me to accept and grieve the loss of the relationship and move on. I felt the Lord remind me again of His promise to "make all things beautiful in its time," so this strengthened my heart to keep trusting God. He was still at work in this area of my life and had the best outcome in mind.

Always the Bridesmaid

By this time, I was living with my friend, Nadia, who herself had gotten engaged as my engagement was ending. With her wedding approaching, I had to find another place to live. I moved in with another friend in East London, but within a few months of living there, our contract came to an end and we had to move. I wanted to be back in West London anyway, to be closer to my friends and church, so I began looking for housing opportunities there. At the notice board in church where people advertise for roommates, I found a lady seeking a flatmate in a lovely two-bed flat in West London. This sounded promising, so I contacted this woman, who was named Pearl, and arranged to view the flat. When I got to the flat, Pearl had a few friends also visiting and I came to find out they were all young women from church. The flat was quite nice. I explained that I wanted a flatmate with similar principles and standards, such as not bringing guys to stay over as a habit, and Pearl agreed and confirmed she shared the same values. Pearl and her friends then explained how Pearl was desperate to get a flatmate to help with expenses, but that it was taking her a while to find someone suitable. They really liked me and wanted me to take the place, so I agreed. There's nothing better than being wanted, and I felt at peace being there, so that settled it.

Pearl and I ended up creating some fun memories in this flat in Acton. Pearl was a South African who had come to study in the UK, so we shared similar backgrounds of being far away from home and family. Therefore, we decided to create our own little family in the flat. Pearl was also single and in her mid-twenties like me, so we both began to pray for our life partners and marriage to come sooner rather than later.

Within a year, Pearl met her husband and they got married the following year. As Pearl was leaving the flat, a new flatmate, Isabel, moved in. She was also single, and we also started praying towards marriage. Within the year, she had also connected with her future husband and started planning to get married. During this time, I had been out with a few guys on dates, but nothing came of these.

It was around this time that I decided that at 29, it was time to pursue buying a place of my own. A friend of a friend offered me a room at her place for very cheap rent, so I moved in there and began to save up for a down payment on a flat. The girl I was renting from told me she was in a long-distance relationship with a guy abroad. Just a couple of months after I moved in, this guy flew to London and proposed to my new flatmate!

My next flatmate, Kelly, told me she was single, but had recently met a guy from church and that there might be some mutual interest. We moved in October 2009, and by December, this guy had asked her out on a date. Within two months, they were engaged! What a whirlwind. Kelly asked me to be her maid of honor, and by the following year, she was married off and I had officially been a bridesmaid for five of my friends in just a few years.

At one point in all this, a friend sent me a message saying that I needed to start charging my flatmates a matchmaking fee because whomever I lived with seemed to meet her husband in no time! I laughed at the time, but as I considered her observation, I couldn't help wondering what was going on. My friends and I were all praying for our husbands, and it seemed that one by one, their prayers were all being answered, while mine was being delayed. I wasn't doing anything different than they were doing. In fact, none of them seemed to really do anything to get these guys' attention or pursue them. They were just following God, working, and living their lives, just as I was. I wasn't living like a workaholic or a nun either. I was actively involved in planning events, attending parties, and going out with friends and had a very active social life where I was meeting lots of guys, but for whatever reason, none of them was my guy.

The Testing Intensifies

In my late twenties, I started praying with a group of lovely young women, and marriage was one of our main topics of prayer. We called forth our future spouses, asking the Lord for amazing qualities in a life partner and in marriage. We cried out to God and at times, prayed all night. One of the ladies sent us an email with her testimony entitled, "God has left me speechless," and somehow this became our way of sharing our testimonies as we prayed together. Sure enough, each of my friends began sending their "God has left me speechless" emails, sharing their testimony of meeting someone. Just like Nadia, Pearl, Isabel, and Kelly, each of my friends from this group began to get married one by one, which was so beautiful. I attended lots of weddings in that season. But month after month and year after year as my turn never came, I couldn't help but feel discouraged that my prayers weren't being answered. Clearly, the young women around me were getting married and even though I prayed earnestly, this hadn't happened for me. I was on this journey of prolonged singleness, and boy did I pray about it. This was probably the area of my most intense prayers. Sometimes I prayed all night to deal with this issue spiritually.

I began to think that this must be a trial or test, and if so, I had to be faithful in trusting Him. I had received answers to prayers in other areas of my life, so why not this area? I began to experience times where my heart felt so broken on the inside over this disappointment and unmet longing. Each time, I would cry out to God. Sometimes this happened in the home cell group I attended, and the ladies would just lay hands on me and pray for me until I felt calm again. These were the times I got a deeper revelation of the verse, "The Lord is close to the brokenhearted." (Psalm 34:18) I did feel the Lord close in those moments of crying out to Him.

In my early thirties, I had my toughest experiences with unrequited love. There was a guy I liked a lot. We were friends and he seemed to like me, but he also had many other female friends, so I couldn't be sure that he felt more for me than the others. I remember confessing my interest in this guy to a colleague at work. After hearing me go on about him, my colleague told me, "Faith, be careful. From everything you're telling me, everything looks great on the outside. He's this very attractive box and it's easy to think that the box is full. But I think that box is empty."

Sure enough, I eventually had a conversation with this guy

about our feelings and he told me point blank that he didn't feel anything more for me than friendship. I was heartbroken, but the difficulty was that he still wanted to keep me around as a friend, even after knowing I had feelings for him. This really did not do good things for my heart, so as much as I didn't want to let him go, I eventually had to break off communication with him. I knew I had to do this to protect my heart and heal from the pain I was already going through. I guess as the waiting gets longer and yearning grows stronger for a life partner, your heart only gets more sensitive and fragile in this area. I remember a friend telling me the vision she saw of the state of my heart, that it was like an egg cracked all around, and indeed, it felt that way. Only the Lord could console my heart in this area of waiting.

My battle with discouragement in this area of my life continued and became so tough, especially when I reached 36 or so. My heart was constantly heavy with silent, unanswered questions. *God, where are You? We started this journey together and when we did it was the most amazing thing. You spoke regularly and my heart was always so mesmerized by You. But now have You forgotten me? Have you forgotten all the work I have been doing for your kingdom? You said if I seek first the kingdom of God and His righteousness, then everything else will be added to me. Well, Lord, where was the "everything else," including my marriage?*

Admittedly, this silence from the Lord was just in this one area of marriage, but for some reason, this area seemed to overshadow all the other areas of answered prayers such as my career and ministry, all I could see was this one area with a big question mark from me to the Lord, WHY and WHEN?

People who met me in this season got the first impression of me being quiet. What they didn't know is that the unanswered questions of life had quieted me. There was so much I couldn't understand and became confused and upset about. No one around me had any real answers either. It seemed there was little real guidance or support for those experiencing prolonged singleness in the church.

My friends and I discussed and debated on this subject a lot. As a result of these questions with little answers, disillusionment, weariness, sadness, confusion, doubt, and fear set into my heart. This was not a good place to be, because it opened me up to considering all the options I would never have considered and wrestling with the many questions and suggestions offered by many.

"What's going on with you and marriage? Do you not want to get married?"

"You gave yourself to church and now what do you have? Were the years you gave to the ministry—your 'flower years,' as some call it—actually 'wasted years?' Other people have lasting things like marriage and children, but what did you end up with?"

"Perhaps you should start going out more. Join dating websites and expand your options. Advertise for a potential husband in the newspaper."

"Think about having a child so at least you have something. Think about freezing your eggs just in case."

All these questions and suggestions were extremely upsetting to me. I kept asking the Lord, "How did I get here? How did I become a statistic in the church?" It seemed like those who had married earlier had made the right choice and jumped in when it was easier to find a good mate, but now the days seemed harder and the options fewer. Especially as I got older, a lot of men my age seemed to be going for younger women.

Many of my family members were also dealing with this issue of prolonged singleness, which made me start to wonder if there was a family stronghold that needed a breakthrough. I ended up going to numerous deliverance sessions to break these strongholds (these are sessions where you are prayed for to be set free from things holding you back). I even had some so-called ministers approaching me and suggesting I sell assets such as my house to sow a heavy sacrificial seed that would break this stronghold. I was being taken advantage of in my vulnerable state. Eventually, I got fed up with all this and shut the door to every one of those suggestions as it became too much. I was no longer so sure of what I was doing and how I was trusting God. I started to lose my sense of who I was and what my purpose was. My voice became very quiet, metaphorically speaking in terms of not having much to say due to the inner struggles I was facing. I became indecisive about many things and unsure of myself, which was very unlike me. My faith was wavering. I still had some faith that the Lord would see me through, but this I would call "managing faith." It wasn't a confident faith anymore.

Sometimes when we have one persistent unanswered prayer, it's hard for us to think about the other areas where our prayers have been answered and blessings have been given. Our vision narrows to the point where that one area of pain – where God's timing is not matching our own – is all we can see. For me, not discerning an answer to my persistent prayer for marriage started to become the whole picture of my relationship with God. In other words, I became tunnel visioned and focused my relationship with God on this one area, which fueled my disappointment with God and meant I began to lose that place of deep intimacy with the Lord. I spent more time complaining and demanding from Him rather than seeking to understand His ways more and go deeper. Walking the walk without intimacy with God can be truly difficult. Little did I know that I would face this trial to ultimately refine my heart and my loyalty to God. I call it the furnace of life. You feel tossed and turned with every wind of doctrine because your faith and heart are no longer solidly rooted in Jesus.

In my late thirties, when men approached me, there was such pressure to settle with one of these guys. In an effort to be more "open," I tried going out with a guy who was a nominal Christian and another guy who frankly told me that he was an atheist. In both situations, these guys actually cut things off with me as they saw more clearly than I did at the time that it was just not going to work between us. I did try going online and meeting guys that way, but nothing came of it but a bunch of first dates that went nowhere. In the end, I gave it up because I really didn't want to date a lot of guys, have to filter through them all to see if they were really Christians, or have to deal with the emotional energy of forming soul ties that I'd have to break.

There was one guy from church who came along and liked me, told me I was the one, and even proposed to me. At this point, I so wanted to be married and it was extremely tempting to think that this could be my only chance. He was a good guy and many people were telling me to just go for it. But I didn't have peace about the relationship, and my anxiety continued to rise as I felt pressure to say yes, reasoning that this was how I would break the stronghold of singleness on my family and I had a duty to make it work. The more I continued with the relationship, the more I felt like I was becoming someone I wasn't—it really started to break down my sense of confidence and clarity in who I was. Thankfully, my friend called me as I was wrestling through this and said, "Faith, I just feel like I need to let you know that it's completely okay if you decide that you don't want to marry this guy. You don't have to marry him. There's nothing wrong with you." What a relief her words were! I broke up with him and began the process of recovering my connection to my heart and my sense of confidence that I was still on the right track with the Lord and in my life.

Corrie ten Boom and Nelson Mandela

Along with the Bible, one of the things that encouraged me in this difficult season of waiting for marriage was reading stories and testimonies of people who had suffered for their faith and came out stronger for it.

Corrie Ten Boom's book, *The Hiding Place*, was particularly inspiring to me. Corrie and her family were Dutch watchmakers and faithful Christians who were sent to German concentration camps for hiding Jews in their homes during the Holocaust in World War II. She talked about the horrific experiences of being in the concentration camp and particularly the impact of this immense suffering on her beloved sister, Betsie. Even through the terrible treatments and beatings, they served God in the camp and gave hope to other women by sharing the gospel with them. Although Betsie became very ill and died due to the conditions and being beaten by a guard, she was never bitter but continued to praise God in the situation and also saw hope through it all. Corrie struggled with all this, especially seeing her sister go through tremendous suffering and eventually dying, but God had a purpose for it all. Corrie was soon after miraculously released from prison and later found out it was a clerical error and that after her release, the women around her age group were all sent to the gas chambers. Corrie ended up being instrumental in helping those wounded from the war heal and be restored. She also had to forgive some of the guards from the prison who mistreated them and contributed to Betsie's death. Corrie ended up becoming a writer and traveled across many nations preaching the gospel of love and forgiveness.

Reading this book, I was deeply moved that two women could be so courageous for the Lord and be obedient through suffering, standing on their faith, and doing what they believed was right. I was encouraged by Betsie and Corrie's faith through the severe trials of their lives and the way they were faithful to the end, fully accomplishing God's purpose for their lives and demonstrating that there is purpose, even in the suffering. God still works through the trials and even when it seems like our prayers are being unanswered, He is still working. Corrie's story inspired me to trust God even when things seemed unclear and helped me "see the woods from the trees," so to speak. There were others who had gone through far worse than I was experiencing and God came through in fulfilling their life's purpose on earth. That perspective was comforting.

Also encouraging to me was the story of Nelson Mandela, who, after spending 27 years in prison for the fight for freedom from apartheid and finally becoming president, encouraged a message of forgiveness and reconciliation between blacks and whites in South Africa. How was it possible that a man who had spent so long in prison, rather than being filled with rage and bitterness, was preaching the opposite with forgiveness, reconciliation, and ultimately love? Nelson Mandela was respected across the world for his stand for justice, for not giving up and seeing his fight all the way to the end. I have been truly impacted by Nelson Mandela's life—first by his uncompromising faith to fight for freedom and refusal to give up or settle for less, and second for his promotion of forgiveness, reconciliation, and love rather than war, bitterness, and hatred.

These stories reminded me that as I surrendered my life to the Lord's purpose without wavering or giving up, He would also fulfill His purpose through my life. Also, these virtues of love, forgiveness, compassion, and kindness amongst others were being developed in me, which are priceless. They cannot be bought with money but can only be instilled in you as you allow your character to be developed through the trials of life. I knew I was in a school of training to build up my character for the call of God on my life. And just like Corrie ten Boom and Nelson Mandela, there was no getting to character and the call without enduring the crucible of suffering.

Friendships

Another way the Lord sustained me through hardships and trials was through the friendships in my life. Friendships have always been important to me, as I love people and relationships. My mom taught me to be friendly and encouraged me to make friends in school, and this has been one of the best gifts from my mom. I also learned to pray for divine friendships from a young age and I have truly been blessed with great friendships through various seasons of my life. From a young age, the Lord began to teach me loyalty and love genuinely, and these qualities have enabled me to build some of these friendships. As Proverbs 18:24 says, *"A man who has friends must himself be friendly, but there is a friend who sticks closer than a brother."*

One of my childhood friends was a girl by the name, Soye. Our parents were friends who became Christians around the same time and attended the same church. Soye's dad was best friends with my Uncle Owuna, so anytime he went to visit Soye's dad, he would bring me along to play with Soye, which I always enjoyed and looked forward to. I didn't see Soye often, as she lived far away from where we lived and attended a different branch of the church.

When we were about eight years old, Soye and I attended a church conference with our families and during the event, we sneaked off to a quiet spot in the building and started talking. As we talked, we dreamed about the future. Soye had been born in the United States and I in the UK, and we both came back to Nigeria as babies. We dreamed about going back abroad—Soye to the US and myself to the UK—and we spoke in detail about how we would both visit each other when we had traveled. I can still remember that day vividly, because though we were kids, we spoke with such passion.

Soye and I both went off to secondary school and I hardly saw her again, yet our friendship continued. After secondary school, Soye went to the US and I to the UK just as we dreamed, and we've been able to visit each other in those countries and even traveled together across Europe. All those years ago as kids, we didn't realize that we were speaking and prophesying into our future, but it all came to pass. I remember being in Rome with Soye for her birthday and reminding her of our discussion as kids and how we were living out what we had spoken back then. This strengthened my faith to keep speaking and declaring into my future, as it was a powerful reminder that I will live out tomorrow what I am speaking today.

In boarding school, I was friendly and made a lot of friends, but there were few that remained friends after we finished school and were waiting to go off to college in the UK. These friends became like a support network during the critical transition year(s) between boarding school and college. Besides those I have mentioned in previous chapters like Otonye and Baa, there was Nneka and Tonye, who were friends from primary and secondary school. We all ended up studying for the Cambridge GCSEs together after secondary school, as we worked hard to get the grades required for our next levels and prayed hard to travel abroad to further our studies.

I have already mentioned Taiye and Bunmi Lambo. Bunmi is like an older sister to me and we became very close when I lived with them and cared for their baby, Joanne. Bunmi taught me to cook some lovely dishes and care for the home. Bunmi was honest and told you things as they were with no sugarcoating. I liked Bunmi for that because I knew I could talk to her about something and she would speak the truth in love to me. Bunmi was also a disciplinarian who gave me certain rules of how to behave—e.g., not coming back home when it was very late—and if I violated these rules, she presented me with consequences like mopping the floors. At first, I got upset about this, but I decided in my heart to be obedient and to submit myself to this discipline to help my growth. I learned the value of submitting to authority, accepting when I had done something wrong, and being willing to correct. Bunmi was also a source of encouragement when things were tough. When I was going through disappointment of not going out with the guy I liked, Bunmi would encourage me saying that mine would come.

Along with my family and long-term friends like Bunmi, my friendships with Sylvia, Esther, and Margaret were especially meaningful to me in those years. I've described Esther and Sylvia a bit already. Margaret was a prayer warrior with a strong passion for the Lord—our friendship grew out of praying together. Over the years, we saw many answers to prayers, and I was always encouraged by Margaret's radical faith and her prayers, believing that God could do anything through our lives. The four of us truly were the "Four Corners" who not only ministered together but had genuine relationships that brought so much strength to me. We prayed and fasted together, went on vacations together, and held each other accountable as we processed our hopes, dreams and preparations towards the future.

Looking back, I know I would have given up in my waiting on the Lord for marriage if not for the grace of God and the faithful prayers of these dear friends, as well as the people of God, ministers, and family members the Lord put around me. I have been blessed by truly beautiful, and in some cases, what I would call covenant friendships that strengthened, encouraged, and inspired me to keep up the faith and endure life's challenges. Some of these friends were also my prayer partners, and we would pray about anything and everything from our hair and skin to more serious issues like sickness and miracles for family situations, financial provisions, and our future. These friends were honest with me, spoke the truth in love, and called me to order when required. I have come to discover that godly friendships don't necessarily just happen; they come as we intentionally pray for divine friendships and we practice being good friends that people would want to be around. I have learned that one of the keys to great friendships is being genuinely interested in others, not for what you can get from them but simply for who they are. As you remain authentic to your life values, you will attract the types of friends that could become lifelong friends. I always aim to be a great friend and as a result end up attracting great friends to myself. Aim to be a great friend! It's amazing how strong friendships can ease difficult days.

QUESTIONS FOR REFLECTION

1. Is anything in your life more important than your intimacy with the Lord?

2. Sometimes it can feel that life is passing you by and you've yet to meet the milestones you expected. Find 3 verses to lean on during your season of waiting.

3. How has your season of testing shaped your character and in what ways has it impacted your faith? If negatively, how can you begin to work towards rebuilding your faith?

4. Ecclesiastes 3:11 says "He has made everything beautiful in its time." What is the Lord making beautiful in your life in its time? Are you in a season of waiting? How can you wait for the beautiful thing the Lord is doing?

5. How did you feel in your waiting seasons of life? How did you stay focused? How did the Lord help you in your times of waiting? How can you make the best of the waiting seasons? What can you do during those times to glorify the Lord?

Chapter 8

THE NIGHT SEASON

Kingdom theme: On the journey of faith, we all walk through a "dark night of the soul" or "valley of the shadow of death," but God will meet us there and bring us through. This is central to our testimony of faith.

As I GOT INTO my thirties, the journey of waiting got heavier. I had no explanation for why I was still single. Year after year, I was praying the same prayers and nothing seemed to be shifting. The books I had read in my twenties about singleness and waiting did not really talk about what to do when the waiting intensifies and you end up in your thirties still awaiting your breakthrough. Keep going and trust God it will happen? Or take immediate action, as this time it could be something you are doing or not doing?

I didn't realize how much this weighed on me. As I longed for this area of my life to be fulfilled, I became desperate to ensure it wasn't my fault that I was still single. My heart became more sensitive, vulnerable, and ultimately wounded by carrying this tension of my lack of answers about still being single while those around me were getting married and picked, even though I felt I was doing all I knew to do in serving God and positioning myself to be seen for marriage.

As my disappointment with God piled on, I carried on with ministry, not always knowing or even understanding how to process it all. By 2013, I was in my mid-thirties. My ministry was flourishing, working with the young adults at Kensington Temple. I enjoyed and thrived in it, and so did the young adults I mentored. I loved working with young women, and so many of them were growing in their faith and enjoying the community we had formed in church. Due to some re-shuffling in KTYM, I had ended up with a lot of younger women to take care of in my cell group. I also, along with my friends Sylvia, Esther, and Margaret and other leaders from the youth and young adults' ministry, became a part of the leadership team of KT women's ministry under the leadership of Amanda Dye, wife of the senior pastor. It was an honor to be in the midst of these older women in leadership and learn from them. Eventually, they began to give us opportunities to speak on the platform in the main church, which was a different kettle of fish to the youth ministry. KT was a big church and very fervent in the Word. Not many people were allowed to speak on the platform apart from the ordained ministers, and there were fewer female ministers who spoke on the platform, so when we were given the opportunity to begin taking segments (offering talks) in some of the services, this was a real honor.

I enjoyed doing the talks, though the buildup before getting to the platform was always nerve-wracking. I found the platform at KT to be really powerful—you felt the presence of God in the church, but more so on the platform. Sylvia and Esther were both qualified barristers and were very good at speaking, and I was so proud of them when they delivered their offering talks. I prepared the best I could with my talks and relied completely on the Holy Spirit to speak to the hearts of the people.

However, as I continued with these talks on the platform, I noticed I was hearing a lot of attacks in my mind about not being qualified to do them or criticizing the talks I had already done. I prayed against this and kept moving forward in boldness, but somehow the pressure mounted from the yet unanswered questions in my heart. When I did a talk, it encouraged me, as it reminded me of God's faithfulness, but deep down, I think I also battled with the question, "Why and when, Lord?" It wasn't a question of whether God could do this—I *knew* He could do it. But that made it worse because I thought, "Lord, I know You can bring my marriage at the snap of a finger, so why are You not doing this?" I couldn't understand why the delay was occurring. I began to hear that these delays were not from God, so I couldn't understand why the Lord would let the enemy do this. Yet again, I had no answer and somehow the feeling of shame began to resurface.

Meanwhile, there were a good number of young women in the cell groups I led who desired to be married and we often prayed about this in our meetings. This was another reason the waiting I was experiencing weighed so much on me. I felt these young women needed to be encouraged that God could in fact answer our prayers in this area by seeing it happen in my life, but since this wasn't the case, I didn't know how to respond anymore. Slowly, shame continued to grow and mock me, as if someone were asking, "Where is your God now? You've served Him so faithfully, but how come you are still single? How can these young women look up to you as they expect to also get married? If it hasn't happened for you, then how can it happen for them?" This was therefore another area of pressure I felt in ministry. The pressure was mounting, especially as the number of young women under me increased and I had to manage multiple cell groups.

By this time, I had devoted 14 years to ministry at KT. I had served and enjoyed my time, but deep down, I began to feel a staleness. As I described, I began to lose my voice as the unanswered questions in my heart mounted. I just didn't know what I could say about God, especially to the young people I was leading. I also recognized that my identity had become wrapped up with my service at KT, and I needed to find myself again. So, by the end of 2014, I felt the release to step down from ministry. This was a very big deal, because ministry had been my life and KT had been my home for fourteen years. I knew this would not be an easy journey of moving on, but I had to do it. I knew it was time to step down to tend to my heart and to explore the new things the Lord was pressing on me. I began to look into more business endeavors, especially as the financial pressure from family needs back home in Nigeria increased.

The Family Struggles

Since I had left home in 1998, I had constantly carried my family in my heart. I loved my family so much, and I wanted the best for my younger siblings, who were quite young when I left home. Lydia, my youngest sister, was only nine years old, and Violet was twelve, so I had missed a lot of their growing up. In my dreams, I still saw them as the little children I had left all those years ago.

As soon as I finished university and got a graduate-level job in 2005, I committed to helping my parents with my siblings' school fees full-time. I also prayed and interceded constantly for my dad for breakthroughs in his business and finances, and for things to get easier for my family. However, despite pockets of short-lived breakthroughs, things got increasingly difficult as crisis after crisis unfolded. I felt the pressure mounting as I stepped in to bear some of the financial burden. Mom and Dad had taught us to be generous, so I was happy to step in to help the family in these times of need. More than that, I was thankful for the strong spiritual foundation laid by my parents for me and my siblings and being away from the family in Nigeria for so long meant the most practical way I could assist was financially. Whenever there was a need, I pulled all the stops I could to meet that need, my family was my priority. However, as the pressure kept mounting and the burden increased, it took a long while for me to realize my limit and by this time, I was emotionally crumbling under the weight of everything else I was dealing with. I was like a ticking time bomb.

In 2014, things settled a little bit at home and I felt it was time to give Mom a break from all the battles she had to fight there, so I bought her a ticket to visit us in London. By this time, Emmanuel, Esther, and my cousin, Bibi, were living with me. Mom hadn't been back to London since the early eighties after I was born, so this was a special time and an answer to prayer. I had always prayed that one day, my family could come to spend time with me in the UK. I wanted to share my life with them. The timing of Mom's visit coincided with my decision to step down from ministry at KT, as well as my decision to transition to contracting. Especially during this season in my mid-thirties, as my unanswered prayers for marriage were lingering, spending those few weeks with her brought a lot of comfort to my heart.

Business Ventures

After I started contracting, I felt the need to step out in business, as I was now making enough money to have significant disposable income. It wasn't the first time I had attempted side businesses. In 2006, I became a distributor for a skincare line, buying products at wholesale prices and selling to friends and family at retail prices, thereby making a modest profit. However, the business was short-lived for me, as I struggled to convince my friends to buy at price points higher than the average prices in the retail stores.

My next venture was selling human hair extensions, which a lot of black ladies wore in the form of wigs, weaves (sewing or gluing the extensions to their hair), or braids. This was when real human hair became a big thing—Indian, Peruvian, Brazilian, Malaysian, and Chinese women sold their hair to be resold as hair extensions. Because the human hair was more beautiful and meant to last a lot longer than the synthetic hair that had been the norm for years, women were prepared to pay a higher price for it. I did some research and decided to delve into this business, ordering packs of human hair from China, so my family could sell them in Nigeria on my behalf. I had a wider market in Nigeria and had a few trips home lined up, where I could help my family manage the business, so this seemed to be a promising venture. The business started off well and the profit margins were quite significant, but soon enough as the family sold the products, the money began to go into solving family problems rather than back into the business, and in time there was no money left. I ended up having to pay back the credit card debts I had used to start the business, and that was the end of it.

Now in 2015, with the resources and flexibility afforded by freelancing and contracting, I was ready to start new business ventures and get my hands on some good projects. I felt full of faith to step out as an entrepreneur. I did a lot of research, attended lots of seminars and networking events, took some classes, and finally decided to take the step to invest in property development. I had saved up a considerable amount of money and built up a squeaky-clean credit rating, so I had many borrowing options available to me.

The first deal I sourced was in north England, where properties were more affordable—the refurbishment of a two-bedroom into a three-bedroom bungalow. I had a deal sourcer who took care of the project, and after praying, I felt confident I was meant to take the deal. Meanwhile, I also looked into investing abroad and found two deals for properties to be developed in Africa. I couldn't get a mortgage to complete the purchases, but I felt I needed to take the step of faith and put down significant amounts in deposits to secure the deals. Unfortunately, by the time I needed to make the remaining payment, I hadn't been able to secure additional funding, and decided to give them up as the liabilities became too much. I was still working on the Northern England property, but there were delays with the completion, and by the time it went to the market for sale, property prices in the area had fallen. Also, in the middle of the project, the project manager decided we should change the strategy from a three-bedroom to a high-end two-bedroom. I agreed before thinking it through properly first, only to discover this was a mistake, as even a nicer two-bedroom property would still be sold for less than a three-bedroom, thus reducing my profit. I also made the major mistake of taking out a really expensive bridging loan to finish the project. In the end, with the delays and the market dip, I had to sell in a hurry to pay off the bridging loan, which meant selling for a much lower price than anticipated and leaving me with a significant loss. Between that and the substantial money I had lost on the deposits for the deals abroad, I found myself facing a mini bankruptcy. My work contract also came to end around this time, so I ran out of money completely.

Understandably, this whole experience was demoralizing. I had started full of faith and ended with four investments that had gone pear-shaped and left me with huge losses and debts to repay. In hindsight, of course, I had made a number of big mistakes along the way, largely because I was in a bit of a rush to profit for the sake of my family. I should have gone a lot slower and completed one deal first before moving on to the next. Thankfully, God was faithful to help me start digging myself out financially (I still have a bit of digging left to do) and learning what I needed to learn from this experience. I don't regret taking on these investments. A lot of it was really fun, I learned a lot, and today I am excited to take more steps in future with the hard-won wisdom I gained through it all. As many have said, faith is spelt "RISK." It involves taking risks and trusting that no matter what happens, the Lord will catch you if you fall, which we all will from time to time. It's important to discover that with Him, our failures and mistakes don't disqualify, but teach us.

To some, it might be surprising that I chose to invest in land and property sales to help get my family out of their financial troubles when it was those very types of investments that had put my family into their financial difficulties in the first place. However, my father had, experienced a lot of success in business over the years, as well as struggles. Like my dad, I also love business and have quite a high-risk tolerance, so it made sense to me to enter this same area of investment. One of my mistakes has now shone a light in this area of my life to encourage me to maintain a healthy balance here. So many of us end up repeating patterns from our parents' lives and this repetition isn't always a bad thing, but what do we do when we see ourselves repeating patterns that we do not want to repeat in our lives? We must start by examining our lives. Reflect on what has been, learn from past mistakes, heal from the wounds of the soul, and begin to dream about the future ahead, plan and prepare to go there. Perhaps one of the most important ways to react to repeating an unhealthy pattern is simply to recognize that we are doing so. Perhaps we have just picked up these habits and behaviors from our parents and need to intentionally work on improving those areas of our lives. On the other hand, this could be an area of attack from the enemy, especially if you and your family have a calling in that area and the enemy is fighting to stop you and the family from answering that call. This situation requires targeted spiritual warfare to break that cycle of mistakes and attacks. This should also be the concern for our children, that they learn the good from us, but avoid repeating our mistakes. Our hope is always that each generation improves upon the last one. Therefore, I view my interest in business and property as a gift from my dad and hope to improve on his legacy by seeking not to repeat the mistakes he and I have made so far.

The Breaking Point

During my research into the property development industry, I explored various business model options to find the right one that fit my situation and the opportunities around me. I engaged the services of a solicitor, got all the legal advice I required, and settled on an "introducer" business model. I would find "turnkey" property investments in the UK and introduce clients from Nigeria and Africa who were interested in investing abroad but had no contacts they trusted.

I started looking for potential investment partnerships in the UK and in the process of meeting and discussing with property developers, I experienced a minor sexual assault at one of these meetings. It was shocking to me how a business discussion could suddenly turn into an assault, and unfortunately it turned out to be my word against his, so I felt I couldn't press charges. As the days and weeks unfolded, it became evident that this incident had traumatized me at a level I had never experienced.

About a week after, I started to have a panic attack at work. I didn't know I was having a panic attack, but I knew something was happening to me and I wasn't breathing properly, so I quickly got into a taxi and headed to Aunty Liz's house, which was only about fifteen minutes away. As soon as I got to my Aunty's, the attack started in full force as I cried out for help. Aunty Liz and her daughters were instantly alarmed and called the ambulance. My Aunty started crying—none of my family had ever seen me like this. To them, Faith was always so strong and the one taking care of everyone, and suddenly here I was in this state.

Aunty Liz called Mom in Nigeria and through tears said, "We don't know what was going on with Faith! Something is happening to her." Mom told Aunty Liz to put the phone to my ear and immediately started declaring the Word of God about who I am in Christ, God's hands upon my life, and more powerful truths. I was shocked by this level of strength and authority coming from my mom in all that chaos. I hadn't seen that side of her before. Her first reaction was not to panic, but to declare the Word of God, which really helped me.

Finally, the ambulance came. After assessing me, the paramedics said I was having a panic attack and began teaching me to breathe. They also asked what I usually used to calm myself. I said my music, which the paramedics then put on for me, and this did the job of helping me come out of the attack. After they left, Emmanuel and Bibi arrived and we all talked and prayed together at Aunty Liz's house. When I felt ready, we got a taxi home.

Though I didn't suffer another panic attack, I did wrestle for weeks with anxiety. I couldn't get on the Tube, couldn't sleep, and lost my appetite. My family became very worried for me for the first time in my life. The trauma I was experiencing seemed quite severe. In retrospect, I think it was the proverbial "straw that broke the camel's back" due to the intense season I had been in—carrying the financial pressure of my family, my unsustainable work schedule, my struggling business ventures, and especially my underlying wounded heart over my prolonged singleness. Suddenly, the world had become a dark place where men could just violate innocent women and take something precious from them in exchange for very little (material possessions), and I just didn't know how to handle it.

At the height of this trauma, I felt like it was time for me to die and go to heaven. This is what I cried out to Aunty Liz when she felt led to call me one day, when I was really in a bad state. I said, "Aunty, I am ready to leave this world and go home to be with the Lord." It felt like I was in a dark hole and I couldn't find my way out. Aunty Liz started praying and encouraging me that "this too indeed will pass."

Ruthann, my mentor, was also a key counselor to me during this time. She spoke with strong spiritual authority into my life when she saw that I was slipping into this dark hole. "Faith, choose to live," she commanded. "Faith, live. There is too much to life to give up. Choose life."

Upon hearing her words, I felt something shift in me and I knew I had to choose to live and come out of this trauma, this dark place. The choice was mostly about forgiveness and letting go. It was difficult for me to forgive the perpetrator, as I couldn't get my head around how he could go scot-free. The police had confirmed that it was indeed my word against his, so I decided to lay it down and not pursue the case any further. I chose to forgive, as life was too big for me to hold on to this. That proved to be the key to my breakthrough in this situation.

After I chose to forgive him and move on, I was well on my way to my healing. Gradually, I continued to recover through counseling sessions, the support of my friends, and family, prayer, and music therapy. I found these Christian instrumentals that were like water to my soul, soothing and healing me. Bibi cooked and waited on me and Emmanuel also took care of me, which was a great help. My experience of healing during this season was part of the inspiration to create a prayer album (more on that later).

Lightening the Load

In 2011 or so, I went on vacation with the Four Corners (Sylvia, Esther, and Margaret). We flew to Florida and took a cruise to the Caribbean. This was my first cruise and it was quite luxurious. We were treated like queens and enjoyed the extravagant food, drinks, music shows, and dress-up nights. However, I couldn't help feeling sad and guilty when I thought about my family back home in Nigeria. A part of me felt they could do with the money I was spending on the cruise, and another part of me felt sad that they were not on the cruise with me. I wasn't sure when I would have the opportunity to go on a cruise with them as they couldn't afford it.

I spoke to the girls about my mixed feelings and they encouraged me to enjoy myself, as I deserved to have a break and enjoy the fruits of my labor. I knew my family back home were really happy that I was going on a cruise and wanted to know every detail of my experience. My mom loved hearing the details and watching the videos I was sending her. I realized that, rather than feeling envious of my experience, my family was experiencing it through me, and that was enough for them. One day soon I know I will be in a position to take my entire family on a beautiful luxurious cruise!

When I reached my breaking point, it forced me to realize that I could no longer carry my family on my shoulders. I needed to give the cares of my family to the Lord and practice Matthew 11:28-30 when Jesus said, *"Come to Me, all you who labor and are heavy laden, and I will give you rest. Take My yoke upon you and learn from Me, for I am gentle and lowly in heart, and you will find rest for your souls. For My yoke is easy and My burden is light."* (NKJV). Thankfully, upon seeing me struggling during this time, my family rallied around to support me and did much to relieve the pressure I had been living under. This helped me begin to lighten the load.

By the end of 2014, we said goodbye to Esther, my sister, as she headed back to Nigeria after her studies in London. I was truly thankful to the Lord for the time Esther and I got to spend together making up for the years we had spent apart.

Although the financial requirements for international students were getting even more difficult in the UK, Emmanuel remained as he had miraculously received a scholarship after praying and knocking on an unlikely door. Emmanuel's life has consisted of breakthroughs. Emmanuel is one of those people who has the type of favor in his life where he gets picked out of a crowd. Once he was on an international trip with Emirates airline flying economy class when he randomly got called out and upgraded to first class. Apparently, they had a spare and decided to choose someone to upgrade, and sure enough, it was Emmanuel.

After completing his master's degree in the UK, we felt Emmanuel had a call in the UK and needed to stay to start his ministry rather than going back to Nigeria. Emmanuel seemed to have brought the fire of God he experienced in India to the UK. We started having small group prayer meetings with friends at our home and the homes of some of our friends, which we called "Fire Starters." We prayed and saw the power of God move in these meetings and this sparked fires in the hearts of various friends to step out in faith and begin living out their purpose. Some launched their ministries and others started businesses that are still going strong. Emmanuel had a heart for people and this became evident as he prayed and ministered over people. We knew Emmanuel's call was in the UK.

Thus, commenced the next challenge—immigration. During this time, I carried the financial load, as legally Emmanuel couldn't work to earn money. It was yet another battle, but I kept trusting God that Emmanuel would eventually break through. Many people tried to get Emmanuel to take shortcuts or even lie in order to speed up the immigration process, and instead, he chose to trust God and wait. Emmnauel chose the path of integrity and standing firm for what he believed in. His experience showed that if we stand our ground in faith and trust God by doing things honestly, in due season, we get to reap the blessings the Lord has for our lives. That's what we experienced with Emmanuel's situation. There were times we received prophetic words on breaking through for this battle; we had to steward those words in the place of prayer until the manifestation. When Angela the woman who would become his wife, first showed up, it was amazing because she was exactly what Emmanuel had prayed for and believed in and even more. He was able to get his leave to remain in the UK, the breakthrough we had been praying for. The Lord was rewarding Emmanuel's faithfulness to God. They are both now leading Nation's Call Church in London together.

Authentic Lives

During this night season of my life, my faith wavered as my waiting season got longer, so I began searching for answers. I was desperate, so this gave room for fear. Fear brought exposure to the things that were deep down in my heart, perhaps wrong motives I didn't even realize were there. In hindsight, my desperation and fear gave room for this and I think the Lord used this to expose the condition of my heart that deep down, my motives were not pure. This was a hard but necessary lesson for me to learn to prepare me for the future.

In 2016, I began searching for purpose and a sense of direction in my life. I found a three-day weekend workshop called Authentic Lives, which sounded just like what I needed. I didn't know anyone involved in the retreat, but feeling desperate, I decided to sign up and book a hotel near the retreat location outside London. I took the Friday off work to get there in time for the first session, curious to know what this workshop would involve.

The first session was an introduction to the workshop and as I listened and participated, I was saying to myself, "Been there and done that." It seemed nothing really new or special was going on. After the session, I returned to my hotel, feeling a bit disappointed. *"Lord, I really had high hopes," I prayed. "Is this just going to be another workshop where I come and go and remain the same?"* I considered all the effort and cost I had put in to attend, giving up a day of work (at a significant day rate then) and paying for travel and the hotel. I decided there was no way I was going to waste all that money by coming and going home the same and made some declarations over myself. "Faith, you will get back all you have put in and more. You are definitely not leaving here the same—no way! You will be open to receive all that there is for you at this workshop." I commanded my ears, mind, and everything else to be open to receive and declared that I was not going back home the same. It was like a warfare prayer I did over myself.

By the time I turned up for the morning session the next day, everything seemed different. Suddenly, everything the speakers and organizers were saying seemed new to me. I was like a sponge sucking in every bit of the workshop. When Andrew Chua, the workshop founder and leader, said the workshop was like a treasure hunt, and whatever treasure you found in yourself was yours to keep, that really got my attention. I needed those treasures to help me continue pushing forward.

The workshop guided us through answering questions like, "Who am I? Where am I going? How will I get there?" Andrew explained that there were no right or wrong answers. Whatever answers I gave were my answers. This was the beginning of the turn-around for me. I felt this release to just express myself as me, Faith, and accept myself. I realized I had not really accepted myself for who I was because I wasn't really like everybody else and sometimes I found it hard to fit in. I loved the Lord and tailored my life to please Him, which was not the norm of our society, so sometimes I felt odd. But for the first time, I felt permission to just be myself without being judged as right or wrong.

I literally saw the authentic "Faith" emerge through that workshop. At one point, we did a name card exercise where you got to talk about your name and what it meant to you. It was validating for me to share how and why I was named Faith. As I pondered the story of how I was named Faith, which my mom had told me, I came to appreciate my name in a greater depth for the first time. Suddenly, I was proud of my name and authentic story.

The Life-Line exercise was also profound. Each of us had to pick seven events that had shaped our life story. As I thought and picked my seven, I was able to share my story with the class. As I did, I began to take hold of my story and saw how to draw strength from the lessons of my life events. When we did the section on Gremlins, the things that stop us, for me, I realized it was this feeling of *"not being enough."* I didn't even realize this feeling had been there all along and I finally identified it, made it into a little round blurb with the play dough we were given, and then smashed it afterwards. I felt a release that finally "*Faith was enough.*" I didn't need anything else to complete me, not one more training or one more thing.

Finally, we had to think of an impactful story in our lives. I thought of our Christmas trip to Lagos in 1985, when my dad paid for all the street kids to see Father Christmas. I had actually forgotten about this story and didn't realize its impact on me until we had to do this exercise. We were asked to brainstorm two words that summarized both the significance of the story and our life purpose—they called this our "core process." This was when I came up with "Lavishing Generosity." These were two words that I felt were my core process, the essence of my purpose on earth. I was here to lavish generosity in the world. I didn't fully understand what this meant or how I would accomplish this, but the words resonated with me deep down, so I embraced them.

Thus began my journey of finding my authentic self. I was so impacted by the course that I connected with Andrew and the team and became a part of the Authentic Lives family. I couldn't wait to share this with my family and friends. Upon returning to London, I joined forces with Andrew and began running Authentic Lives workshops in London. We were given access to the beautiful Jireh House on Chancery Lane, from where we held the London workshops. I invited everyone I could, including all my friends and family members living in London. They all ended up attending and now have their core processes. One of my friends, Pam, identified her core process as "Unveiling Pearls," and went on to set up her own workshop for women to discover the beauty inside of them. Pam is already making an impact in the world through Unveiling Pearls. Andrew Chua, the founder of the Authentic Lives workshop, has his core process as "Transfiguring Lives" and his goal is to help people discover their purpose and live it out, which starts by being authentic.

The impact of the Authentic Lives workshop was significant in my journey of transformation, especially coming as it did as I was healing from the season of trauma, loss, and heartbreak. From then on, my confidence grew in who I was without having to apologize to anyone or trying to be somebody else. More than that, I saw a way to help others find what I found. I continue to offer Authentic Lives workshops in my travels around the world. To date, I have run the workshop in London, San Diego, California, and Florida and look forward to all the other countries I will have the privilege of taking this to. The workshop itself, through the effort of Andrew and the team, has already spread to many nations of the world.

Another key piece of my restoration journey came in May 2017, when I began attending a wonderful ministry called Jesus House. After leaving KT in 2014, I had visited a number of other churches to expand my horizons, learn new things, and hopefully find a new church home. I encountered all sorts of ministries and doctrines that tried to address my issue of waiting. I attempted to be open-minded and tried some of their proposed solutions because I felt I needed to prove that I wasn't the cause of this delay due to some stubbornness of mine. However, I only ended up more hurt and broken. I also lost money, as this was where I met those who implied giving a sacrificial seed to the Lord would break this stronghold of delay and give me my breakthrough. These experiences contributed to me feeling like I was losing myself and moving away from the confident Faith I had been. Sylvia and Bunmi were my voices of reason during this season, reminding me of who I was in Christ and urging me not to be swayed by those who would manipulate me while I was in a vulnerable, desperate state.

In the end, I decided to walk away from these ministries and trust the relationship I had built with the Lord and His voice. It was time to go back to the basics and simply trust God without trying to "help" Him in any way. I knew I had to build up my faith again, as even my place of intimacy (time spent in prayer to the Lord) had suffered a lot. I had replaced this by escaping with Netflix binging. I could literally watch Netflix 24 hours at a time, only stopping for little breaks here and there and sometimes putting a wet cloth over my exhausted eyes and carrying on watching. As I've described, I can be quite extreme and have the tendency to overdo things. I had to pull myself back. I had become spiritually stale, and I needed a jerk back to fervency.

Jesus House provided that place for me to sit and be ministered to, while I reconnected with the Lord and my own heart. There I just sat under the ministry and covering, basking in the beautiful worship and praise from the platform. Soon, I began to exercise my prayer muscles again. Interestingly, I found the baby dedication services particularly healing as I watched families in colorful outfits dance up to the platform to dedicate babies to the Lord with so many family and friends joining in the celebration. The thanksgiving services also greatly blessed me. Just watching the colors, beauty, and joyfulness of these ceremonies was soothing to my heart and helped me just relax and begin enjoying my relationship with God again.

One particular inspiration amongst many I also got from Jesus House was that a number of women in church had written books, which were being promoted and encouraged by the church. I was really inspired that these women were doing great things, and this awakened me to dream again as I went through my healing process. I also needed in this valley season to know that the sun would shine again and there was light at the end of the tunnel. I particularly remember when the senior pastor talked about a young lady who had just released her book, *A Young Woman's Guide to Seeking God,* at the age of 26. This was so inspiring and encouraging that I went and spoke to this young lady, whose name was Ayo Awotona, after the service. Ayo shared how she had accomplished this and that I could do the same and even shared some of her contacts who had assisted her in the process. This planted a definite seed in my heart that my dream of writing a book was not so far off anymore. Now here we are, the book finally completed. I am grateful to the seeds sown in my heart at Jesus House for all Nations Church, London.

Going through Authentic Lives and finding Jesus House caused me to reflect on the various ministries and workshops I and my friends had participated in over the years preceding KT, as we sought breakthrough and success in various areas of our lives. In some cases, we were promised help to achieve great things, but ended up more wounded and broken. I realized that there are no shortcuts to the breakthroughs of life. You just have to diligently go through your process, trust God, and be obedient to His voice. This period taught me to stay in my lane—not just to desire anything that would bring me a measure of success, but to go on an adventure of finding my authentic calling and assignment and following that path without allowing good things to distract me from the right things. Like Dr. Myles Monroe said, *"Right is not defined by what is good. Right is defined by vision."* There are many good things out there to do, but what is in line with your vision is what is right.

QUESTIONS FOR REFLECTION

1. Have you had times in your walk with the Lord where it's been asked, '"Where is God?" How did you get through it?

2. Recall a time when you felt disconnected from God and your purpose or you went through a particularly tough season. How did you come out of this "dark night season"? How did God speak to you during this time?

3. Who have you had to forgive in your life to receive healing? What was this experience like?

4. Are you choosing life? Are you listening to His voice as you wrestle over life and death situations?

5. Did you know that music can invite the presence of the Lord into your environment? Do you deliberately put on music in times of trouble?

6. Everyone born of the Spirit must learn to discern and trust the Lord for themselves. Nobody can walk your journey for you and even prophetic words given to you from others must ultimately resonate with you, at the core of your being. How are you learning to discern the voice of God for yourself? How do you steward the prophetic words given to you by others?

7. Psalm 139:14 says that ""You are fearfully and wonderfully made." What is your authentic self? What is your authentic story?

8. What scriptures can you write down on index cards to place around your home or work area to declare or take authority over any negative emotions, such as fear, anxiety, or moments of discouragement?

9. How can you pray, plan, and prepare to welcome or maintain divine friendships into your life?

Chapter 9

KALEIDOSCOPE

> **Kingdom theme:** Jesus said to seek first the kingdom, and all the things we need will be added to us. This is the true path to personal fulfillment.

In the midst of my church "wanderings" after leaving KT, my brother, Emmanuel, observed something that struck me as true. "Faith, you need to really be in a prophetic environment," he told me. "The prophetic is what catapults you to the next level."

I had always believed in prophecy, received many prophetic words over my life that have guided my prayers and actions, and engaged in prophetic ministry for others. However, in that season of disappointment and struggle, the prophetic had just become less prominent and active in my life. It was no coincidence that I also felt a bit stuck and lacking direction or vision for where my life was going. A prophetic lifestyle of listening to God's voice and meditating on and declaring His Word is critical to our ability to view our lives with faith, hope, and expectancy for what God is doing in our lives. But, as Proverbs 13:12 says, *"Hope deferred makes the heart sick"* (NKJV). As my heart became more wounded, it became difficult to even want to hear another prophetic word or promise. I had heard it all before, and it seemed nothing had come of it. Now, as my heart was recovering and reconnecting with my authentic self and with the Lord, I began to hunger once again for fresh words, hope, adventure, and vision. So I took my brother's words to heart and began to pray for the Holy Spirit to speak to me again and lead me to prophetic environments.

At the time, my contract job was coming to an end, so I was particularly praying for God to provide me with work. As I shared in Chapter 5, it was in this season that I remembered a prophecy someone had given me about a job that would open the door to more traveling. This led me to my current company, where I secured a permanent position. One of the many significant things about this job was that when they hired me, it was more about my soft skills than my hard skills. I had been nervous that I wouldn't stand out for the job due to the competitive nature of the London job market. But they explained that they ultimately chose me for my soft skills—my character, people skills, and communication skills—as those are much harder to teach. This experience was a lesson in the truth of the kingdom: If God gives you a job to do, you don't have to be afraid that you're not qualified. He is the one who qualifies you.

A year or so into this job, I felt in my spirit that change was coming. I also received another prophetic word about international relocation. I began to pray about this, and through a series of many more words, prayers, signs, and breakthroughs, the door opened for me to go on a work trip to the United States for three weeks.

When I first mentioned to my brother, Emmanuel, that I may be going to San Diego, California for work in 2019, he replied, "Oh, I hear that's the land of milk and honey." Immediately, I thought, *I am going to my Promised Land.* I received this as a prophetic sign that there was something waiting for me in California and that indeed it would be my Promised Land.

Although I had been to the US many times in the past, I had never been to California, so the West Coast of America was a new adventure for me. The beach town of San Diego was gorgeous and it was summer, so the weather was also beautifully sunny. As I usually did when my work travels took me to a new town, city, or, in this instance, country for work, I quickly found a church near me on Google. This one was called C3—now Awaken Church—and I immediately liked it from my first visit. It was a vibrant church with a crowd of young, Spirit-filled, and even more important, really friendly people. On my first day after church, I was running late to catch a train to downtown San Diego. Ken, the first person I had met from the welcome team, saw me waiting for an Uber that wasn't getting there anytime soon and kindly offered to give me a ride to the train station. What a great first impression of the church!

I got to make more friends in the church by the second and third time I visited. I quickly realized that my British accent was like a magnet to the American ear. It was amazing. My accent became the ice breaker into this new world. Literally everywhere I went, not just in church, Americans only needed to hear me speak and we would converse like I'd known them for a long time. I realized that by moving from Nigeria to the UK and spending 22 years in preparation for my transition to the US, I had received this God-given key to the hearts of the people in my new Promised Land. Who would have ever thought that?

As I got to know my new friends at Awaken Church, I shared my story and desire to move to the US permanently with them, explaining that I needed the job assignment, visa, and resources to make that happen, and none of that was on the horizon yet. A group of them laid hands on me and prayed over me that the Lord would make a way for me to move to America.

Later, I went for a prayer walk on the beach one evening. Prayer walking was something I had done for years in London. During the spring and summer months, I would walk about six miles (it took me just more than two hours) from home to work or back home as my regular exercise regimen rather than going to the gym, and during these walks, I would just pray and talk to the Lord about the future. Therefore, this was a normal practice for me. On this particular walk on the beach in Carlsbad, California, I began the process of "breaking ground" in my new Promised Land, the US. I quoted Joshua 1:3: "Every place that the sole of your foot will tread upon I have given you." I began to declare that the Lord had given this land to me because He had an assignment for me here. I poured out my heart to the Lord concerning the things He would do and blessed the land of California and the United States.

I returned to the UK at the end of those three weeks, feeling expectant for what the Lord was about to do. In a matter of two months, I miraculously got granted everything I needed to go on regular work trips to the US, including a visa and a project team. I spent the rest of 2019 back in San Diego before heading back to the UK for the end of year and Christmas at the end of 2019. While I was there, I celebrated Emmanuel's wedding at the end of 2019 and threw my grand 40th birthday celebration at the beginning of 2020. As I shared in the introduction, this was an incredible time to stand back and bear witness to the faithfulness and goodness of God to me and my whole family, but even more significantly for me, it marked a dramatic moment where it was as though God began to lift the veil for me to see my entire life with new eyes—more on this in a moment.

Within a short time, my prayers were answered again, and I got all the resources needed to move back to California for a year. I was still a UK employee and it wasn't a long-term plan, but it was the next step toward getting settled permanently in the US. It was also significant because I was given this opportunity at the beginning of the COVID-19 pandemic, when many people were losing their jobs or being furloughed. Walking on the wave of the prophetic (standing on the words the Lord had spoken to me, believing they would come to pass), I kept doing prayer walks over the land and declaring the word that America was where the Lord was planting me. I also got more involved at Awaken Church, San Diego, and stepped into what felt like a new level of authority and effectiveness in prayer, intercession, and prophetic ministry. Multiple people I met at church told me I had an anointing for prayer. Obviously, these people didn't know where I'd come from, but I knew this was happening as a result of all I had sown through my years of walking with the Lord.

The weekly women's prayer at Awaken Church was the highlight of my week. We met and prayed, speaking prophetically over each other and seeing mountains shift in our lives. One thing was for sure, the women at Awaken were on fire for God and I was glad to be a part of it! I met and befriended so many amazing women of God, who provided me with the spiritual strength and community I needed at this time. I was told that the lead pastors Jurgen and Leanne Matthesius, who had moved from Australia to start the church in San Diego, saw themselves as "spiritual midwives" to help people birth their dreams and visions. When I heard this,

I knew this was the place for me. I knew I was coming into a birthing season, so this was the place for me to be and this proved to be absolutely right! Someone once said, "When you are in the right place, at the right time, with the right people, great things happen." This was my experience with Awaken.

I was also blessed that this anointing and season of prayer was shared by my whole family. After the pandemic hit, we started organizing weekly prayers via Zoom. Mom was especially fervent about keeping up this practice. I remember one week I didn't schedule our weekly call, as I thought we had agreed to take a break, and Mom asked me about it. "Why are we taking a break?" she asked, surprised. "Is the devil on a break?" I immediately scheduled the next call. Despite being on three continents, it was such a gift to be able to stay connected in prayer. It's a testimony of the Lord's faithfulness that all my siblings are walking with Him, and I believe praying together has kept us united and fueled in our faith.

One amazing opportunity that arose during 2020 was the chance to create my first spoken-word album, "Speak the Word," in which I declare my favorite promises, prayers, and prophetic words from the Scriptures. I also began the process of writing this book as a vehicle to process all the understanding and insight that continued to unfold in this "lifting the veil" season of seeing my life with fresh revelation.

As that year and assignment came to an end, I was praying yet again for the Lord to open the door to a permanent job and place in America. By this point, I had a number of friends in California who were also prayer partners standing with me in agreement for this breakthrough. Their united message to me was, "Faith—obviously, your name is Faith. And we feel like we are learning to walk by faith by watching you right now in this season. You're demonstrating the process to us right now. We can't wait to see what is going to happen next."

Well, what happened next was that I received notice from work that I was going to be made redundant—the complete opposite of what I was praying for! I have had this experience more than once, and I know it's a common test to see what we are going to do. Will we stand in faith on the word we have from the Lord, continue to operate in the prophetic, and trust in what God is doing in the unseen? Or will we focus on what things look like in the visible realm, lose our faith, and become discouraged and hopeless?

I told the Lord, "Lord, You make a way where there seems to be no way." I kept speaking that and standing on that word. In God's perfect timing, the breakthrough came. Not only did I get a new job offer, but I also ended up with *two* offers. When this happened, I had the strangest sense that these offers had already been prepared just for me by God and had been waiting in the unseen for the moment of breakthrough. God is so amazing!

My new role required me to move to Florida, where I am now settled and leaning into the next season of what God wants to do in my life. I'm learning to walk in the prophetic more than ever—to take God's words, pray over them, and take steps of faith as the Lord leads. I now attend Winter Haven Worship Center church where I am serving and building a strong community around me. I have been greatly encouraged by the teachings from this church, some of which have inspired revelations and insights I share in this book. I also recently started a small group of women at my new church where the primary focus is learning to pray and declare the Word of God over our lives and the world.

The Missing Piece

In many ways, my new life in Florida hasn't changed my primary pursuits. I'm still growing in my career, still working on various ventures, caring for my family, involved in church community and volunteer ministry, and hoping and praying for marriage and children in my future. However, what has changed, is my perspective. Leading up to this change, I had three series of dreams.

One night in 2008, I had a dream that I had a huge, human-sized egg, which cracked open to reveal a baby. However, instead of crying like a normal newborn, this baby could already talk. In the dream, I was introducing everyone to this talking baby. When I woke up, I immediately knew the dream was significant and shared it with a friend, who agreed that it had something to do with what the Lord was doing in my life. My first hopeful interpretation was that it had something to do with the promise of marriage. I thought it was a picture of some kind of miraculous rapid development that would make up for all the time I felt I had lost in the waiting. I remember feeling very encouraged thinking that God knew I had been waiting. He hadn't forgotten me, and maybe there was some kind of reward coming.

Six years later, in 2014, after I stepped down from ministry and entered my soul-searching season, I had another dream. In the dream, I met a woman who was praying and quoted Ecclesiastes 3:1 to her: *"To everything, there is a time and season."* Then the woman prayed for me and I realized I was heavily pregnant and gave birth. Emmanuel was the first person I told about this dream, and his response was, "Faith, I think that you've had an angelic visitation." It was so powerful, so strong. Yet again, I felt like something was growing inside me that would be born, and I still hoped that it had something to do with my desire for marriage. In 2019, I had a similar dream yet again of being heavily pregnant and getting ready to give birth. In this dream, I was being given gifts to help with the birth and one of the gifts I was given was a pair of glasses.

In 2020 as I experienced the moment of revelation that changed my perspective, I realized these dreams were symbolic to my rebirth and transformation. It was significant to me that this process had taken 40 years to complete, and the year 2020 can be represented mathematically as $20 + 20 = 40$. In the Bible, the number 40 symbolizes a period of testing or quarantine, trial, and then triumph, a transformational and paradigm shift. It also signifies supernatural sustenance and is connected to the fulfillment of God's promise. In the Old Testament, the children of Israel wandered in the wilderness for 40 years, after which they came out of the wilderness and into the Promised Land, the land flowing with milk and honey, Canaan. In the New Testament, Jesus went into the wilderness and was tempted for 40 days and nights before emerging to commence His ministry.

According to Cindy Trim in her book, *The 40 Day Soul Fast*:

> In biblical numerology, the number 40 relates to the period of probation before the fulfillment of a promise. It is the product of the factors *four* and *ten*, which represent "completion" and "divine order," respectively. It seems fitting that 40 is also the gestation period for a human. In short 40 weeks, a microscopic seed planted in the womb transforms into a baby full of world-changing potential. But this new being must first let go of the safety of the womb by pushing through the confinement and darkness until at last emerging into the open and light.

The year 2020 has brought with it a paradigm shift in how we do things, imposing on us all a transformation of some sort.

Transformation Is About Vision

My favorite metaphor for my own transformation is that of the butterfly. There are many aspects of the butterfly's metamorphosis that I relate to, but the first and most important is that the central thing that changes in us when we go through a transformation process is our *perspective*. The caterpillar's range of vision is small, as it must crawl on the ground and can only sense its surroundings via antennae. The butterfly has fully developed eyes that can see and wings that can carry it high into the air, where it can view the world from a much wider vantage point. This is what the journey of transformation is about—becoming a person who can see reality through a certain lens, from a certain perspective.

This is also the journey of *faith*. On one level, faith is, or at least appears, blind. And it can often feel blind to choose to trust God even when nothing in your five senses is registering His presence or activity. But on another level, faith is about seeing and knowing the superior reality beyond our five senses, which is the realm of the Spirit, the realm of the kingdom of God. Our transformation as believers is ultimately about learning not only to see the kingdom, but live from that kingdom.

This was the great "Aha" I received upon turning 40. For so many years, I believed my journey of faith was about waiting to see the specific breakthroughs I had dreamed of for so long in different areas of my life. Instead, what happened was God took me higher, so I could see what my life was actually about and who I was becoming. I finally understood the meaning of the pair of eyeglasses I was given in my dream to help me give birth. It was as though He took all the pieces of my life and showed them to me through a new lens, and as I looked through it, I realized it was a kaleidoscope. The word *kaleidoscope* comes from Greek words meaning "to look at a beautiful shape." For so long, I had held on to the promise that He would make all things beautiful in their time, and now from this new vantage point, I saw the beauty that He had created in my life. I didn't have to wait for a husband, a better job, greater financial or ministry success, or whatever else I thought was "the missing piece" to complete the beautiful shape of my life. It was already beautiful!

We all have a missing piece in our lives and as we learn to view our lives through God's kaleidoscope, we will get to see the beauty in our lives as it is.

According to Merriam-Webster.com, a kaleidoscope is "an instrument containing loose bits of colored material (such as glass or plastic) between two flat plates and two plane mirrors so placed that changes of position of the bits of material are reflected in an endless variety of patterns." A kaleidoscope has been made into a children's toy which you look through to see changing colorful beautiful patterns as you rotate it and shake it up. God gave me a kaleidoscope of faith to look through to see my life as beautiful.

An article by Author Ken Mavosky says, "When you look into a kaleidoscope, you see something beautiful. But after you shake it up, destroying what is there, and hold it up to the light again, you will see something new and different, but equally beautiful. Life is much the same as the kaleidoscope. After being shaken, it will always reveal something new and beautiful, but only if we take the time to hold it up to the light and look inside."

Mavosky concluded, "Thus, the kaleidoscope has taken on a new meaning for me. It represents the initiative we all must take to sustain beauty in our lives and land in the right place, as life continues to change and we are continuously challenged. Things fall apart sometimes, but they can always be put back together again, achieving ultimate beauty with a new look, but only if we 'hold it up to the light and look inside'."[5]

What a *revelation*. We must refresh our perspective in the light of God's word continuously to see the beautiful patterns God is making of our lives over and over again as we progress through the highs and lows of life. Rather than being crushed by the challenges and pressures of life, we must renew our perspective by holding up our lives to the light of God's word to get His perspective of our lives and through that, we are transformed. This is what I call God's kaleidoscope, the gift He is giving to us for transformation after which we begin to view the constant changing patterns of our life as beautiful.

What's more, everything beautiful in my life was an expression of how I had learned to live in the kingdom of God. It was the fruit of prayer, intercession, meditating on and declaring the Word, living a holy life, and loving God and others. It was the overflow of walking with the Lord, choosing to trust Him, align my heart under Him as King, allow Him to guide my life, and honor His design and call for how to live my life. All of that had transformed me and radiated out to countless others. All of that had turned my life into an adventure. I didn't start out thinking it would be an adventure—I simply made a commitment to walk with the Lord. On that 30+ year journey, I have built a history with Him of highs, lows, and countless testimonies that prove He is worthy of my faith in Him.

The adventure of life in the kingdom is that we are not simply living our lives according to the world's script, where we hustle to advance in our career and rack up whatever accomplishments we desire. We are servants of the King who serve at His pleasure. On one hand, there is a cost to this way of living. We must forsake

---

5 Ken Mavosky, What Kaleidoscopes Communicate (https://www.forbes.com/sites/kenmakovsky/2013/06/06/what-kaleidoscopes-communicate/?sh=28c42f4c36c9)

doing life on our terms or timing. But the reward is that when we are living in the center of God's for our lives, fulfilling the assignments He has given us, then *we cannot fail.* No matter how the circumstances look, no matter the qualifications or resources we lack, He makes the way. In fact, He loves to perfect His strength in our weakness and do the impossible, because that is where we see Him most clearly at work and our faith in Him grows.

It is difficult to adequately express the joy I felt when I finally emerged from my chrysalis and saw that the story of my life was not what I had wrestled with for so long. Before I could see it through God's kaleidoscope, I thought something must be wrong that marriage, kids, career, and other milestones weren't happening like they seemed to be for everyone else. But once I saw the beautiful patterns God had been forming through this long journey, I realized that I had been living out His plan and purpose for me all along. I hadn't missed out on anything.

As I began to enjoy my newfound perspective, one of the first things I noticed was that so many people around me had not yet received or experienced this profound gift of sight and vision to see their lives through the kaleidoscope of divine purpose. Dr. Myles Monroe pointed this out in his powerful talk on vision, which gave me so much clarity and understanding of what I was experiencing. He explained that God has put vision inside us like a seed, but that a lot of people, even after many years, still haven't allowed that seed to germinate and grow to full term in their lives. In some ways, these people are like The Walking Dead, going through the motions of life but asleep to their vision and purpose. To emphasize this point, Munroe said, speaking to those who had not yet come to the realization of their God-given vision, "Congratulations, you're all virgins. A virgin is someone who has never done it before." The tragedy is that some people will die virgins to their vision if they never wake up to, cultivate, and fulfill them. And now that I have come awake to my own vision, I have also become passionate about helping others wake up to theirs.

No matter what your deepest dreams and longings are, I can promise you that nothing compares to the joy and fulfillment you will experience if you seek the Lord for His vision for your life, choose to follow His lead, feed on Him and His Word, allow Him to form you in the chrysalis of waiting and testing, and finally emerge with this powerful ability to see your life from His perspective, with eyes of faith. No matter how confusing, apparently meaningless, or disappointing your life may seem, there is hope when you surrender to Him and His transformation process. There is so much more to see than what you have seen.

The Small and Unseen

I have discovered that one of the themes in the journey of faith and living in the kingdom is that we are learning to see what is happening when it seems that nothing is happening. When we are waiting on God to fulfill His word and his promises, we are not merely being passive. Something powerful is forming us into who we were created to be. We are participating in the work Jesus is doing within us and through us to bless the world. I love how The Message puts it in Romans 8:22-25:

> All around us, we observe a pregnant creation. The difficult times of pain throughout the world are simply birth pangs. But it's not only around us; it's within us. The Spirit of God is arousing us within. We're also feeling the birth pangs. These sterile and barren bodies of ours are yearning for full deliverance. That is why waiting

> does not diminish us, any more than waiting diminishes a pregnant mother. We are enlarged in the waiting. We, of course, don't see what is enlarging us. But the longer we wait, the larger we become, and the more joyful our expectancy.

Those of us who give our lives to the Lord are pregnant with purpose. Even when it looks like something isn't happening, it is growing in the unseen, and eventually, it will break through into the seen. And the evidence of things unseen is our faith. The more we trust Him, the more our faith grows in strength and confidence. Like Abraham, we learn to "hope against hope" because we know that everything God promises He is able to and will perform.

Growth, influence, and success in the kingdom all operate according to this "unseen" principle. Jesus talked about the kingdom of God being like a mustard seed, which is the least of all the seeds, but when planted and grown, is greater than the herbs and becomes a tree where birds can nest in its branches (see Matthew 13:31-32). The kingdom of God tends to start out really small to the human eyes and understanding, but later exceeds all expectations and human thinking. A recent interpretation of this parable said, "God is crazy about small things and when we are consistent in the little things, it leads to the big things." Also, "small things open the doors to big things."

I believe this principle applies to each of us at an individual level. In fact, I have come to see us human beings as different types of trees that bear fruits in different seasons. One type of tree may bear its fruits within a few years of growth, and another tree may take many years to mature. So we cannot compare ourselves to others, as we are all made differently to serve different purposes and our life spans differ from person to person. All we must do is stay diligent in the path laid out for each of us, so we can accomplish the purpose for which we are here on earth.

I have come to see myself like an oak tree. Oak trees take about 30 to 40 years to grow to full maturity, because it takes this long to develop their root system, which can spread hundreds of miles at maturity and enable them to endure over a thousand years. I felt the Lord speaking to me that this is what He has been doing in my life. Though there seems to be this delay on the surface, He has been working on my roots underneath the surface and growing those roots of character development and virtues to sustain me for the life He has ahead. The Lord has been building in-depth character in me for 40+ years. Though things seem to have taken longer and been much harder than I expected, I have come out with virtues that cannot be bought with money–love, kindness, compassion, generosity, empathy, wanting the best for others, and authenticity.

This is the treasure of the kingdom—the riches God first develops inside us (the kingdom within) that will eventually manifest through us to bless those around us. Many of us get discouraged as we wait on God for certain promises to be fulfilled or disappointed when things don't happen the way we think they should. But this is often because we are measuring our lives and dreams according to our own standards or worldly standards of meaning or success that aren't necessarily aligned with the values of the kingdom. We may feel that we are working so hard and doing all we can to do everything right, but have little to show for it. What we can't yet see, but must learn to trust, is that God is working in the unseen to build a kingdom in us that far surpasses anything we could ask or think. Our expectations, hopes, and dreams pale in comparison to His plans for us, and if we will simply continue to put our faith in Him, we will see the fullness of those plans.

I once heard a sermon about the cross. When Jesus was dying

on the cross, the disciples watching were completely heartbroken, because from their perspective, there was no hope. The enemy had conquered. The Messiah was defeated. But of course, the Lord had a master plan. He was building His masterpiece of redemption, and this moment was just a snapshot. Because the disciples could only see the snapshot, all they could see was Jesus dying. But seen in the context of the full redemptive masterpiece, that snapshot didn't show Jesus being defeated—it showed Him achieving victory over death itself. Only through that moment could Jesus be resurrected and bring us eternal life and salvation.

That sermon really encouraged me. So often in our lives, all we can see is a snapshot. We can't see the bigger picture of what the Lord is saying or doing. If we could see the bigger picture, we would immediately say, "Ah, now I understand." But we don't get to see the full masterpiece until it's complete. However, what we do get—which not even the disciples got—is the assurance that God is faithfully building that masterpiece in our lives, just as He did with Jesus on the cross. The snapshot of today may not look very beautiful, but it will be in the end. God will use everything—the delays, the obstacles, and anything else the enemy has tried to throw at our lives. He makes all things beautiful in time.

Central to our journey of faith is learning to see the snapshots of our lives through this assurance and perspective shaped by God's masterpiece, His story of redemption in Christ. When we can't see *how* God is working all things for good in our present circumstances, our faith rests on *who* He is, revealed in Scripture, in the lives of countless believers who have walked a journey of faith, and in our own lives to this point. This is why we study Scripture and the lives of the saints, and gather with other believers to share what God is doing in our lives—so we can learn to see our lives through the testimonies that reveal God's masterpiece unfolding from the beginning up to the present, because He promises that He is also building a testimony in our own lives.

Hebrews 11:2 (NKJV) says that *by "faith, "the elders obtained a [good] testimony."* What is a good testimony? In simple terms, a good testimony is the life we live when we choose to truly believe in God and surrender fully to Him and His call on our lives. Everyone who says yes to this life signs up for a journey with the Lord that will be unique to the circumstances of our lives, but will contain certain elements—a God-sized promise or mission impossible for us to fulfill alone, testing and trials that prove our character and strengthen our trust in Him, and breakthroughs and fruitfulness that not only bless us, but nourish and impact many others. It is by taking this journey that we grow from immature to mature believers who look, think, and act like Jesus.

So how do you walk out this journey of faith and transformation? In the next chapter, I'll unpack some of the most important lessons I've learned on my own journey.

QUESTIONS FOR REFLECTION

1. Where is your 'Promised Land?' Have you taken the time to respond to God's call to walk and pray through and over it, in line with the scripture quoted? If not, can you plan a time to do that? [Joshua 1:3]

2. Do you think you are awake to your purpose and vision or just going through the motions like the Walking Dead? How can you begin to pray for this area of your life?

3. Do you think you have a 'missing piece' in your life? How have you dealt with it so far?

4. Do you ever compare your timeline with other people's timelines? How does this make you feel? What can you do to appreciate the timeline you have that it is beautiful as it is?

5. Where are you on the 'transformation journey' of life? Have you ever taken a moment to plot out your experiences along those lines? Could you take some time to reflect and draw this out? What has impacted you in each butterfly stage of life? Egg, caterpillar, chrysalis, and butterfly?

6. Who are some of the heroes of faith that have impacted your life? What areas of their lives have inspired you?

7. Are you meditating on and declaring His Word? What verses could you start meditating on and declaring into your situations?

Chapter 10

THROUGH THE FURNACE

Kingdom theme: Testing is what refines our faith like gold, so we can take hold of the treasure of the kingdom.

HEBREWS 11:1 SAYS THAT *"faith is the substance of things hoped for, the evidence of things not seen."* In his first epistle to the church, Peter likens the substance of faith to *gold* (see 1 Peter 1:6-9). Like all precious metals mined from the ground, gold must be purified before it can be of use. When a metallurgist wants to refine gold, they put it in a furnace where the high temperature causes the ore to melt and the impurities to rise to the top. In our own lives, we too must pass through the "furnace" of testing and trials, so that our faith can be proven and purified.

Testing and trials aren't exactly fun, but there can be no genuine faith or transformation in our lives without them. Every single person in Scripture or church history with a testimony of partnership with God experienced testing. Even Jesus Himself had to be tested and tried. A test of faith exposes what we really believe. It's easy to trust God when life is comfortable and our prayers are answered quickly. It's much tougher to trust Him when life is difficult and the things we're praying and believing for just don't seem to be happening. But it's in that place of tension between the seen and the unseen where our faith grows, where we begin to develop the ability we need to transform from the caterpillar, whose vision is so limited, to the butterfly who can see and perceive with much greater vision.

I once came across a quote by Jennifer LeClaire that resonated deeply with my own journey of faith: "The devil will put you in the furnace of affliction, but the Lord will use it to refine you (see Isaiah 48:10). The furnace of affliction will either birth a personal prayer movement in your life or you'll just be miserable and die trying to fight God."

LeClaire makes two important points here. First, many of the tests we face in our lives do originate in the enemy's attacks, which we all experience living in a fallen world. For example, after 20 or so years of waiting for marriage, I have concluded that prolonged singleness for those who desire to be married, like poverty or sickness, was never intended by God, but is in fact a result of the fall. He said, *"It is not good for man to be alone"* (Genesis 2:18 NKJV). Prolonged singleness for most people is connected to many factors in the culture, families, and our own personal lives, and many of them are effects of sin and brokenness. However, like all realities we face in a fallen world, we can be sure that God's heart is to redeem it and use it for good in our lives.

Secondly, the purpose of every test of faith is not just to drive us towards better theology or knowledge of Scripture, but towards God Himself. Faith is trust. It is putting our lives fully in God's hands because we are confident in His heart toward us. The real gold–the treasure that forms in our lives through testing and trials–is our history with God. This is our testimony–our story of God's faithfulness in our lives–and the only way we get that story is by being willing to follow Him into situations where He has to show up.

Joseph and the Journey of Testing

Growing up reading the Bible, I have always been familiar with the story of Joseph, the son of Jacob, but in recent years, I have paid much more attention to certain aspects of his life. I have also received several prophetic words that draw parallels with Joseph's faith and calling and my own. One person told me I had a "Joseph mandate," that God had sent me from my homeland to another country so that I could ultimately bless my family and many others. So many of the lessons I have learned about faith show up in Joseph's journey. In particular, Joseph is a profound example of what it looks like to successfully pass through seasons of testing God uses to refine our hearts, deepen our trust in Him, and ultimately prepare us to see our dreams, purpose, and destiny fulfilled.

In Psalm 105, we find a reflection on the story of Joseph in which the psalmist makes this statement: *"Until the time that his word came to pass, the word of the LORD tested him"* (Psalm 105:19 NKJV). Joseph's "word" was the dream he had as a young man that one day his family members would all bow before him. As soon as he announced this word, he found himself plunged into a journey of testing in which, by all appearances, nothing like his dream could ever possibly happen. In these tests, we clearly see the attacks of the enemy and evil at work. His brothers sell him into slavery and lie to his father that he is dead. As a slave, he is falsely accused by his master's wife and thrown into prison. As a prisoner, he is forgotten by the butler whose dream he interpreted. Yet God is also clearly at work in all of these situations, protecting Joseph, granting him favor and success, and ultimately giving him the opportunities that prepare him to step in to fulfill the word of the Lord for his life.

Through this journey, we see Joseph's faith and character being tested, proven, and refined like gold. We also see that he is developing his history of trust and relationship with God. He refused to be seduced by his master's wife because it was a "sin against God" (Genesis 39:9). In prison, though his own dream had not yet come to pass, he became a dream interpreter, first for Pharaoh's butler and baker, and then for Pharaoh himself, because "interpretations belong to God" (Genesis 40:8). And when his brothers finally stood before him and his dream of twenty-some years earlier was finally fulfilled, he held no bitterness toward them, but finally saw the truth: *"But as for you, you meant evil against me; [but] God meant it for good, in order to bring it about as [it is] this day, to save many people alive"* (Genesis 50:20 NKJV). It is by continuing to trust and obey God, even when it is costly, that Joseph became a truly great man, a man whom both God and Pharaoh could trust with the authority, wisdom, and generosity to save not only Joseph's family, but an entire nation from a deadly famine.

Undoubtedly, Joseph, like us, did not know that all his difficult seasons of testing would lead him right to where he needed to be to fulfill the word of the Lord. But thousands of years later, we have the benefit of being able to look at Joseph's story and see that even as a slave, a servant, and a prisoner, Joseph was on target to become prime minister as God had always intended. We too can be confident that if God has given us a dream, word, or promise about the desires, purpose, and destiny He has placed in our hearts, then He is working in every circumstance to prepare us to receive those things. And the way He prepares us is by teaching us to trust Him—specifically, to trust Him in the face of *temptation* and the process of His *timing*, which is always different from what we expect.

The Test of Temptation

As we see from the beginning of Scripture with the story of Adam and Eve, the enemy tempts us to sin by inviting us to take something apparently good and desirable, but in the wrong way, at the wrong time, and for the wrong reasons. I remember the temptation in my early twenties to lie to the university, so I could qualify for home student fees. Obviously, getting into university was my first priority in moving to the UK, as my goal was to provide for my family and be a good steward of the opportunity God had given me in bringing me to London in the first place. But I knew I couldn't get to this good end through dishonest means, and chose to trust that God would make a way, which He did.

Though, by far, my greatest temptations have come around my deepest heart's desire for marriage and family. As I've shared, there have been many men I have been attracted to, or who were attracted to me, who were not God's choice for me and would have led to some kind of compromise either in or out of marriage if I had chosen to pursue or give in to them. In Songs of Songs 8:4b (NIV), it says, *"Do not arouse or awaken love until it so desires."* This means we have a choice to manage our desires and longings and decide what we will allow to grow or not. Throughout my twenties and thirties, as I met guys and was attracted to them, I had to choose how to manage that attraction. I had a pretty strong conviction that it was not my role to be the pursuer in the relationship, and I had made a firm commitment of purity and abstinence before marriage to the Lord in my early twenties, so I wasn't going to get involved with someone who didn't share that standard. Many Christians today seem to think that they can surrender their lives to the Lord but hold back just one area, often their sexuality, from Him, but I've always known in my heart of hearts that this is a compromise that won't work.

For me, the real temptation was to feed the attraction and crush to the point where I was starting to imagine that the guy had feelings or was pursuing me on some level. This is where staying accountable to my close friends who would speak the truth to me proved to be a lifesaver. I had to learn to love the truth and not be afraid to hear it, because the truth is what sets us free. In each situation where I was nursing hope that a certain guy would return my feelings, my friends sat down with me and said, "Faith, look at the evidence. There's no evidence that he likes you. We're not going to sugarcoat it. This is the truth and you've got to get over it." Of course it wasn't fun to hear in the moment, but that truth truly did set me free from holding onto an illusion that was only going to lead me into heartbreak.

Of course, attraction wasn't the only thing I was wrestling with in these scenarios. As I've described, there was also pressure to compromise. The message I often heard was that for those of us dealing with prolonged singleness, it was somehow our fault that we were still single. People told me I was too picky, pushy, or religious. They also said that I wasn't open enough, that I didn't look or dress right or show enough of my legs. I was told that I needed deliverance, that I should sow more money to receive my breakthrough, that there may be a curse stopping this from happening, that I ought to go and have a child so that I don't miss out as my biological clock ticks (or freeze my eggs just in case), or that I should just pick a guy and go home with him. Over the years, I have observed many Christian singles give into these messages, try to take shortcuts, and practically do whatever it takes to get married and have children. But after considering these options, trying some of them, and watching others try them, I don't believe these are God's solutions if that's not what the Lord has told you to do. Somehow, people tend to suggest that those of us that are single have done something wrong and that's why we are still single. Or that we have to take dramatic steps to correct the situation. So how do we respond when people imply that it's your fault, you're still single, that you're not trying hard enough or "putting yourself out there" in the right way? It is in God's hands and up to His timing. God has not forgotten us or the fact that we are single and wish to be married, but it's not something that we can make happen on our own.

God is true to His word and I believe that when we follow through on God's leading, He will also come through for those that wait on Him.

Another aspect of temptation in this area of my life were the many opportunities to compare myself to all the women around me meeting their husbands. I had to make the choice not to allow shame, jealousy, or bitterness to enter my heart as I asked, "God, why not me?" Holding on to the truth I embraced at seventeen—"My life is not in the hands of any man. It's in the hands of God"—helped me guard my heart, so I could respond to others from a place of love. It was this truth that helped me shut the door to jealousy when my friend Jane ended up dating the guy I liked, or as friend after friend met their husband and got married. I didn't fall into blaming or resenting others for getting the blessing I desired. Because my life is in the hands of God, I have always believed that what is mine will be mine, and no one will be able to steal it. I don't have to compete with anyone for my blessing.

Over the years, I have had several people comment to me, "Faith, it's amazing how you're able to genuinely celebrate your friends." It was true that I got a lot of chances to practice this. At one point, a friend's mom called me and told me off for agreeing to be a bridesmaid for so many of my friends. "Faith, this is ridiculous," she said. "You have to stop doing this. It's costing you a fortune. Who is paying for the dresses?" But I gladly paid for the dresses and loved celebrating with my friends because I was truly happy for them. Why shouldn't I celebrate their breakthrough? I knew, and still know, my breakthrough is going to come, and if anything, their breakthrough is a testimony that God will bring my breakthrough in His perfect time, just as He did for them.

God brings our breakthroughs turn by turn. A friend had a dream about this. She saw us all in a bank standing in line waiting to be served. As the people ahead of us were served, the line got shorter, which meant that our turn was approaching. Seeing other people served only increased our anticipation. That's the way I choose to look at it when a friend gets their breakthrough. It means the Lord is answering prayers and the line is getting shorter, so my turn is coming soon. I'm going to rejoice with them when their turn comes, because when my turn comes, I want them to rejoice with me! The Bible tells us to rejoice with those who rejoice, because when one person gets a breakthrough, it's also a collective breakthrough. The list is getting shorter because people are getting served, and our promise is coming.

I have certainly felt my share of frustration, disappointment, and the temptation to fall into shame as I have watched my friends getting married, having children, and living lives that look so different to mine. Some years ago, I attended my friend, Jennifer's, tenth wedding anniversary and vow renewal celebration. Before the event, I struggled with thoughts of comparison and disappointed expectations. Jennifer and I had also started praying for our husbands together in our early twenties. Now she had been happily married for ten years and had four beautiful children, and I was still waiting. I never imagined that I would be showing up for an event like that, still single. During the celebration, Jennifer and her husband told the story of how they met, got me to stand up, and explained to everyone that I was instrumental to their meeting. I felt honored and touched in the moment, but later, my negative thoughts returned as I imagined the audience looking at me and wondering why I was still single. I also reflected that in addition to Jennifer, at least four of my other married friends had met their spouses through me. In the end, I had to just take all of these thoughts and feelings to the Lord, put it all in His hands, and say, "God, I don't understand why I have always been the matchmaker and the bridesmaid and not yet the bride. But You're in control, and You're going to make everything beautiful in its time. That was the word You gave me."

The Test of Timing

In 2014, when I had the dream of being pregnant and giving birth, I had this overwhelming sense that, "This is it! My breakthrough is finally here." Soon after that, in early 2015, I picked up a book by Dutch Sheets called *God's Timing for Your Life*. In the book, Sheets explains the difference between the Greek words for time—*chronos*, *kairos*, and *plēroō*. *Chronos* refers to the general passage of time, the clock, and the calendar. *Kairos* is connected to the timing of certain events, the opportune time for them to occur, and *plēroō* is the "fullness of time" in which those events actually come to pass. To use the analogy of childbirth, the 40-week term of pregnancy is the *kairos*, and *plēroō* is the moment of birth.

After reading this book, my first thought was about my dream of giving birth. *I need to do something to move this breakthrough from the* kairos *to the* plēroō, I thought. *I don't want to miss this "fullness of time" or let anything abort this baby.* I decided to call my friends and ask them to start fasting and praying with me. For several weeks, we had a call every morning to pray what I called "birthing" prayers. I was so expectant to see something happen. But as the days and weeks rolled on and nothing did, we began to lose our motivation and eventually stopped our morning prayer sessions.

Five years later when I turned 40 and finally saw what God was birthing in my life—my own personal transformation—I reflected on my well-intentioned effort to affect the timing of God's breakthrough. The Lord led me to consider the story of Elizabeth and Zacharias, the parents of John the Baptist. Scripture says that they were an older couple who hadn't been able to have any children. In those days, people commonly assumed that if you were barren, it must be a consequence for sin in your life, but the Bible specifically emphasizes that they were righteous people (see Luke 1:6). Zacharias was a priest who received a unique privilege to go before the Lord and burn incense in the temple. It was during this likely once-in-a-lifetime event that the angel of the Lord appeared to Zacharias and announced, *"Do not be afraid, Zacharias, for your prayer is heard; and your wife Elizabeth will bear you a son, and you shall call his name John"* (Luke 1:13 NKJV). I don't believe the angel was referring to a prayer that Zacharias had been praying that day or even in that season. Most likely, he and Elizabeth had prayed for children when they were younger, but once Elizabeth passed childbearing age, they probably stopped praying. So the Lord heard and answered their prayers, but the timing had to be right because they were going to give birth to John the Baptist, who was the forerunner of Jesus.

What this story showed me was that prayer and fasting do not change God's timing for our spiritual breakthroughs or the fulfillment of our promises and destiny. His timing is set, and as we see not only with Elizabeth and Zacharias, but also with Joseph and so many other heroes of faith, that timing is connected to a much bigger story that He is telling, in which we simply play a role along with many others, albeit a unique and important role.

This is not to say that prayer and fasting are not important. The angel clearly told Zacharias that Elizabeth's pregnancy was a response to their prayers. Jesus told us that the Lord wants us to *"always pray and not give up"* (Luke 18:1 NKJV). I think of Hannah in 1 Samuel 1:1-28, who cried out to God desperately for a child because she had been barren and was being ridiculed by the other wife of her husband. As she poured out her heart to the Lord and made a vow to give her firstborn son over to the service of the Lord, the Lord heard and granted her request and soon after, she received her breakthrough, a son Samuel.

So, prayer is necessary for breakthrough, but it is really more about *positioning us* for the breakthrough. Yes, I do believe there are times where there are delays because the enemy has come in and is blocking the answer to our prayers, and when we fast and pray, it can break that, and then the manifestation happens. But even that is subject to God's timing. Prayer and fasting ensures that the promise comes to pass in God's timing and that we don't miss it because it is possible to miss God's timing.

Undergoing the test of God's timing is designed to bring us to a place of rest where we can be confident that we have done our part by praying, trusting, and positioning our hearts to receive what He wants to do, and we know He will do His part. So often, I have felt this pressure or panic, like I'm not doing something I should be doing and will miss out as a result. But time and time again, I have seen that anything I might do to "help" God fulfill His promises according to my preferred timeline just falls by the wayside. Consider Joseph in prison. After interpreting the butler's dream, he took the initiative to beg him, *"But remember me when it is well with you, and please show kindness to me; make mention of me to Pharaoh, and get me out of this house. For indeed I was stolen away from the land of the Hebrews; and also I have done nothing here that they should put me into the dungeon"* (Genesis 40:14-15 NKJV). Yet after the butler returns to Pharaoh's court, he forgets about Joseph and only remembers him *two years later* when the time comes and Pharaoh needs his dream interpreted. God kept Joseph where he needed to be till the appointed time, and nothing Joseph did or didn't do could change that.

When you're enduring the test of timing, like the test of temptation, it's uncomfortable. It's confusing. Life isn't happening the way you expect, the way you hoped, prayed for, and worked at. It makes you feel frustrated and powerless. But when you finally realize that all you can do is trust God and you make that choice, you've broken through and passed the test. He is in control. Your times are in His hands, and He is making them beautiful, no matter how things look in the moment. You haven't missed His plan for your life or messed it up. You're still on target to receive His promises and fulfill your purpose. All you need to do is trust His timing, embrace what He's doing, and position your heart with expectancy, so you can reap in due season. Now, when moments come where I feel that familiar sense that "Maybe I should be doing something to make this happen," I will pray and fast, not out of desperation to see a breakthrough, but to reposition my heart back in the place of trust in God and His timing. That is the true breakthrough I need—the breakthrough of putting my heart at rest in His promises and timing instead of being tossed by fear and doubt. His timing is of the essence, and my job is to wait for it in the place of faith and prayer, believing that He is faithful who promised.

Guarding the Heart

As I have come through the tests of temptation and timing in my own life, I have concluded that God is after one primary thing: *my heart.* Proverbs 4:23 (NKJV) says, *"Keep your heart with all diligence, for out of it spring the issues of life."* The greatest commandment is, *"You shall love the LORD your God with all your heart, with all your soul, and with all your strength"* (Deuteronomy 6:5). Loving God is the fundamental thing, the foundation of our life, and love flows from our hearts. However, because the human heart is *"deceitful above all [things], and desperately wicked"* (Jeremiah 17:9 NKJV), we must go through a process of refinement, so God can expose any area of our hearts that could lead us to betray our commitment to Him and into compromise.

Consider the story of God asking Abraham to sacrifice his son Isaac to Him on the altar. Isaac was the miracle son, the fulfillment of the promise God had made to Abraham. Yet God asked Abraham to give Isaac up to demonstrate that Abraham fully trusted God and his heart was loyal to Him above all. In response to Abraham's surrender and obedience, God makes this stunning statement:

> *"By Myself I have sworn, says the LORD, because you have done this thing, and have not withheld your son, your*

> *only [son]--blessing I will bless you, and multiplying I will multiply your descendants as the stars of the heaven and as the sand which [is] on the seashore; and your descendants shall possess the gate of their enemies. In your seed, all the nations of the earth shall be blessed, because you have obeyed My voice."* (Genesis 22:16-18 NKJV)

Significantly, Isaac was not Abraham's "only son"—he also had Ishmael. Yet Isaac was the son of promise, the one chosen by God to carry on the bloodline of God's covenant people, and in that sense, he is a counterpart to Jesus, God's "only begotten son," whom the Father would lay on the altar on our behalf. God did not ask Abraham to sacrifice something that He Himself was not already planning to sacrifice. He simply wanted to know He had Abraham's heart for His own sake, not for anything he would get from God.

Scripture is clear that God knows the desires of our heart and wants to give them to us His way. The Psalms say, *"Delight yourself also in the LORD, And He shall give you the desires of your heart"* (Psalm 37:4 NKJV). When He asks us to give something up that we really want, or wait on Him to give our desire to us, He is not trying to deprive or punish us. He is trying to protect our hearts, so we can be whole and able to enjoy Him and all the good things He wants to give us. Are these sacrifices of trust painful? Yes. This has certainly been true in my journey of waiting for marriage, and my heart is much more sensitive than it used to be as a result. Like Job, I often ask, "Why, God?" and don't really receive any good answers. I know that I still need healing from certain aspects of this process. At the same time, after paying this price for 20 years, my heart is committed to seeing this journey through, no matter what it takes.

Some people think that after waiting so long, I should just give in, compromise, and try to make something happen, but I see it the opposite way. I've waited this long for God's best for my life and I'm not going to stop now. I understand that could mean I never get married. In the "hall of faith" in Hebrews, it says that those who received a good testimony of faith didn't all receive their promise in their lifetime because God had something better for them. Of course, I hope I receive this promise sooner than later, but I know that what matters most is trusting God and waiting for His best. I am also confident that despite the pain in the journey, trusting God has saved me from much worse heartbreak and wounding that would have come if I had compromised myself with one of the men I met on my journey. I know so many people who carry painful baggage from broken relationships, and hearing their stories helps me feel gratitude that I haven't had to carry that. The truth is that whether we choose God's way or our own way, we will pay a price, and I believe the price of going our own way is steeper in the end. Trusting God can be painful, but in the end, it protects and saves us from destruction.

It's not as though I'm coming through this journey of testing empty-handed. Yes, I am continuing to hope and pray for the promise of love in marriage. But I am also delighting in the love I have found now, the love that is always with me. We all desire love above all, but what we must all discover is that the love we are created for is found in God Himself. He is the source of the love we need and long for. As I have surrendered my search for love in marriage to the Lord, I can truly say that I have received His love in return, and even if I don't get marriage in the end, I have this intimate relationship with God that is beautiful and fulfilling and has been my safe haven through every struggle and storm. The center of every beautiful love story is uncompromised love—two people who are fully loyal and committed to each other. That's the kind of relationship the Lord builds with us as we learn to love Him more deeply.

The Treasure in the Field

Though I would have loved for God to fulfill my lifelong desires for marriage and family when I turned 40, in the end, He gave me something infinitely more precious—the revelation that my story has not been about a career, ministry, or marriage, but about His kingdom. This is my purpose in life—to live in the kingdom of God, to advance it, and *be* the kingdom of God. As Jesus said, *"For indeed, the kingdom of God is within you"* (Luke 17:21b NKJV).

I wrote in a previous chapter about a message that impacted me significantly on the parable of the hidden treasure: *"The kingdom of heaven is like a treasure hidden in a field, which a man found and hid; and for joy over it, goes and sells all that he has and buys that field"* (Matthew 13:44 NKJV). Jesus was emphasizing that a person should be willing to part with all he or she has to possess the kingdom. As I said, I decided that day to "buy the field," though I didn't yet know what that meant. What I discovered was that "buying the field" isn't just a one-time decision, but a lifestyle of choosing to continually lay down our lives like Jesus did. Self-giving and sacrificial love is what being the kingdom is all about—which is why it is upside down to the kingdom of the world, which is all about self-serving.

Consider some of the sayings of Jesus that capture the generous, loving, sacrificial way of life in the kingdom. First, He said that to be the greatest in the kingdom, you must be the servant of all. This is where we get the concept of a "servant leader." In other words, you lead by serving the needs of those around, below, and above you. Worldly thinking, which is self-promoting, says to be the greatest, you have to fight your way through to the top and maybe trample on others, if need be, to get there. Also, you should be served by those below you. This is quite the opposite to how the kingdom of God operates. Consider how Jesus, the King of Kings, embodied this from the moment He came into the world. Most earthly kings are born into wealth and privilege—the world waits on them. Yet Jesus was born in the humblest circumstances to humble people, and He grew up serving them and became the servant of all. This is how greatness and authority operate in His kingdom—by serving others.

Another important principle in the kingdom of God is generosity, which says *"Give and it shall be given to you"* (Luke 6:38 NKJV) and *"There is one who scatters, yet increases more; and there is one who withholds more than is right, but it leads to poverty"* (Proverbs 11:24 NKJV). These words stand in direct opposition to our human thinking, which says the way to increase is to take and accumulate for ourselves. Forgiveness is perhaps the most difficult form of generosity we are called to practice in the kingdom because it means instead of demanding a debt owed to us, we allow the debtor to go free. From a human, worldly point of view it makes no sense to forgive those who have deliberately hurt you, perhaps in a very terrible way. But Jesus tells us to forgive because we have been forgiven an impossibly huge debt by the Father, so how can we hold a grudge against our fellow humans whose debt to us is insignificant by comparison (see Matthew 18)? Forgiveness does not justify what the person has done as being okay—it is simply you releasing them from your judgment and handing them over to the Lord. Forgiveness really does set you free to move forward, which is probably why Nelson Mandela used this strategy in South Africa to promote unity and progress.

Jesus also said, *"Most assuredly, I say to you, unless a grain of wheat falls into the ground and dies, it remains alone; but if it dies, it produces much grain"* (John 12:24 NKJV). There is no growth, multiplication, or fruitfulness in the kingdom of God without sacrifice and even death. Everything good we receive in the kingdom of God is connected to someone else's sacrifice—obviously, Jesus' sacrifice for us on the cross, but also the sacrifices of countless men and women who have followed Him by laying down their lives in sacrificial love and obedience.

In 2020, I was reminded of this profoundly when I received a newsletter from The Prayer Foundation in England and read an account by Julie Anderson, one of the leaders who helped to organize and put on The Call England, which I had attended in 2002. Julie explained that obeying God in leading this event required sacrificial obedience and radical faith to rely on God and see Him do what seemed overwhelming and impossible. She said:

> I wanted to run from all my responsibilities when leading The Call England, whether I led from the rear, or the head, it seemed like such a lot of responsibility. I first learned to grow in God's grace when I understood it was the way forward. Each morning I awakened to obey how to serve God and know what He wanted me to do for Him—I knew we had to pray for everything that should happen . . . I learned each day to obey with what God was giving.

As I read this, I realized that this event–which I saw as my "making" that launched me into intercession for the nations–had happened through the sacrifice of others. I had never really appreciated that my blessing had cost someone else. Humbled and grateful, I reached out to Julie to thank her, and received this reply:

> Thank you so very much for your lovely testimony from The Call, England. It was the best and the worst time I went through—and probably dragged everyone else through who was around me then. God came and dealt with the unity of hearts of all the leaders we were working with, and everyone who came and did not—but heard about it all. The vision was paid for in full and God was certainly all over everything. I made some lifelong relationships, and certainly lost a few significant friendships and relatives! as people saw things in a new light. However, it was a huge call of obedience for us all.

When I read this, I was even more shocked and grateful. Sometimes obeying God will cost money, friends, family members, jobs, opportunities, and even our very lives. Yet whenever we choose to lay these things on the altar, we can be sure that He will take them and use them to bless us and so many others through us.

I remember some years ago in London, I came out of the Underground station by Arsenal Stadium just after a football match. The crowd of people coming into the station to get on the train was like a tidal wave and I was the only one going against the traffic. *How on earth am I going to get through this humongous crowd of people?* I had to put my head down and push hard to make my way through the flow of traffic, which was a challenge indeed. When I finally got to the front of the station, I heard someone behind me say, "Thank you!" I turned to see that a line of people had followed me as I forged a path through the tide of people.

It's never easy to swim against the tide, but whenever we do, it doesn't just help us. We become pioneers and trailblazers for those who will follow behind us. One of the main reasons I decided to share my story of waiting for marriage is that I believe I and others who long to be married and are trusting God in our season of prolonged singleness are called to be pioneers, showing others that there is another option than simply going with the flow. It can be tempting to feel that you are all alone on this journey and that there are few people who share your conviction that you are doomed to be alone forever. It can feel daunting to look for role models and mentors in the church and come up with few. This is why people end up saying, "If you can't beat them, join them." But joining the world means losing ourselves. At some point, we must choose to become the change we wish to see in the world, to be the role model for others we wish we had for ourselves. This is how all change happens.

Some years ago, I did a study on the life of Kathryn Kuhlman, one of the great revivalists of the 21st century. She was known as the woman who believed in miracles because she believed in God. Miss Kuhlman's ministry received international fame for the numerous healing miracles that took place during her meetings where thousands attended from far and wide within the United States. Her success was attributed to her close walk with the Holy Spirit, but according to her, this did not begin until after her "death to self" experience, as she called it.

In 1938, Miss Kuhlman married a divorced Texas evangelist, Burroughs Waltrip, who left his wife with two small sons. The years she was married proved to be her "wilderness" years, during which she lost her ministry and felt she had chosen her husband, whom she referred to as "Mister," over God. The marriage ended six years later when she had her "death to self" experience in Los Angeles, California:

"I had to make a choice. Would I serve the man I loved,

> or the God I loved? I knew I could not serve God and live with Mister. No one will ever know the pain of dying like I know it, for I loved him more than I loved life itself. And for a time, I loved him even more than God. I finally told him I had to leave. God never released me from that original call." [6]

After this "death to self" experience, Kathryn Kuhlman went on to build a very successful ministry in Pennsylvania as she partnered with the Holy Spirit. Such was the impact of His power over her life and ministry that during her meetings before or while speaking, people received great healings, such as blind eyes opening, the mute speaking, tumors and cancers disappearing, and the crippled walking out of wheelchairs. She began holding regular miracle services at Carnegie Hall in Pittsburgh, where people flocked in their thousands to experience the great miracles, as well as medical professionals who verified some of the healings. Miss Kuhlman's ministry became one of the greatest in her era until her death on February 20, 1976. At the height of her success, she held meetings with a capacity of well over 18,000 people and experienced many great miracles.

For me right now, death to self means letting go of the timing of the promise for a husband rather than letting go of the promise itself, but I also recognize that, as Miss Kuhlman's example shows, we have to continue being open to God's word in our lives, even when it's not what we want to hear. Sometimes we discover more of what it means to die to self as we go deeper with God. I know that I have to always be learning more about how exactly God is calling me to be obedient.

Moreover, if we truly undertake the journey of faith, we will

6 Buckingham, Jamie. Kathryn Kuhlman Daughter of Destiny (Bridge Publishing Inc. Copyright 1976), pg. 88.

all undergo a "death to self" process because that is an essential ingredient of spiritual transformation. This isn't just for "super" Christians with platform ministries—it's for all of us. For instance, I recently got to know a lovely woman at my church in Florida named Barbara. She told me she had been widowed and was grieving the loss of her husband, who was her best friend. In the end, she chose to submit the pain of her grief to God and ask Him to lead her through this "death" season. Barbara ended up starting a connect group to minister to other widows and began to see them encounter the love of God in profound ways, which in turn brought her so much joy. When I spoke to her, we both agreed that when we surrender to Jesus, out of death comes life, and out of pain comes healing. Just like the caterpillar dies to give birth to the butterfly, so dying to ourselves will lead to a rebirth and resurrection that will cause us to become even more fruitful and effective in who we were created and called to be.

In my own life, I have seen this to be true, specifically regarding my voice. As a teenager, I first found my voice in the secret place interceding to come to England and went public in a big way with my voice at The Call England, then lost my voice during the "dark season" of waiting and unanswered questions. As I emerged from that season, I not only recovered my voice, but also discovered that God was stirring me to use my voice in new ways, and that I had stepped into a new anointing and authority to declare His Word and promises over my life and others.

One of the books I read in this time of recovering my voice was *Decrees That Make the Devil Flee* by Jennifer LeClaire, which is an excellent resource on our authority as believers. She lays out the biblical truth that Christians are called to be kings and priests. However, many of us don't know how to operate in our kingly anointing. More of us understand that we have a priestly anointing to minister to the Lord and people through prayer. But our kingly anointing is an anointing to *make decrees*. When a king makes a decree, then it is established. In the kingdom of God, we are not merely the King's subjects. We are His delegated authorities with a kingly anointing to decree what He is saying "on earth as it is in heaven" and see them happen.

When I read this book, I was so stirred to start making more decrees and walking in my spiritual authority. I felt a deep conviction in my spirit: "Lord, I need to prophesy Your words over the land, over the nations, people, and my life." I ended up recording and producing an album that was entirely made up of declarations of promises and prayers from the Scriptures. I also started a connect group in church for young women called "Young Women Learning to Speak the Word." The sole focus of the group is learning to use the power of words and walk in the authority Christ has given to us. A few weeks after we started meeting, our pastor began preaching about the power of the Word of God one Sunday and literally used the Scriptures we had just gone through in our group. The ladies were amazed at the confirmation in what they were learning.

As I've shared, in 2020, I also received a fresh anointing for prayer and was inspired to release a spoken word album in March 2021 called *Speak The Word*. This is an album of prayers, Scriptures, declarations, and meditations connected to my walk with God over the years. This album is available on all the major media online platforms like Spotify, iTunes, Amazon, Apple music, and YouTube. I wanted to make these prayers readily available, so they could be played to those in hospitals, quarantines, and even in prisons. I still have yet to see the fullness of this vision, but the testimonies I have received thus far have been so encouraging to me. They have confirmed that when we are obedient and pay the price, God uses us to impact others.

People have told me that the power of God has touched them through this album. I have read testimonies of healing, peace of mind to sleep well for those struggling to sleep, encouragement to step out in faith, and many more. You can scan the QR code at the end of this chapter to listen and download the album. Testimonies and details of the album can also be found in Appendix 3 of this book. You can also go to my website, www.faithhailsham.com, for more details. One particular testimony I want to share with you here is from Kathy, a friend in Florida:

> I recently went through a scary time when I ended up in the hospital with COVID-19 pneumonia. I was transported to the hospital via ambulance from an ER center. While en route to the hospital, I kept thinking, Am I going to die? Am I that bad that they have to take me by ambulance?
>
> By the time I got to the hospital, I was shaking with fear. I was put in a room by myself at the hospital and after being connected to oxygen and plasma was left alone in the room for what seemed like forever. I began to think the situation was hopeless and I thought about dying.
>
> Eventually, I realized that this was a spiritual battle in my mind and I decided to fight in the spirit with the Word of God. I started playing recordings on my phone created by Faith Apiafi-Hailsham. I listened to Psalms 91, 23, 34, and 103 and possibly others. I began to gain hope that I would live and overcome all these things.

Each morning at around five o'clock, I would listen to Faith speaking out these scriptures and as a result, became spiritually and physically stronger each day. I thank the Lord for Faith's *Speak the Word* recordings. I overcame my fears and won the victory over this disease."

- Kathleen Cole, *Florida, USA*

After I got this testimony from Kathy, I was overwhelmed with joy at the manifestation of His power to heal and restore through prayer. The vision I had that these prayers would be played in hospitals had begun. *Speak the Word* album has now earned me my first nomination for Best Spoken Word Artist by The music and media platforms awards (TMMP) UK. How encouraging!

When Jesus prayed and made declarations, supernatural things happened. His authority as the King of Kings is superior to the kingdom of darkness, which produces sin, sickness, disease, demonic torment, and death. So when He spoke, the power of those things was broken and people received salvation, healing, deliverance, and life. The reality of His kingdom manifested in their life as He decreed it.

Jesus is the model of a kingdom lifestyle. As we see in His disciples, He intends us to walk in His authority and experience and release the supernatural reality of His kingdom wherever we go. This is not just for some super-spiritual Christians, it is for all of us! When Christians don't live supernaturally, we are like "The Incredibles" (The Disney movie) when they had to live like everybody else and were miserable. We have the supernatural power of God inside us, but too many of us have either become lukewarm and worldly, gone into hiding, or just not tapped into that power. We must activate the fire and the supernatural power of God inside of us through faith. When we do this, we will enter into our true calling and become effective as the end time army of God to defeat the plans of the enemy and bring the kingdom of God to earth. That said, God is not a magician to simply do whatever we say or want. Our authority only works when we are fully aligned with His plan and strategy to advance His kingdom. So we must draw near to Him in the secret place and align our hearts, minds, and words with what He is saying. Jesus said He could only say and do what the Father was saying and doing—that is our standard for walking in spiritual authority and the supernatural.

Many believers love the idea of seeing the supernatural demonstrations of the kingdom of God break out through our lives—to see the blind see, the deaf hear, the lame walk, and the dead rise. I believe all of those things are absolutely available for us and that God wants to see His kingdom come in miraculous ways in and through us. However, we must understand that our greatest power, fruitfulness, and impact can only come when we are willing to pass through the furnace of dying to ourselves and living fully and only for the Lord. We must be willing to allow Him to help Himself to our lives as He desires.

A minister once prayed for me and said, "You have been poured out like wine before the Lord." I later found the song lyrics for "Poured Out Like Wine," an American folk melody arranged by Michael R. Green, which got me meditating on what this phrase really meant. I think that's a good expression for my life, and for everyone who chooses to walk through the furnace of life for Jesus' sake. I'm not saying I even deserve to be described this way; it is a privilege if the Lord truly thinks this of my life. I know that there are others who have paid a higher price than I have. I am grateful to have made it thus far, and to be able to say with complete conviction that though the furnace is painful for a time, it is worth it. When we buy the field, we get the treasure.

QUESTIONS FOR REFLECTION

1. "Testing and trials aren't fun, but there can be no genuine faith or transformation in our lives without them." What testing or trials have you gone through that produced faith? How did they produce faith?

2. "The real gold, the treasure, that forms in our lives through testing and trials is our history with God." What has been your history with God? What treasures have you gained? Describe your relationship with the Lord.

3. "This is our testimony, our story of God's faithfulness in our lives, and the only way we get that story is by being willing to follow Him into situations where He has to show up." How has God been faithful in your life? What is your testimony of His faithfulness? What situations are you following Him into that you need Him to show up in?

4. How can you celebrate the breakthroughs of others while trusting the Lord for your own?

5. Where do you need "a death to self" experience?

6. Buying the field is a lifestyle of choosing to continually lay down our lives like Jesus did. How can you "buy the field" daily? What are you laying down in your life to own this treasure?

Scan for *Speak the Word* Album

Chapter 11

REACHING THE SUMMIT

Kingdom theme: The journey of faith teaches you to take one step at a time, unload unnecessary baggage, and surround yourself with faithful companions.

IN 2015, I HAD the opportunity to climb Ben Nevis, the highest mountain in the UK. It was truly an unforgettable experience. The trek took the better part of a day and was quite grueling yet rewarded you with incredible views of the Scottish Highlands, most spectacularly from the summit. However, most of the hike required you to look down at your feet, so you could safely navigate the steep and rocky path without tripping. Also, the length of the journey forced you to travel light. I had brought a pack with me full of various supplies I thought I might need, but as the journey progressed, I discovered that many of these were not so critical and I was better off without their weight slowing me down. In the end, the thing I was most thankful to bring along was a friend. My friend, Kiruba, did the hike with me, and during the climb, especially the tough bits as we ascended higher and higher, teamwork was essential. I struggled with my energy level going up the mountain, and Kiruba supported me through this. Coming down the mountain was tougher for Kiruba, due to rocks and the impact on the knees, so I got to support her on that leg of the journey.

After completing this feat, I concluded that the three most important pieces of advice for climbing a mountain were to 1) take it one step at a time, 2) don't overthink it, and 3) don't go alone. The same advice holds true for us as we embark on a journey of faith in God and seek Him for the unveiling of His vision and purpose for our lives. We all want to get to that summit where we can finally look out and see the complete view of where we've come from and where we're going. But we won't get there unless we are paying close attention to the steps we are taking along the path and letting go of everything that will weigh us down or hold us back. This is why Proverbs exhorts us, *"Let your eyes look straight ahead, and your eyelids look right before you. Ponder the path of your feet, and let all your ways be established. Do not turn to the right or the left; Remove your foot from evil"* (Proverbs 4:25-27 NKJV). And the way to really be successful at this is to surround ourselves with the right people who can help us see the things in our path that we can't see.

I don't believe the unveiling of my vision and purpose I experienced in my fortieth year was the only summit I will reach in my lifetime. Rather, it's the basecamp from which I have now set out to reach new heights and vistas of revelation of who God is and the story He is telling through my life in the years ahead. But having succeeded in gaining that initial vantage point and being able to reflect on the first 40 years of my journey, I do want to leave you with some final thoughts to encourage you as you take each step in faith to your own mountain of vision and purpose. I consider these pearls of wisdom, and offer them not because I know better than you, but because these truths have been formed in my life in the midst of trials and difficulty and have brought me through them. They have kept my feet on the path and strengthened me to keep climbing my mountain. I share them with you in hopes that if you take them to heart, they will do the same for you.

You Are an Original

When it became obvious in my late twenties and thirties that my life was not following the same track and timeline as so many of my friends, particularly when it came to marriage and family, it was painful not only because I wanted these things and couldn't seem to get them, but also because it felt like something was wrong with my story being so different. It wasn't until I emerged from my "night season" and discovered my authentic self that I came to see the uniqueness of my journey as a good thing. The discomfort of being different pointed me toward the truth that awaits us all if we will allow God to unveil us to ourselves: *I am an original. And so are you.*

Our stories aren't supposed to look exactly like anyone else's. In the incredible, complex, yet beautiful redemptive story God is writing in human history, each of us has a unique role to play, which means that our stories will have plenty of similarities to others who are also part of that story, but also points of divergence from the rest of the crowd. This is why we all have two basic core needs that are often in tension with each other—the need for belonging, and the need for significance. As social creatures, we long to be liked, accepted, and fit in. We want to belong. At the same time, as individuals, we also want to do something that matters, something that distinguishes us and demonstrates that our life has a unique and valuable purpose. As we navigate these two desires, most of us are looking for that sweet spot where we stand out in the crowd enough not to feel invisible, but not enough to feel alienated.

The problem is that most of us are looking to others in the crowd to help us meet these deep needs for belonging and significance. We are comparing ourselves to others and either trying to be like them or differentiate ourselves from them to find our authentic selves, and it simply won't work. Only the One who created us in the first place, the Author of our stories, can reveal who we truly are and meet our deep needs for belonging and significance. But in order to discover this, we must stop chasing the approval of others or even our own self-approval, and surrender our lives and stories fully to Him. This is the paradox Jesus spoke of—*"For whoever desires to save his life will lose it, but whoever loses his life for My sake will find it"* (Matthew 16:25 NKJV).

C.S. Lewis concluded his classic work *Mere Christianity* with this very advice:

> Your real, new self (which is Christ's and also yours, and yours just because it is His) will not come as long as you are looking for it. It will come when you are looking for Him. Does that sound strange? The same principle holds, you know, for more everyday matters. Even in social life, you will never make a good impression on other people until you stop thinking about what sort of impression you are making. Even in literature and art, no man who bothers about originality will ever be original: whereas if you simply try to tell the truth (without caring two

> pence how often it has been told before) you will, nine times out of ten, become original without ever having noticed it. The principle runs through all life from top to bottom. Give up yourself, and you will find your real self. Lose your life and you will save it. Submit to death, death of your ambitions and favorite wishes every day and death of your whole body in the end: submit with every fiber of your being, and you will find eternal life. Keep back nothing. Nothing that you have not given away will ever be really yours. Nothing in you that has not died will ever be raised from the dead. Look for yourself, and you will find in the long run only hatred, loneliness, despair, rage, ruin, and decay. But look for Christ and you will find Him, and with Him everything else thrown in.[7]

The New Testament calls us not simply to a moment of surrender to Christ, but to living in surrender as our way of life. Paul describes it as being "led" by and "keeping in step" with the Holy Spirit (see Gal. 5:18, 25 NIV). Instead of following the voices of the crowd or our flesh, we are following the voice and direction of the One who now lives inside us and is continually leading us into truth—the truth of who He created us to be, how He created us to live, and what He created and called us to do.

Here's where we must count the cost. Will the Spirit lead us into uncomfortable situations or instruct us to do difficult things—things we don't want to do and that may not feel at first like "us?" Yes. In fact, it must be this way, and not just because these are necessary for our growth and transformation. These moments that require our trust, obedience, and willingness to "die" to our own

7 C.S. Lewis, Mere Christianity (San Francisco, CA: HarperCollins, 2001), 250.

wishes and desires are the proof that we are truly in a surrendered relationship to Him and not following Him only as long as it's comfortable and rewarding. Yet every time we do choose to trust Him, we can be sure that it will be rewarding, though maybe not in the way we originally envisioned.

Again, in my own story, I kept hoping and anticipating that following Jesus would lead me to the external rewards I desired—a husband, family, successful career, and fruitful ministry. In the process, while I still desire those things, I now understand that the Lord has been giving me something deeper, the internal rewards of coming to know Him and who He authentically created me to be. I have also seen in my own life and the lives of others that every time we resist the voice of the Spirit and what He is calling us to do, there is also a cost. By taking our own path to fulfillment, we may indeed receive the external rewards we sought, yet they will not satisfy us like we hoped. Sadly, many people end up miserable because they keep chasing fulfillment that can never come the way they're trying to get it.

Jesus calls us to the road less traveled. *"Enter through the narrow gate. For wide is the gate and broad is the road that leads to destruction, and many enter through it. But small is the gate and narrow the road that leads to life, and only a few find it"* (Matthew 7:13-14 NIV). It can be so tempting to want to follow the crowd, to do what everyone else is doing, to take the easy and obvious path everyone is taking. It takes a lot more work and courage to be a trailblazer, to go against the grain, to swim upstream. In society, we love pioneers and innovators *after* they have produced something original that benefits us all, but for most of them, the journey to get there was full of sacrifice, loneliness, ridicule, opposition, and persecution. Many people venture down the road less traveled, but turn back when it becomes difficult and painful. We will only persevere when the courage and conviction that we are doing what is right—what we were created and called to do—outweighs and overcomes our fears of what we might lose by taking this road.

Yet here is the unexpected gift of taking the road less traveled. Though fewer people take this road, it is not a road where we are doomed to isolation and loneliness. We may face lonely moments and periods—that is a universal experience, even when we're following the crowd—but in the end, choosing to be our original, authentic selves positions us to become *visible* to certain people whom I call our "destiny helpers." I believe God has appointed certain people in our journeys to help us fulfill our calling—and appointed us to do the same for others. Some of these people may be solitary encounters, while others may become dear friends, but what matters is that these people find us, and we find them, because we are pursuing the unique God-vision for our lives, which makes us recognizable to one another in the spirit.

When I think back over my life, I see that the Lord put so many destiny helpers in my path to help me get to my next level in my career, ministry, finances, personal growth, and every other area of life. Some of these destiny helpers were previous bosses or managers who employed me. Though we didn't have a close relationship, it was clear that I had a divine appointment with these people. They believed in me and opened doors for me that would have otherwise been harder to open on my own. I am truly grateful to them and hope to be destiny helpers to those who are coming behind me, just as they have done for me. Each of us could well be someone's destiny helper, and I want to be positioned to help others the way that I have been helped and believed in.

Another destiny helper in my life was my Aunty Liz. When I took the step of faith to travel to the UK without having a place to stay, it was so clearly the favor and provision of the Lord that

Aunty Liz saw me for the first time and decided to take me in. Much later, I learned how Aunty Liz had come to know and be friends with my Aunty Data. In the early eighties, Aunty Data was studying for her PhD in Southampton, England, and while there, she met a young lady who was about eighteen, had just come from Nigeria to join her husband in the UK, expecting their first child and needed help to adapt into a new country. Aunty Data immediately took her in and began to help her adapt and settle until she was acquainted with Southampton and had her baby. This young lady was Aunty Liz. When Aunty Liz met me in London for the first time and found out I was Aunty Data's niece, she remembered Aunty Data's kindness and decided she had to show the same kindness to me by taking me in to live with her family. I wasn't aware that this was something Aunty Data had done—in fact, I never heard or knew about Aunty Liz until I got to Heathrow Airport. Sometimes, we take steps of faith not knowing how it's all going to come to pass, but we must trust God to pave the way. Often, we find that seeds have been sown by those before us, and are just waiting for us to take that step to bear the fruit we need in due season.

My friends, Esther, Sylvia, Margaret, and I—the Four Corners—were all "destiny helpers" in one another's lives. Early on, it became obvious that each of us was on our own "road less traveled" journey with the Lord. For example, both Sylvia and Esther always knew they were called to practice the law. In the UK, at the time of their developing career, most people who work in law become solicitors and work outside the courtroom. This path is fairly straightforward and leads to a well-paying position rather quickly. The other, more difficult path in the law, is to become a barrister who litigates cases before a judge. This path is extremely competitive and requires lots of courage and hard work to build your career and reputation. Both Sylvia and Esther decided to take this tough path and become barristers. There were moments when the challenges they encountered on this journey caused them to question whether they had made the right choice. In these situations, they called the Four Corners together to pray, encourage each other, and contend for breakthrough. Wonderfully, we saw God come through for Sylvia and Esther again and again and ultimately bring both of them success in their careers.

One of the more dramatic breakthroughs we experienced together on Sylvia's journey took place while she was in law school. She took a qualifying exam for a certain part of her studies, and when she received her results, her scores weren't as high as she needed them to be. We called the Four Corners together, laid hands on those results, and prayed, "God, we ask for your favor. Let her results be picked out and let them be changed." Incredibly, that was exactly what happened! Sylvia received a letter stating that the testing board had decided to review her results and score them higher—right where she needed them to be. This happened without any intervention from Sylvia to the board—a miracle indeed!

Another significant breakthrough we contended over together was both Sylvia and Esther getting a pupillage, the year-long apprenticeship that constitutes the final step in a barrister's training before they can be called to The General Council of the Bar, also called the Bar Council in England and Wales, and start practicing professionally. Getting a pupillage is extremely competitive, with many candidates for very few spaces available nationally. After completing a post-grad course in law, one had five to seven years to secure a pupillage or you had to go back and take the bar exam again, which was very expensive.

Esther and Sylvia both worked extremely hard building up

relevant experience to become competitive candidates for pupillages, but year after year ticked by with no success. There were times where they felt discouraged, especially when they saw their mates getting pupillages and going on to thrive in their careers, but they kept at it, knowing this was the path they had been called to. As Four Corners, we encouraged Sylvia and Esther not to give up on this road less traveled because we could see that they would be brilliant barristers, forces to be reckoned with. Just in the nick of time, the doors miraculously opened for Esther and Sylvia to undergo their pupillages. Esther had waited five years and Sylvia seven years for this breakthrough—years of pushing, believing, praying, doing numerous volunteer hours and advocacy work, and receiving numerous rejection letters. What a road to travel along!

Sylvia once commented that we were like Daniel and his friends in the Bible. The four of them were all taking the road less traveled as captives faithfully serving the Lord in pagan Babylon, and their faith and friendship gave them the courage to stay on course, even when it was life-threatening. If any of them had been facing the same situation alone, it would have been overwhelming and impossible, but together, their friendships gave them the spiritual, emotional, and moral sustenance they needed to not just survive, but fulfill the purpose for which God had placed them in the king's palace. Likewise, I believe God brought the Four Corners together at a critical time to be destiny helpers on our journeys. There were so many times when we came together to cry, pray, make declarations, and encourage each other as we each paid the price to run after the thrilling, yet challenging path to which God had called us—and then so many times when we celebrated the incredible testimonies of breakthrough we had contended for together. These are the kinds of divine friendships I believe God has for all of us on the road less traveled.

Don't Sell Yourself Short

One Sunday, my pastor shared some fascinating quotes from a book titled *The Day America Told the Truth* by James Patterson and Peter Kim. The book presents and discusses the results of an anonymous opinion survey designed to gain a picture of Americans' moral beliefs, attitudes, and practices. The book is 30 years old now, so the findings are a bit dated, but even so, they are shocking. Most sobering was hearing people's responses when they were asked what they would do in exchange for millions of dollars. For $10 million, 7% of people would kill a stranger (36 million of the population), 25% would abandon their entire family, 25% would abandon their church, 23% would become prostitutes for a week, 10% would withhold testimony and let a murderer go free and 3% would put their children up for adoption—all for a lot of money. [8]

"For what profit is it to a man if he gains the whole world, and loses his own soul? Or what will a man give in exchange for his soul?" Jesus asked (Matthew 16:26 NKJV). According to Him, nothing is more precious than our souls. Most of us are rightly horrified at the thought of sacrificing the integrity, wholeness, or growth of our souls by doing extreme acts of wrong or evil. On the other hand, do we properly value our souls like Jesus does? Do we treasure them so much that we refuse to entertain the small compromises that ultimately invite shame, guilt, division, bitterness, unforgiveness, discouragement, despair, jealousy, fear, pride, and deception to violate our souls?

In today's society, we hear many messages like "love yourself," "you're worth it" and "you deserve it." Yet often what these messages

8 James Patterson and Peter Kim, The Day America Told the Truth (First Plume Printing, June, 1992), 65.

are encouraging us to do is to give in to our temptation for comfort, compromise, taking the easy road, or taking shortcuts. When was the last time you heard an advertiser, leader, or influencer encouraging you to love yourself by doing hard things, practicing self-control and self-discipline, and refusing to compromise or take shortcuts, even when the road to the fulfillment you're seeking seems too difficult or long? Yet this is actually how we most truly love ourselves and honor the worth of our souls and lives—by staying in the difficult process of soul formation and life transformation.

If you have successfully engaged in any kind of health and fitness improvement program in your life, you may have discovered this truth. The more you exercise and stick to a healthy eating plan, the better you feel, because you are actually giving your body what it needs to thrive. Eventually, the pain, discomfort and hard work becomes associated not with deprivation, but with the rewards of becoming healthier. You are loving yourself. The same is even more true for investing in any area of your life where you want to grow, learn, develop skills, and really improve your life. Growth simply never happens by indulging ourselves. It always requires an investment of focus, work, discipline, time, and often other resources. It costs us something, and when we pay that price, it signifies that *we are worth it*. So, whether it's your physical health, mental health, spiritual health, career, relationships, finances, or any other area of your life, don't sell yourself short. Learn what it takes to thrive in these areas and develop your gifts. Then do the work without shortcuts or compromise.

I realize this is easier said than done. The world around us doesn't merely fail to encourage us to love ourselves in these ways—it actively tempts, pressures, and outright bullies us into compromising our souls and our value. Consider Joseph once again. As a young man, he knew he was called to greatness and leadership, then spent 13 years in slavery and prison. During that time, his entire world saw him as the furthest thing from a great leader. So many people in such powerless and humiliating circumstances would have fallen under a victim mentality, chalked up their youthful dreams to delusions of grandeur, grown cynical and bitter at the hand life had dealt them, and disqualified themselves from ever becoming more than who the world insisted they were. Yet Joseph refused to allow his circumstances or what others did to him to define his identity, value, purpose, or destiny. This is why he never compromised who he knew himself to be—who God had called him to be. We must be convinced that who God says we are is true, no matter what the world, our circumstances, or even our own minds or feelings tell us.

The Bible plainly tells us, *"Do not be deceived, God is not mocked; for whatever a man sows, that he will also reap. For he who sows to his flesh will of the flesh reap corruption, but he who sows to the Spirit will of the Spirit reap everlasting life"* (Galatians 6:7-8 NKJV). This means that no one is going to get away with anything. It's easy to find people who seem to be taking shortcuts and compromising and getting away with it, but that is not the end of the story. In the end, they will reap what they have sown.

This doesn't mean there is no room for repentance. If you have compromised, sold yourself short, and violated your own soul by actions you have taken, there is mercy, forgiveness, and restoration waiting for you at the foot of the cross. God is absolutely brilliant at taking the areas where we have failed most and turning them into our greatest gifts to offer the world. The kingdom of God is a kingdom of redemption and restoration. We all come into this kingdom broken and in need of salvation. And it is precisely the will of God that all of these areas come under the influence of His rule and reign and become transformed through His power and love.

God is the God of second chances. In fact, He's the God of third, fourth, fifth chances and many more. He's always beckoning us to come to Him no matter where we are or what we think we've done. And here's the nature of His redemptive work in our lives: He always makes things more and more beautiful. That means that even if we think we have messed up Plan A, He has a Plan B that will be even better and more powerful than Plan A ever would have been. It's not like we go to Him and say, "Okay, Lord, I've messed up. I'm coming to You to repent, but I'm not going to get anything near what You originally planned for me." It's just the opposite. When we come to God and surrender ourselves and our mistakes to Him, He will do something even greater, because now it's a completely new plan, and His plans only go higher and higher.

Part of my story is that I have been protected by the Lord and kept from making much worse mistakes than I could have made. He put friends in my life who were brave enough to call me out and give me warnings when I was starting to head in a dodgy direction, especially in the realm of dating. I remember once my friend, Bunmi, called me from America to tell me that she'd had a dream that I was physically crossing the line with a guy I had started dating. I wasn't doing this, but it was a warning I took to heart by putting the brakes on the relationship.

In the area of business and financial investment, I have made some mistakes—not willful sins, perhaps, but costly errors in judgment that have been discouraging because I truly believe there is a call not only on me, but on my whole family to walk in lavish generosity and make wealth that will bless many people. Over and over, it seems, the enemy has tried to steal this call. Yet with every loss and setback, I return to the truth that God is the God of restoration. No matter how impossible it may seem at the moment for this call on our family to be fulfilled, our story is not over until God says it is over, and He is the God of the impossible. I don't know how and when He will do it, but I believe that He will restore *"the years that the swarming locust has eaten"* (Joel 2:25 NKJV).

None of us are perfect—we all make mistakes. But we mustn't look at what we have or haven't done, but at the mercy and grace of God, His love for us and the fact that we are His beloved children. He wants to beautify our lives, so that people can see His beauty through our lives. His redemptive love is the true source of our value, and the more we encounter that love, the more we will value ourselves the way He does, and refuse to sell ourselves short.

Take the Adventure

The two places I have lived in the United States—Southern California and now Florida—are famous for their theme parks featuring rides and rollercoasters. I certainly understand their appeal. They are one expression of our natural human longing for thrills and adventure. While many people seek their thrills at Disney or Six Flags, or in many other forms, I have found that the greatest thrill of all is the adventure of *faith*—following God on this wild, unknown, terrifying, supernatural, romantic, and rewarding journey of revelation and transformation.

Someone recently showed me a set of pictures and asked me to pick the one I found most compelling. The one I chose showed a person standing at the top of a cliff about to jump off it. Again, I am the last thing from a daredevil, so this kind of physical risk is something I would never take, but it is the perfect metaphor for the spiritual risk of faith. God invites us to jump off the cliff, to leave the place that feels secure and familiar and put the whole weight of our trust on Him to catch us and carry us into the unknown. And the best part of the adventure is that we don't remain in that place of unknowing, but that God gradually reveals His epic purpose for our lives, like the best mystery writer leaving clues for his readers to solve.

This adventure is the heart of living in the kingdom, which is why the Christian life should be anything but boring. If we ever become bored as believers, it is a sign that we have stopped truly living by faith. We have lost the plot of what our lives are all about. So many of us go to the movies and love watching epic adventures full of cliffhangers, high-stake thrills, romances, and battles, then return to our lives and judge them as mundane and relatively meaningless by comparison. How could our everyday life that may seem so ordinary be part of changing the world, saving someone's life, fighting evil, achieving something significant, or having a transcendent love story, something someone might write a book or make a movie about someday?

Yet this is the very invitation God gives us. If we truly say yes to Jesus, He will lead us on an adventure of faith that will include every type of thrill and epic experience we can imagine. Every story we love to read in a novel or see in a film was first conceived in people's imagination as an expression of our dreams, longings, and search for meaning in our lives and in the world. But God is the source of all reality, and He promises to do *"immeasurably more than all we ask or imagine"* (Ephesians 3:20 NIV). The real story He is telling in our lives is better than any fantasy we can come up with for ourselves. Of course, that means it will also be far more terrifying, moving, and ultimately transforming than any book or film might be. Flights of imagination can stir our longings, scare, provoke, and fascinate us, but it is on the adventure of faith where we must move into action, take real risks, make decisions, face tests and challenges, wrestle with our desires and fears, and ultimately grow and transform.

The key is to understand that what makes it an adventure is doing it *with Him*. You've probably had the experience of doing something alone and feeling anxious about it, then doing the same thing later with a friend and feeling perfectly relaxed. Something scary can become fun, depending on whom you're with. There's a reason we see so often in Scripture God exhorting people not to fear, for "I will be with you." There's a reason Jesus called the Holy Spirit the Comforter, the One who comes alongside us. So often we think we need to know what's going to happen or how God is going to work out a certain situation, when what we actually need to know is that God is with us, fully present, aware of what we're going through, and wanting to lead us into deeper intimacy with Him through this experience. This is what calms our fears, comforts our hearts, and restores our sense of joy, hope, and adventure for what He has in store.

Intimacy with God is the ultimate purpose and vision for our lives. It is the purpose of the kingdom of God. Our lives with God are meant to be a great romance. I have always loved watching beautiful romantic movies where the hero falls in love with the girl and loves everything about her, even her imperfections. He serves her sacrificially, offering his help and strength where she is weak or in need. He rescues her from danger. He makes her feel beautiful and desired. Nowadays, society can hardly believe that such a story could happen. Yet one day I realized there's a reason I love this type of romance story because that's exactly the story I am in! Jesus loves me in my imperfections, saves me from my sins, rescues me from my enemies, perfects His strength in my weakness, provides for my needs, and makes me feel loved, cherished, delighted in, and beautiful. I am living in the love story I have always longed for—it just took years of climbing the mountain and jumping off the cliff in the adventure of faith to find His love waiting for me again and again.

This is the love that is waiting for you in the journey of faith. So don't give up. Stay on the road less traveled. Be the original, authentic self He has called and created you to be, without compromise. Stop looking for a map to your story and look for Him, the One who is writing it. Draw near to Him, surrender to Him, and let Him take you on the greatest adventure you will ever know—your own life.

QUESTIONS FOR REFLECTION

1. 'You are an original.' Let that sink in! What are things about you that you love about yourself and your story?

2. Do you have divine friendships? If not, pray the Lord will bring them to you!

3. What have you been carrying that you need to let go of that has been weighing you down?

4. Who has God placed in your life as "destiny helpers" to help you in your journey? How were they "destiny helpers"? Who are you a "destiny helper" to? How have you helped them?

5. "The kingdom of God is a kingdom of redemption and restoration." What are you needing redeeming and restoration from?

6. What new commitment(s) can you make to begin or take this great adventure of your life to the next level? What practical steps can you take to enjoy this adventure?

7. What parts of Faith's story did you connect with the most? How has this book encouraged or inspired you in your own spiritual journey?

Prayer for You

Dear Lord, I commit this precious reader into Your hands as they have been reflecting on their own life and reading this book, that they may know You are right here with them and cheering them on. The Lord will have me say to you: Son/Daughter, your life is about the kingdom of God! You have been placed here for such a time as this to establish God's kingdom on earth. That's how important you are, child of God. You have been designed to bring heaven to earth through the destiny and purpose given to you by your heavenly Father. Your calling and purpose are unique and you are special to God. May each step you take from today on your journey of faith be purposeful, intentional and take you closer to your God-given destiny. The Lord says,

> "Behold, I am doing a new thing;
> now it springs forth, do you not perceive it?
> I will make a way in the wilderness
> and rivers in the desert." Isaiah 43:19 (ESV)

The Lord is doing a new thing in your life and making a way where there seemed to be no way. As you emerge in this new season of your transformation, may the Lord grant to you the spirit of wisdom and revelation in the knowledge of Him and the eyes of your understanding be enlightened to receive new depths of revelation and intimacy with God (Ephesians 1:17-18 NKJV paraphrased). Let hope arise within you. You will begin to experience new levels of freedom, healing and deliverance. The old has gone and the new has come. The Lord is restoring all that the enemy has stolen from your life (Joel 2:25). May the Lord ignite a new fire in your heart to burn ever so brightly for Him, that all may see and glorify God. I pray for a fresh passion to be birthed in your heart to desire and love God more deeply than you ever have. Let this new revelation of His love for you take you on the greatest adventure of your life to date, A NEW ADVENTURE OF FAITH!

Note from the Author

If this book has inspired or encouraged you in any way, I would love to hear from you. Please drop me an email using the email below to tell me how all about your experience reading this book and I will personally respond to you. My email is **faithhailsham@gmail.com**. Please also consider leaving me a review on amazon, thanking you in advance. You can also connect with me on social media using my handle @ladyfaithhailsham or through my website www.faithhailsham.com.

Acknowledgments

THIS BOOK HAS BEEN two years in the making and now finally published. I would like to give all thanks to God my heavenly Father who has loved me unconditionally and granted me the grace to share this testimony of faith with the world. I would also like to thank all those who have contributed to who I am today, firstly my parents, Hon. Bishop J. Apiafi Hailsham and Elder (Mrs.) Violet Hailsham, for bringing me up in the way of the Lord, so that my roots have been firmly planted in the Lord. Without you, Mom and Dad, there would be no me. To my six siblings, thank you for your love and prayer support that I can always count on. To my extended family, aunties, uncles, and cousins, much love to you all for being a part of my upbringing and making my story what it is today. To Dr. Elizabeth Achinewhu-Nworgu, thank you for opening up your home to me, believing in me and mentoring me through the early stages of my career. To my wonderful friends, sisterhood, and prayer partners, thank you for always being there for me. I appreciate you deeply because where would I be today without your friendship, prayers and counsel?

To all the church ministries that have contributed to my spiritual growth, teaching me to understand the place of the Church in our society as one of the significant spheres of influence in our world, I honor you. From Greater Evangelism World Crusade, Nigeria, where I took my baby spiritual steps, to Kensington Temple, London City Church under the leadership of Rev Colin and Amanda Dye, where I was discipled through my 14 spiritual caterpillar years in a deeply rooted and spiritually rich environment, I honor and thank you and all the pastors and leaders who contributed to my growth.

Jesus House for all Nations, London, under the leadership of Pastors Agu and Sola Irukwu, thank you for strengthening my prayer muscles through the tough season of my faith journey. Awaken Church, San Diego, with lead Pastors Jurgen and Leanne Matthesius, the vision the Lord had conceived and nurtured through the years in my life had finally been granted a place and a people that would receive and bless it into expression and life, thank you. My current church, Winter Haven Worship Center, Florida, thank you Pastors Jeff and Kim Connor and the leadership team for giving me a new spiritual home and community to continue to grow and develop the call of God for my life. To Pastor Felix Young of Greenfield Ministries, thank you for being an incredible prayer support to the Apiafi-Hailsham family over these many years.

To my spiritual mentors - Bishop Victor Uzosike (Kingdom Life Gospel Outreach Ministries Int'l), Rev Ruthann Cannings (Arise Ministry), Pastors Praise & Funke Olatona (Rivers of Life Church, KTLCC, London), Pastors Tayo & Toyin Awoyera (Agape Christian Centre, KTLCC, London), Marilee Pierce Dunker (International Ambassador for World Vision) and Liliana Williams (Missionary/Entrepreneur), you have been my spiritual warriors taking me through battles and into victories, I honor and thank you.

To my career mentors - Carol Carmichael Edmunds, Daniel Cronin, Cassie Gold and Jason Davies, you have been destiny helpers in paving the way for me as a Finance Professional and I am most grateful.

Finally, to my editorial team, Treasure Frank, Allison Armerding, Julia Roller, Lambo Publishing, Oluwole Emmanuel and Alexis Ward (The Visual Republic) who worked tirelessly to birth this dream of getting published, thank you for your wisdom, guidance and patience with me as a first-time author.

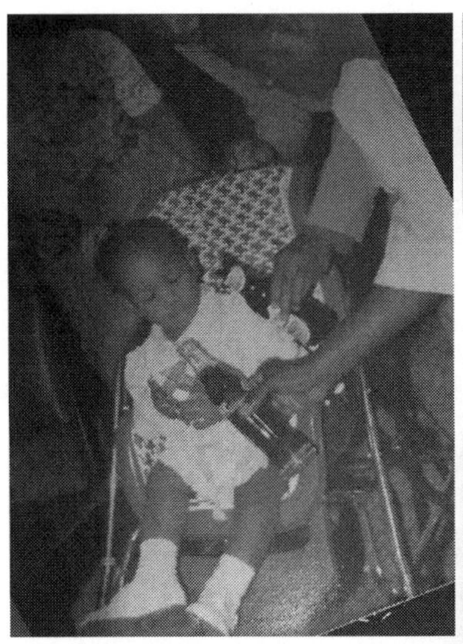

Me as a baby - One of the few baby pictures I have left as most of our baby pictures were destroyed by water/rain

Dad and Mom at the Peace Resort - 1998

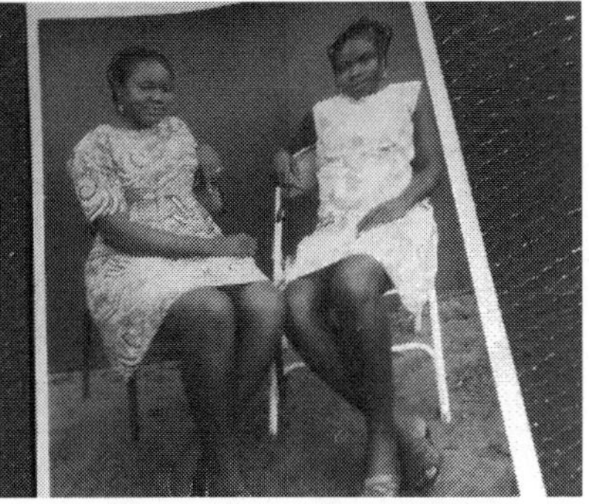

Mom to the left and her friend Professor Jessica Ezekiel-Hart in Nigeria. This was 1970 just after the Nigerian civil war.

My parents, siblings and I at the Peace Resort just before I left Nigeria in 1998 From far left standing - Emmanuel (Daddy's Gogo), James (The Chairman of Council), Esther (Esi Daddy's daughter), Me (in green - Dabotuwo), Violet (The Queen), Lydia (The great lady), Mom, Dad and David (David the boy).

Mom with Apostle G.D. Numbere and some members of Greater Evangelism World Crusade - London, mid 70s.

My maternal Grandfather - Late Mr. Alexander Barrasitamunopiri Hart. The academic heritage set by him and my grandmother Mrs. Violet Alex-Hart set the pace for high levels of academic achievements in the family for generations to come.

My Senior Uncle and Aunty - Roland Owuna Alex-Hart and Prof. Alexandra Data Hart – during their studies in the UK in the late 70s. They inspired my desire to study abroad.

My Paternal Grandmother (Granny) – Mrs. Jane Nwafor Gilbert Colten Agbanibo Hailsham Banigo. During her years as a Prison Wardress.

Granny at her funeral –
Mrs. Jane Nwafor Gilbert Colten Agbanibo Hailsham Banigo.
A strong woman and inspiration who lived a full life to 101.

In loving memory of my first Spiritual Mentor -
Late Elder Mrs. Esther Amiso Alatoru was one of
my role models of faith.

Boarding school classmates of FGGC Abuloma in their school uniform in the early 90s.

Me and my classmates in boarding school uniforms and Sunday wear, after a Sunday church service - mid 90s

My early days in London - 1999.

Me in my 'Beyond Beautiful' dress at my 40th birthday Celebration

Mom and Dad at my 'This is Your life' 40th Celebration

Pastor Emmanuel and Evangelist Angela Apiafi-Hailsham of Nation's Call London Church, England. 2019

Mom and her siblings in recent years. From left sitting – Professor Alexandra Data Hart, Pastor Roland Owuna Alex-Hart (this was his 70th birthday - 2019), his wife Mrs Victoria Alex-Hart, Pastor Sodienye Alex-Hart (Mom's second elder sister), Standing from left – Dr. Julius Apiri AlexHart ("Chief Hart"), Mom and Hon. Abinye Alex-Hart.

My sisters in recent years. From left Angela (Emmanuel's wife), Lydia, Esther and Violet.

My brothers in recent years. From left James, David and Emmanuel.

The Borokiri neighborhood of Port-Harcourt City in 2020. Situated just south of the Old GRA area. The neighborhood is bounded by Ahoada street to the north, Okrika Island to the east, Orubiri oilfield to the south and shipbuilders road to the west. Borikiri is where I spent my early childhood years in the 80s. Picture by @Pixpectiv

The Nigerian Port Authority (NPA), Port-Harcourt, Rivers State in 2022. This is a factory district with huge tanks that produce food items such as pasta, sugar and flour. Picture by @Pixpectiv

Port-Harcourt Mile One Park Flyover (overhead bridge) with a popular market running along an old railway line. Each stall is sheltered by an umbrella and the market stretches out for miles. Picture by @Pixpectiv

Bonny Island is situated at the southern edge of Rivers State in the Niger Delta region of Nigeria in 2022. The St. Stephen's Cathedral as it is named dates back to 1889 and started as a school chapel, a parish and graduated to a cathedral on request by the Amanyanabo (King) of Bonny.
Picture by @Pixpectiv

Bonny Island in 2022 hosts the Nigeria Liquefied Natural Gas Limited (NLNG) project with six-train plants that has produced and transported liquefied natural gas globally over the last 20 years with the new train 7 plant about to commence construction.Picture by @Pixpectiv

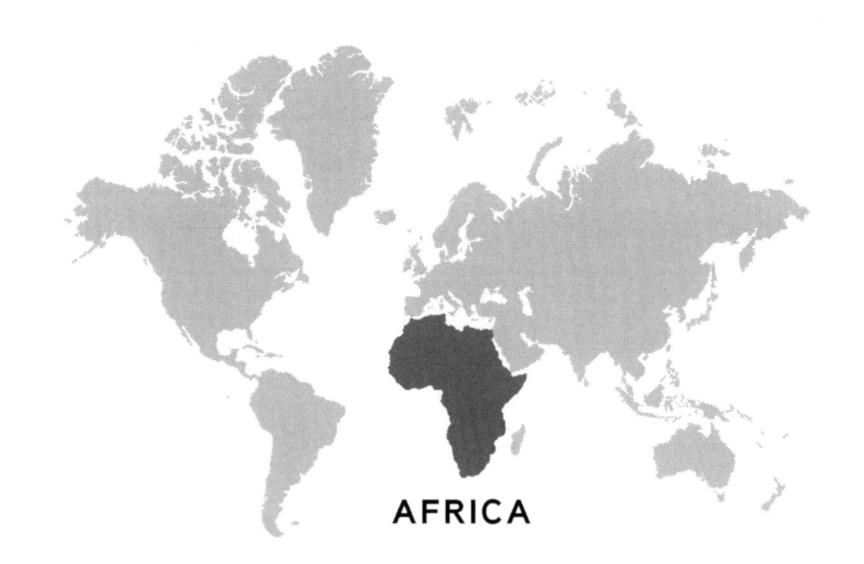
AFRICA

ALGIERS
TUNIS
RABAT
TUNISIA
TRIPOLI
MOROCCO
CAIRO
ALGERIA
LIBYA
EGYPT
MAURITANIA
MALI
NIGER
SUDAN
NOUAKCHOTT
CHAD
ERITREA
DAKAR
SENEGAL
KHARTOUM
ASMARA
GAMBIA
BURKINA FASO
NIAMEY
BAMAKO
OUAGADOUGOU
DJIBOUTI
NIGERIA
CONAKRY
GUINEA
BENIN
SOMALIA
SIERRA LEONE
ADDIS ABABA
GHANA
SOUTH SUDAN
FREETOWN
LIBERIA
YAMOUSSOUKRO
CENTRAL AFRICAN REPUBLIC
ETHIOPIA
MONROVIA
ACCRA
COTONOU
CAMEROON
JUBA
BANGUI
YAOUNDE
EQUATORIAL GUINEA
UGANDA
KENYA
MOGADISHU
GABON
CONGO
LIBREVILLE
KAMPALA
NAIROBI
D.R. OF THE CONGO
RWANDA
BURUNDI
BRAZZAVILLE
TANZANIA
KINSHASA
DODOMA
LUANDA
ANGOLA
MOZAMBIQUE
ZAMBIA
LILONGWE
LUSAKA
HARARE
MADAGASCAR
NAMIBIA
ZIMBABWE
ANTANANARIVO
BOTSWANA
WINDHOEK
GABORONE
ATLANTIC OCEAN
PRETORIA
MAPUTO
SOUTH AFRICA
CAPE TOWN

NIGERIA

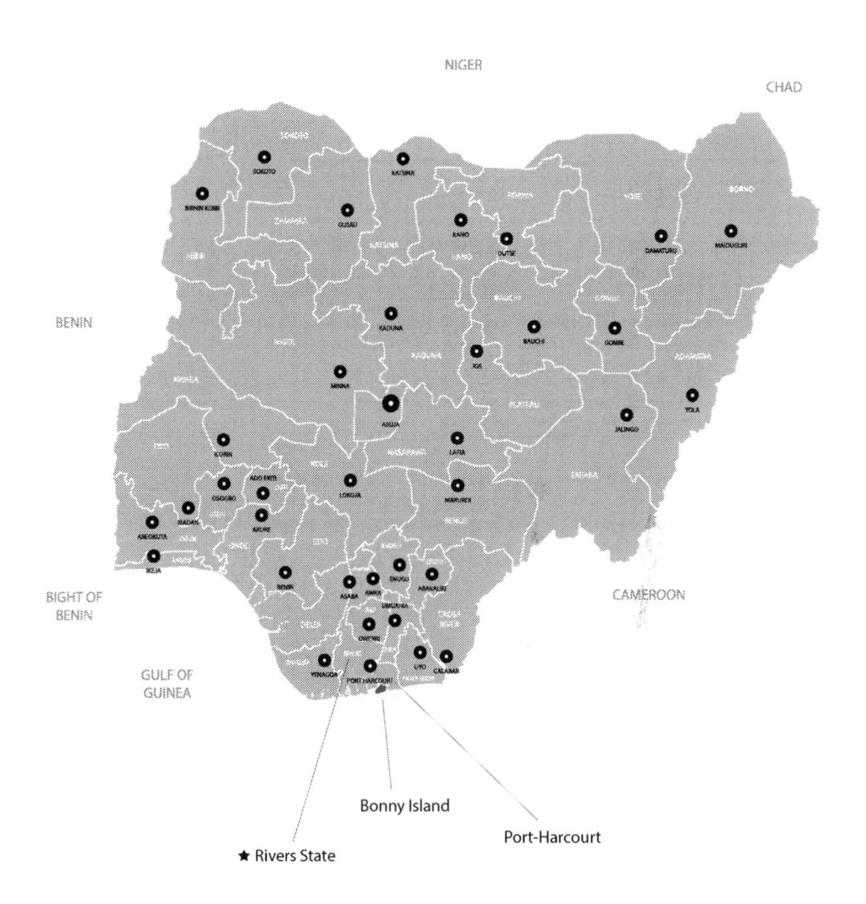
NIGER
CHAD
BENIN
BIGHT OF BENIN
GULF OF GUINEA
CAMEROON
Bonny Island
Port-Harcourt
★ Rivers State

Disclaimer

This is a book written from my experience and memories, and some may have different recollections of the events I describe here. Some names and places have been slightly changed for reasons of privacy. Any mistakes are mine alone.

Appendix 1

Appendix to Introduction - This is Your Life

By popular demand, I have included a few testimonials from family and friends for my 40th birthday "This is Your Life" Celebration.

Questions asked:
Name
Relationship with Faith?
Where did you first meet Faith?
How long have you known Faith?
Please give details of two of your most favorite memories of or experiences with Faith.
What makes Faith so special?
What are the special qualities that she has?
What do you most admire about Faith?

Name: Naomi Smith

Relationship: My cell group leader at KT and good friend

Where did you first meet Faith? Kensington Temple Church

How long have you known Faith? Since 2009

Please give details of two of your most favorite memories of or experiences with Faith. Cell group sleepovers!

What makes Faith so special? Her innocence and her pure and caring heart.

What are the special qualities that she has? She's always positive.

What do you most admire about Faith? Her faith, diligence, obedience and love for God!

In what way has Faith been a blessing to you? Please give examples. Faith was always there to intercede for me in prayer when I first became a Christian and that really encouraged me and helped me build my faith.

When I was first placed in Faith's first cell in Kensington Temple, there were between 4 and 6 of us but many people didn't come and the group wasn't very interactive. Eventually, that cell ended as we couldn't all make it on that day anymore. I stopped going to the cell for a while, then when I decided to be placed in a cell group again, KT administration sent me back to Faith. During this time, little did I know Faith had been fervently praying for cell group members to the point where she would pray over the empty seats in her meetings. Boy did God answer her prayers!

When I rejoined her cell, it became a group of strong women who were thirsty for more and more of God who came together and formed an amazing sisterhood where we saw breakthrough after breakthrough and where we were able to confide, encourage, and pray for one another. Something I have never found again in any church. It was truly an amazing season in my life and a gift of friendship with 12 amazing girls that I will always cherish.

If you could describe Faith in one word, what would it be? Proverbs 31

Name: Nneka Barber

I have known Faith since she was 10 years old. The tales of such a long friendship cannot be adequately expressed in words but I will say some of the things that drew me to Faith.

We attended primary and secondary school together. We were in different classes in our primary years, but in the same class in secondary school. I joined the latter in my second year - it was an unfamiliar and intimidating experience as I was new, quite shy and reserved. I remember that Faith stood out to me as one of the familiar faces and one of the first people to make me feel welcome and comfortable. She was such a friendly and emotionally intelligent young lady from even back then.

At that age and in that culture, we were surrounded by each other and we were quite opinionated young women with sometimes inflexible and juvenile ways of thinking. I remember, casually eavesdropping on some of the academic conversations and arguments she would have around various topics and being impressed by her ability to not only put her points across, but also to hear a different point of view. This quality of being tolerant while still being firm, was emphasized further by her ability as a young vibrant Christian, to interact easily with "non-Christians" in such a comfortable and non-judgmental way. This was noticed by a few of us who privately joked that this was due to her being of English birth (as she was born in England).

Hence, Faith was very popular with all types of girls - however, she remained immune to any pressures and influences that might detract from her faith and good character. She has really lived up to her name, in all the years that I have known her. She represents for me: Christianity by example; she demonstrates the love and light of Christ by being unshaken in her faith and principles, while also being caring and inclusive, all by her actions. I believe that this is her special form of evangelism. She epitomizes the often quoted "Do as I do, not just, Do as I say" and has always been supportive, offering great advice and encouragement since I have known her.

I am honored to know her and Blessed to see her reach this great milestone at 40. Faith is one of my dearest and forever friends, and I am thankful that God has brought her this far. I know that her amazing light will continue to shine as she is specially favored by God. I pray for another 40 years and counting - years that will be even more extraordinarily Blessed. Congratulations faithful Faith. May your star shine even brighter.

Abu Girls for Life ...... Nneka Barber

Name: 'Olu Olabode

Your relationship with Faith: Former work colleague turned friend.

When did you first meet Faith? 2010/2011

Please give details of two of your most favorite memories of or experiences with Faith. Very committed, Conscientious, dependable and hardworking. Always happy, smiling and brightens any room she walks into.

What makes Faith so special? What special qualities does she have? What do you most admire about her? Always happy, smiling and brightens any room she walks into. Faith is an inspirational woman!

In what way has Faith been a blessing to you? Please give examples. Being there always, in challenging work situations to listen and roll up her sleeves! Happily stands in for others. A great team player! A problem solver and solution provider!

If you could describe Faith in one word, what would it be? Inspiring

---

Name: Obed Hailsham

Faith is my Aunty. I met her first in 2006, but I have known her all my life.

She is so special because first she is my Aunty Faith and then she is very patient and loving and she is always willing to show the love of Christ to others.

The thing I admire most about her is her selfless love for her family. She is always ready to make sacrifices for her family and that is very admirable.

She has been a blessing to me in so many ways I remember when I went through a traumatic experience. Immediately, Aunty Faith heard that I was unwell, she came straight to the hospital and was there with me and she encouraged me through that period. I remember this because she was there when I really needed her and God used her to actually make that experience less traumatic.

Two of my most favorite memories with her are:

1. The time during her visits in 2016 when she remembered that she was almost leaving and we had not done anything really fun together, so she decided we should go to the cinema together. We went to Cinema at Port-Harcourt mall and 9D movies just

came out in the mall. We went in for the movie and during the movie, we sat in the front row. I was so scared of the thrill of the actions, so she kept holding my hand all through and that is something I'll never forget.

My second favorite memory is a more recent one. It goes back a month ago when I had been without a phone for close to a year and I kept using my parents' phones and that really affected my business, so I got the bright idea of calling every family member and asking them to contribute any amount no matter how small. I called everybody and I also called Aunty Faith and she responded by telling me it has been on her mind and she would definitely get back to me about it. So I waited a few weeks and I called her again and this time, she said that I should give her about a week to think about it and to my greatest surprise, I woke up the next morning and my mom told me that Aunty Faith had just sent some money see her account and it was for me to get my new phone and that was it she sent more than I even wanted to collect from everybody put together and I was just surprised and speechless about the whole thing.

Name: Anita Duabo-Theophilus

Relationship with Faith: We are cousins.

How long have you known Faith? I have known Faith since she was about 6 years old.

Most favorite memory of Faith: Faith and I reconnected in Secondary School in 1992.

I was in Senior Secondary and she just came in (Boarding School). We were at the dining hall having dinner and I was one of the school prefects on duty that night. I went outside the dining hall to see the students who were late for dinner and she was one of them.

I wasn't too sure it was her because I hadn't seen her in ages. I walked up to her and asked for her name, when she mentioned Faith, I took her to the dining hall and talked for a while. I asked someone to get her dinner from the kitchen since she was a new student and hadn't been assigned to a table. It was so good to see her again after a long time.

What makes Faith so special? She's caring, godly, firm and responsible. Secondly, what I admire the most about Faith is her love for God.

In what way has Faith been a blessing to you? Faith has been a blessing to me in several ways but she did something in 2015 which blew my mind. My husband passed on that year and one unique thing she did was to send me comfort scriptures. She took time to pick them out and she actually typed out the verses, replacing some names with my name, and making them my personal scriptures. She sent me some money which I spent but I still have that sheet (one of my treasures).

Describe Faith in one word: If I could describe Faith in one word, I would say she is adorable.

Appendix 2

Appendix to Chapter 6 - The Easy Fruit

The Young Adults Encounter Weekend Testimonies

Here are testimonials from some of the attendees:

1. God delivered me from committing suicide. I have been feeling like this for the past six years and trying to do things on my own and in my own strength and nothing going the right way. Before I came to Encounter, I was saying to God if You don't meet with me, I would commit suicide. I even packed paracetamol in my bag ready to take an overdose and die. On Friday night, one of the leaders said someone needs prayer for committing suicide. One of the leaders prayed for me and gave me Scriptures to meditate on. Also, in the Holy Spirit session, one of the leaders prayed for me and I felt a weight lift off my shoulder and can now say I am free!!

2. God has appointed me to come on this Encounter and I finally have my breakthrough! I was living in defeat, condemnation, and extremely low self-esteem. God has delivered me from this demonic oppression and has also opened my eyes to all forms of deception. Praise God!

3. I want to thank God for bringing me back to the place where I remember His goodness, His love, and power. God reminded me especially of His love and the way He has preserved me all those years because of this. He showed me vividly in a dream I had on Saturday evening and confirmed to me through prayers on

Sunday. God be praised!

4. God taught me how to depend on Him concerning my finances and reassure me of His presence and how much He loves me. For the first time, I could imagine something and see it. Before, when I closed my eyes, I only saw darkness.

5. I came here with a million pounds of emotional and spiritual baggage, and this encounter was God's way of dealing with my baggage and emotional trauma. Through this encounter, I've been made to feel special by God and have strongholds and unforgiveness removed from my life. I AM FREE INDEED BECAUSE I HAVE HAD AN ENCOUNTER WITH GOD!!!!

6. This encounter has really helped me get to the root of my problem, sexual abuse, and abortion. I have finally been able to forgive those involved. I feel free, light, happy and confident about God's love.

One of the young people also gave us leaders this feedback:

I loved the unity amongst the Encounter leaders, as well as the delegates. There was a huge sense of readiness, expectation, and hope, which determined the strong breakthrough atmosphere. Even the worship and praise was very different, very bold and warfare-like . . . if there were no teachings, we literally could have continued praising for hours.

Appendix 3

Speak The Word Album by Faith Apiafi-Hailsham

(nominated for Best Spoken Word Artist
by The Music and Media Platforms Awards)

You can download the album and access testimonials by scanning the QR code below or going to the links listed below

www.faithhailsham.com

Distrokid HyperFollow

(Links to music on all platforms)

www.tinyurl.com/UnveilingFaith-Distrokid

Spotify

www.tinyurl.com/UnveilingFaith-Spotify

Apple Music

www.tinyurl.com/UnveilingFaith-AppleMusic

Shazam

www.tinyurl.com/UnveilingFaith-Shazam

Amazon

www.tinyurl.com/UnveilingFaith-Amazon

Deezer

www.tinyurl.com/UnveilingFaith-Deezer

iHeart Radio

www.tinyurl.com/UnveilingFaith-iHeartRadio

Tidal

www.tinyurl.com/UnveilingFaith-Tidal

Musixmatch

www.tinyurl.com/UnveilingFaith-Musixmatch

YouTube

www.tinyurl.com/UnveilingFaith-YouTube

Testimonies

FROM 'SPEAK THE WORD' ALBUM

This album has been such a blessing to me and my husband, Shawn. I had been praying for Shawn, who has suffered from traveling joint pain and inflammation for several years. After I listened to track #4 Healing Prayer, I knew immediately Shawn and I needed to listen to this together. This track ushered in the Holy Spirit and began our time of deliverance. Shawn and I prayed together over all of his joints, we also listened to track #2 Fear Not, track #5 Arise Come Alive, and track #6 Restoration Prayer. Each of these prayers ministered to us in such an intimate, personal, and powerful way! Through these prayers and power of the Holy Spirit, Shawn has been delivered from a spirit of infirmity, torment, and pain. We are so thankful for Faith and her new album, Speak the Word. We experienced breakthrough, healing, deliverance and complete restoration in Jesus' name! Glory to God!

- Rufina Walker
California, USA

Faith's beautiful voice speaking the word over my life through this album is a timely gift that I'm incredibly grateful for. I met Faith at my church, specifically in our weekly women's prayer meetings. Every time she spoke or prayed, I felt God's spirit moving in my heart. Her passion to speak out the Word was something that I've always been encouraged by in real life, but now I have it in the form of this direct audio and it has proven to be such a blessing, especially in my season right now. I've needed to stir my faith and cling to the Word, through the ups and downs. There is something special about this album that's different than just a Bible reading. It carries Faith's convictions and revelations of the word in her voice. It carries her authority. You can feel the battles she's faced and overcome with the Lord's word in her heart and on her tongue when you listen. You can sense the worshiper that she is, in spirit and in truth. She speaks from a genuine faith in her walk with God. Because of this, alongside the music that plays underneath her voice, makes for a stunning project that brings God's presence and peace through His truth straight into your heart. The Bible tells us that faith comes by hearing the Word of God. Thank you Faith for this weapon against the enemy, to stir our faith.

- Heidi Lakin
California, USA

I had skull pain near my left ear and neck for over a week and was considering going to the doctor to check it out. But after listening to Faith's healing prayer and receiving it by faith, the pain is now gone!!

- Charity Patty Keungm
Hong Kong

I listened to your healing words and was deeply moved and encouraged. I need to listen to it again and let the Holy Spirit really show me the root of my pain. But your beautiful voice speaking the promises of God in such a powerful yet comforting way is truly anointed! I know your album will be a great blessing to all who listen. And God will use your "voice" to call many people to a new and more powerful walk with Jesus as the Word

of God comes alive in their hearts as they listen to your powerful declarations of truth! I know I felt the Holy Spirit speaking to me through you! So proud of you! Thank you.
Big hug!

- Marilee Pierce Dunker
International Ambassador for World Vision, USA

While abroad, I had an issue with an abrasion to my eye which was excruciatingly painful due to the eyeball being the most sensitive part of the body! I had had this issue a number of times before when home in England & had to go to the emergency eye department, but it would still take a long time to heal. With this recent episode, I was prayed for by Christians who were full of faith for healing and I felt a measure of healing. However, a few days later, it flared up even worse. I still knew that Jesus was my healer. As before, due to the pain, I needed to lie in bed in a dark room but this time, I decided to play your spoken word album (which I had listened to before) and guess what, even before the album finished, I got up fully healed!!!! My eye feels amazing, no flare ups, I have been miraculously healed!

- Toyin
England, October 2021

I was so touched by Faith's spoken word she released over healing! The Holy Spirit moved me to tears as I listened, touched my heart greatly, and used Faith's word to answer a prayer I cried out over my health and physical healing just the night before. How personal and good is our God! I felt the love and power of God through her words and God's Word in her mouth, like a personal message made only for me. I also decided to share with some family and friends immediately! The next day, my grandmother was being taken to the hospital in a scary emergency with Covid complications and on the way, my mom thought to play Faith's spoken word I had just sent her over Grandma. Although she is not a believer, my mom shared how impacted she was as the power of God filled that car and saw her deeply touched and moved through different spoken words Faith had released. She played several all the way to the hospital and my grandmother received great comfort, ministry, and hope for healing. Grandma later returned home and is now doing well! I'm so thankful for the seeds planted in her heart through God's Word because of Faith's obedience and her faithfulness to step out and not only record these, but to send them out in the exact timing she did! These are powerful and so needed, "for such a time as this!"

- Mrs K.R.
California, USA

I strongly recommend Faith's album. When I was going through a particularly challenging time with poor sleep, Faith's voice emerged as a soothing, nourishing balm - rhythmic, beautifully paced, helping me to regulate my breathing and gently speaking God's Word into my soul. There is a rich, lyrical timbre to her voice that, speaking God's words of comfort and truth, brought a flow of relaxation and peace to my mind, body, spirit and soul and helped me to feel deeply held. Thank you, Faith!"

- Debbie Chua
England, UK

Appendix 4
Salvation Prayer

After reading this book, if you would like to become a christian or renew your commitment to God, you can pray this prayer below. You have to truly believe in your heart that Jesus died on the cross for your redemption (salvation) and pray this prayer sincerely.

> *Lord, I commit my life to you, I give you my heart and repent of all my sins. The bible says if we confess our sins, He is faithful and just to forgive us our sins and to cleanse us from all unrighteousness (1 John 1:9 NKJV), therefore I confess my sins before you Lord and ask that you cleanse and wash me clean with the precious blood of Jesus. Come into my heart as my Lord and Savior and take complete control of every area of my life. I make a new commitment from today henceforth to live for You, help me to walk in obedience to Your word and use my life for Your glory. I begin a new chapter of my life by choosing to walk with you Lord to advance your kingdom on earth. Thank you Lord for saving me and accepting me into your kingdom.*

If you prayed that prayer from your heart, congratulations you are now a Christian! The bible says there is joy in heaven over one sinner that repents than over 99 christians who are already saved. You have therefore caused a great rejoicing in heaven, that's how special you are.

Look for a good bible believing church near you to attend and let them know you just committed your heart to the Lord. I would also like to hear from you so you can write to me on faithhailsham@gmail.com so I can be praying for you.

Other useful resources:
The bible gateway - www.biblegateway.com. To start reading the bible if you haven't got one. You can also download the bible app on your phone.

Made in the USA
Columbia, SC
28 March 2023

e11c25d9-5e69-406e-86d6-f2a7276e7df6R01